a memoir

MW00562389

SMASH
a memoir

RITA KAMPEN

AWAKEN ✿ VILLAGE

—— PRESS ——

This is a work of nonfiction.
The events and the heart of all the conversations
in this book have been recreated
to the best of the author's ability,
and some names, details, and
timelines have been changed to
respect the privacy of individuals.

The content of this book is for
inspired (fingers crossed) enjoyment only.
The ideas shared in this book are not intended to replace a
reader's relationship with their counsellor, physician, or other
mental health professionals.

Copyright © 2021 by Rita Kampen

All rights reserved.

Printed in the United States of America.

Editing by Awaken Village Press
Cover illustration and interior design by Laura and Micah Hill
Author photo by Sara Wong

ISBN 978-1-7356582-4-7 (paperback)
ISBN 978-1-7356582-5-4 (ebook)

Library of Congress Control Number: 2021918662

Published by Awaken Village Press, Reno, NV
www.awakenvillagepress.com

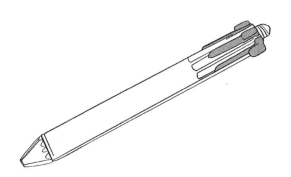

DEDICATION

In memory of my father—

You have been my lifelong champion. The quiet courage of your convictions and your enduring love supplied me with a compass to venture out and find my own way home. For all the times you asked how my book was coming along, my heart breaks that I can't tell you in person that it's finally complete. Perhaps it all worked out for the best, however, as you might not have enjoyed reading the kissing parts.

A NOTE FROM
THE AUTHOR

Writing a memoir has required more courage and commitment than I could have guessed. I thought it would be like doing a puzzle—having lived all the pieces, I would simply write them into place. The process was much more like dredging the flowing river of my current life to decide which rusty events and treasured keepsakes will tell the most interesting, authentic story.

While it may seem obvious to state that my experience of an event may not fully match the experiences of the individuals who lived it with me, I feel it's important to say that I'm trusting my memories and my heart on what I share here. And it is for this very reason—because this story is *my* rendition—that I've changed many of the names and a few details to provide anonymity. Also, on occasion, I have used composite events and characters. Months of counselling, for example, were compressed into one conversation to reveal the heart of what I learned about myself in those sessions.

Writing this book felt like telling deeply personal stories to someone I know well. As I got to the end of the project, however, I found myself wondering why I thought it was a good idea to write my life into the shape of a book for anyone to hold. By nature, I am a private person, and publishing a book creates an open door for others to wander like tourists through the intimate rooms of my life. Fortunately, I also trust in the human spirit and the way we are eternally connected to each other and, therefore, to the universal heart of each other's stories. I cling to the belief that my story doesn't have to be salacious enough or worthy enough by a critic's standards to be told, but precisely because I'm the only one who knows the intimacy and immediacy of my own parade, it is mine to lead. And so, my words march onward to the centre of town, where I hope the townsfolk will be kind and celebrate this accomplishment with me.

I was surprised at the stories and people who did not make an appearance in this book. However, those dear to me do not lose their special place in my heart because they aren't pinned onto the clothesline of memories from this particular basket of clean laundry (yes, I'm aware I'm beating this metaphor against a rock). And those mentioned in this book are included because, without their presence and their own pain, I simply couldn't have walked the peculiar and rather perfect winding path to where I am today.

My prevailing motivation for this project is my two daughters. When I was diagnosed with breast cancer a few years ago, I realized it would be my biggest regret if this book wasn't finished before I was. I desired to capture what I experienced in one especially transformative decade of my life so my girls and I could talk when they arrived into their forties, even if I wasn't here anymore. Writing this for them ended up being a lavish gift to me. I met myself, often to remind myself what I had forgotten I knew, under the luminous moonlit skies of my memories.

MOONTALK

Partially clad she hangs low in the night
Clouds on their journey slowly drift out of sight
Shining soft truth that reveals ancient awe
Cloaked in her moonlight we speak our souls raw

~Rita Kampen, 2002

CONTENTS

GRUFF

November 2013

Dim lights kiss the rough stone walls and spill a welcoming glow onto small wooden tables huddled together in anticipation. The hum of the dumbwaiter at the back of the restaurant signals to my taste buds that my order of sea bream could be up next. The owner skips down the stairs from the kitchen and smiles my way. "Our customer of the month is writing while eating again?" he teases in a Cretan accent that makes his English sound ancient yet playful. "We have live Turkish music tonight. You will like it," he gestures enthusiastically.

"I already know I'll love it," I echo back, hearing the impassioned voice of a woman who has recently fallen deeply in love with her life. Just as I'd felt while floating effortlessly in the clear, salty Mediterranean only hours earlier, I feel buoyant and open to whatever comes my way.

I scribble words onto the page in front of me, chasing thoughts that could easily be snatched away in a gust of distraction. My tall, silky-haired server places a glass of "inspirational wine," as he calls it, next to my well-worn journal.

Musicians, crammed under the stairs like obliging sardines in their can, tune their exotic-sounding instruments as the waiter clears my plate. Having eagerly accepted his offer of dessert, I return to recording reflections of my day and notice how they so perfectly match what brought me here from Canada in the first place.

My decision to celebrate my forty-ninth birthday in a foreign country finds me in Chania's Old Town on the island of Crete for the whole month of November. I wander the enchanting cobblestone streets of this preserved ancient world during the day and feast amongst the locals every evening.

The owner greets two older men like family and seats them at the table in front of me. In profile, the younger of the two, likely in his sixties, reminds me of a proud mountain goat with a high, flat nose and coarse, silver hair. He barks out his side of the conversation in Greek to the older man. His commanding voice gallops faster to the end of each sentence to drive home his point. I secretly name him Billy Goat Gruff, a character from a child's fairytale, as my pen makes quick notes about this new stern-faced curiosity in front of me.

I assume the lights are being dimmed as my words begin to fade on my page until I realize that, in fact, my pen is running out of ink. I'm attempting to revive it with a hard shake when I hear a low, smoke-fueled voice simply utter, "Here." Like a woman in an old black-and-white movie who holds a cigarette to her lips and a stranger appears out of nowhere with a light, I look up to see Gruff holding out a pen. My pulse quickens at the unexpected intimacy of this exchange. From the safety of my table for one, this keen observer was caught being observed. I accept his offer and mumble my thanks. The thick, black exterior of his pen feels bold between my fingers and smells of exotic smoke.

I am mesmerized by the trail of green ink on my page as I write about Gruff and his pen, with his pen. The older, gentler man across the table from Gruff turns in his chair and asks what I am writing about. I tell him that I have come to Greece to celebrate life in a place where civilization was born. When he asks to hear more, I share a sweeping outline of the Year of Jubilee, the concept that is guiding my celebration.

"The Year of Jubilee is a practice where an ancient tribe—not as old as the Cretans," I interject with a smile and receive one back in return "—was instructed to rest and celebrate for an entire year every fifty years."

He shuffles his chair closer, and Gruff looks over but doesn't seem interested in joining the conversation. "I just began my fiftieth year of life a couple weeks ago here on Crete, and I created my own personalized version of Jubilee," I tell him, then ask, "Where are you from?"

"Here," he answers. "My mother was a Turk, but our father was Greek. We're half-brothers."

With the music getting louder, I lean in and ask him for an insider's perspective on what remains of the spirit of the mighty Minoans from the first civilization on Crete.

"Nothing." He shakes his head wistfully. "It has vanished. The mountains no longer have the essence of the original spirit in them. The gods," he muses, "are all gone now."

As the music swells, making it impossible to continue talking, I allow his words to add another layer to the backdrop of my life. *Which old beliefs need to die in order to allow new ideas to emerge?* I write in my journal.

When I'd told my parents of my plan to travel alone to Greece, it hadn't surprised me that they thought it sounded dangerous and completely unnecessary for a divorced woman to venture alone so far away. I had lived a predictable life for the first forty years, sticking close to home and the faith I was raised in. As the ache of disconnection from myself had intensified, it had torn a hole in my spirit—and then, in the decade leading up to this night in this restaurant, the hole had ripped my life wide open to allow a much larger, more interesting world in.

After one and a half pages of green ink musings, this pen runs dry too! I look up and notice the musicians are on a break and Gruff is eyeing me suspiciously.

"I've run the ink out of your pen as well," I tell him, shrugging bashfully.

"Give it to me," he growls. I hand it over, and he pulls out a piece of paper to test it for himself. The older brother proudly announces, "Don't worry. He is a man of many pens." On cue, Gruff pulls out another pen from a concealed inside pocket in his jacket. This time it's a tri-colour plastic click pen. He presses down the tab on the blue ink option and passes it across the table. "Keep writing," he instructs and just as quickly turns back to the conversation with his brother.

I blush when I consider whether it's possible that, like the browsing history stored in a computer, a borrowed pen might capture what it scrawls and Gruff will know everything I wrote about him when I return his pen. Then I laugh and chide myself for this ridiculous thought as I savour the last sip of my raki, a strong digestive elixir served after dinner in every restaurant in Chania.

Young locals have streamed into the restaurant and are moving in time to the undulating music as it starts up again. The waiter makes his way through the crowded room and presents me with a container of the potent raki. I lift my empty glass to remind him I've already had my complimentary serving, but he simply nods his head sideways in the direction of the two brothers. "It's from them," he yells over the music. Gruff bellows from his seat, "It will give you more ideas."

This gruff man, far from friendly, hasn't asked one question about my life or heard what I'm writing about yet has single-handedly made it possible for me to continue to record my evolving story for another night. After a single enchanting evening, my journal pages tell a tale beyond the words they contain as the black ink I arrived with morphs into hope-filled green rows of shared history and then a blue pool of looping, dancing, raki-infused sentences in which anything seems possible—a feeling that is perfectly supported by the fact that I'm sitting alone in a restaurant on the other side of the world telling locals how I'm taking a year off to learn how to celebrate, all of which would have been utterly inconceivable at the start of this decade.

The brothers rise to leave. The older one, smiling and full of life despite the fact that his gods have vanished, wishes me well on the rest of my journey. Then Gruff approaches with his towering presence, and I quickly extend his tri-colour pen to him. With a flick of the wrist, he shoos it away. Then, as if Gruff was the mighty Zeus himself, he booms for all to hear: "Keep the fucking pen! Use all the colours. Run it out of ink, and KEEP WRITING!"

BUCKLE UP, BABY

November 2004
(9 years earlier)

I swipe a stray hair from my face as I follow my husband into the upscale pub known for its impressive stock of imported beer. (I don't drink beer.) We snake our way past tables to the area in the back that he reserved for my birthday party and are greeted by rows of beaming faces. I respond with a look of mock surprise that dissolves into mock delight, which I deem an appropriate reaction to arriving at a party that's only half a surprise.

I wink at Kerrie, my neighbour, who is chatting with a couple of friends I've known since I was a teenager. There's a group of church friends laughing in a huddle, most of whom are members of the music team I've been a part of for almost ten years. Another small cluster near the back wall are parents from my daughters' school who have become good friends over the years. By the impassioned looks on their faces, they're probably discussing the latest unwelcome changes in the curriculum or their least favourite teachers.

These snapshots of my life anchored by the faces of those present don't include any members of my family, who plan to celebrate with me tomorrow, or my two daughters, who are too young to enter a pub. I wander from group to group to say hello and thank them for coming. One irony of attending one's own birthday party is the responsibility to work the room on a day I'd prefer to soak it all in. If I've had the same lighthearted conversation with every group by the end of the evening, then I have been a good birthday girl—but am I a woman who feels she has truly celebrated her fortieth birthday?

Birthdays are becoming increasingly depressing. It's not the getting older part; I actually like the idea of turning forty. It's the fact that birthday celebrations are supposed to feel, well, celebratory—and they don't. They haven't for a long time. It could have something to do with the fact that my birthday falls at the beginning of November, just as Canada's West Coast rains refuse to let up and days are noticeably shorter and darker. This sounds like a perfectly logical explanation, except that other notable celebrations throughout the year—Christmas, Easter, Mother's Day, Thanksgiving—all seem shrouded in the same fine mist of sadness. I blame it on all the hoopla, the extra time and effort it takes to plan food and organize people and decide on the right gift. I find it all exhausting, but I know that is still only part of the answer since I didn't have to do any of that today. If I am honest with myself, I just don't like my life that much. Although I have actively created the life I am living, it feels like I am slowly being flattened by the blows of simply being alive.

When I caught wind of a surprise party being planned, similar to the one I had organized for my husband four months earlier for his fortieth birthday, I knew immediately that I didn't like the idea. There was a familiar niggle of discomfort around the expectations that come front-loaded in celebrations, so I let my husband know that a full surprise party would not be appreciated. I didn't need to know the exact location or even the guest list, but I asked for just enough details so I could prepare myself a little for the event. I seem to require a small life raft of certainties at a time when things feel increasingly uncertain.

I can't remember when I first noticed this growing aversion to celebrating. As the years passed, events I once enjoyed began to leave me numb around the edges. Somewhere along the way, I concluded that if I can't access the feeling of celebration at an event, perhaps I'm just not capable of celebrating. From all my experiences, celebration has one thing in common: It requires people to gather. Celebration also leans hard on tradition and ritual. For birthdays, this usually means cake, candles, singing, and presents. For all the ways rituals help us know we're celebrating, even the overly sweet frosting on the cake cannot cover the ever-deepening cracks that disconnect my heart from the motions my body goes through during these events.

I notice I can feel the slightest breeze of celebration in the air when I'm with one or two others in a more intimate setting, but today there are considerably more than that at my party. Feeling ashamed of my resistance to a perfectly loving gesture, I admonish myself for not being more grateful that I have people in my life who are willing to plan a party for me. And since I didn't have any better ideas for how to celebrate this milestone birthday, I bought a new sweater, coloured my hair a fiery reddish brown from a box, and gave myself strict instructions to rise to the occasion. At a minimum, I knew I could make it appear like I was enjoying myself. That last part I had gotten pretty good at over the years.

I don't know it yet, but the sensation of slowly feeling drained by even the idea of a large group doesn't make me selfish or strange; it makes me an introvert. The rules for social engagement—and therefore celebrations—must have been created by those who are energized, not exhausted, by a room full of people. The rest of us make the necessary internal and external adjustments to get through the event with a plan in place to recover later.

I excuse myself and escape to the privacy of the restaurant bathroom. I push through the door of an empty stall and release a shaky exhalation. I am able to measure how much pretense I am using by how quickly the smile drains from my face the moment I turn and walk away. I'm not surprised that all the extra attention and expectation stacks the odds in favour of calling on all my acting skills rather than being able to be fully myself today. I also assume that the experience the guests I just left chatting around the tables are having isn't my inner experience, since they all appear genuinely happy and relaxed. I've learned to replicate it, through a well-placed smile and the tone of my voice, but I can't seem to locate it in the rest of my body. And for the record, it's not that I don't like people. I'm pretty sure I just don't really like myself most of the time.

I've gotten particularly good at hovering above my life and noticing how things look from a distance or from someone else's point of view. I can see that my light has dimmed over the years. I received the manual on how to do life from the Mennonite faith community I was born into, and while even from a young age I didn't always agree with what was presented to me, I knew it by heart—which meant my heart was busy doing all the things I was supposed to do instead of what might have felt more true for me. All these years later, there's a thick layer of dust and neglect on my inner light, making it difficult to feel into or out of my own heart most days. I remind myself that I'm starting a new decade, which offers a dollop of hope that I'll find a way to clean off the grime and start fresh.

Earlier in the day, I'd sat by a river a short drive from my house. With the river flowing by, I'd jotted down some ideas to share at the party. I'd wanted to prepare for the inevitable request to say a few words at the end of the evening. Someone is bound to yell "Speech!" and I'd prefer to avoid the awkward "I don't know what to say, but thanks for coming!" jumble of emotions and platitudes. I don't like being put on the spot, so I figured I'd prepare something to share even if I don't end up saying anything.

My time at the river had offered solitude, which seems to be my only way of gathering in the thoughts that dangle almost out of reach at the far edges of my mind. It had given me time to decipher what this birthday means to me so that I could figure out what it wants from me.

When my body has a hard time feeling, my mind compensates by generating a lot of ideas. I pull down as many lofty thoughts as I can grab, then line them up and glue them down so I can see where I stand. Once I've figured out what something means to me, then I can polish it to a high shine and wrap it with a bow for general consumption.

Sitting by the river, I'd reflected on the cliché that someone who's reached the age of forty is "over the hill." It certainly feels like I've spent a lot of energy clambering up the mountain of my life. But have I reached the top? Is this as good as it gets? Looking back on my life, each decade seems like a helpful "trail marker" I can use to corral my thoughts and discern my current location on this mountain.

The end of my first decade put me at my tenth birthday, which wasn't much different from other birthdays in my childhood. Since my older brother's birthday is six days after mine, it was decided that despite our two-year age difference, having one party would be more practical. My mom knew that whatever she did for me and my brother, she'd eventually have to reproduce for my two younger siblings, so she kept it simple. Parties and people seemed to exhaust her, but she pushed through and then usually seemed unwell for days afterwards. It didn't even cross my mind to request a party just for myself, since that would surely be asking too much.

Our default birthday cake every year became a cookie-sheet slab of homemade brownies. Slathered in chocolate icing, it always provided more than enough acreage for any number of candles and any amount of guests. Hot dogs, Old Dutch potato chips, and a bowl of colourful Jell-O topped with whipped cream adorned the kids' birthday table every year. The celebration was always planned for the weekend that landed closest to our actual birthdays. Some years our cousins were invited over along with their parents, and sometimes a few kids our age who lived near our farm were allowed to join in. We didn't know there was any other way to celebrate until we started to get invitations to our school friends' parties during the week on their actual birthdays with a curated group of friends from school. It seemed extravagant to celebrate during the week, but I certainly didn't mind getting out of doing chores those days.

My second decade moved as quickly as the lines notched into the trim around the kitchen door that charted my growth. I went from a small, skinny kid to a tall, lean adult. My hairstyles, most of them accentuated by the extra lift and curl from perms, were the undeniable proof in all my high-school yearbook pictures of my adherence to this popular hair treatment from the seventies.

I fell in and out of love with the latest pop star or cute boy in school faster than fashion changed the width of the pants legs on my school jeans. In the fifth grade, I couldn't see my shoes poking out from under my denim dome, but by eighth grade, everything worn below the belt was very short and very tight. I could eat anything and couldn't gain a pound even if I tried. Although I didn't struggle with weight, I made up for it in a war against acne that I didn't win until well into adulthood.

The completion of my second decade, my twentieth birthday, was overshadowed by my engagement a few months earlier. Between attending bridal showers and planning a wedding that would be attended by 350 people, my birthday slid right off the calendar. With four months until the wedding and organizing the move out of my parents' home into a tiny rental house just down the road, there was a lot to do. Birthdays come every year, I reasoned, but a wedding is a once-in-a-lifetime event, and there are only so many big celebrations one can reasonably expect to have in one year.

My third decade found me squarely in the role of soccer mom. I had birthed two daughters in my twenties, and we moved into a townhouse in the suburbs. I was essentially solo parenting during the week because my husband, Tom, consistently worked extra hours to make ends meet for our family. My extra-large scheduler lay open on the kitchen counter beside the corded family phone, showing weekly church commitments, multiple volunteer shifts at my daughters' schools, and almost-daily sports practices or dance lessons that required me to shuttle my girls, and often their friends, to and from. It was also a time when I was transitioning off the medication that I had been prescribed since the grand mal seizure I had right before the birth of my second daughter. The medication made my mind feel sluggish as I shouldered the strain of keeping up with my family's schedule. All the other moms seemed to be able to juggle their busy lives and even add full-time jobs into the mix, so I pushed harder, assuming this was just what living felt like.

With a start, I realize I've gotten lost in thought and my party guests are probably wondering what's happened to me. I coax my mind back from the river to the present moment at the pub while still clutching the realization that tonight I am completing another decade. Forty feels old but also young in the scheme of a full life. As I open the door to the bathroom stall, I feel relief when I see there's no one else standing at the row of dimly lit sinks. I have a few more moments to buoy my spirit in this quiet space before I head back to the glare of lights and expectant eyes of those who have come to celebrate. I really want to enjoy this day and to feel the experience. I don't like pulling out an assortment of pre-approved antics from my bag of tricks, like maintaining a permanent smile to signal to myself and those gathered that all is well. But it all comes so automatically that it's tempting to believe this is just who I am and how life works.

I consider that the guests who have shown up today have come to celebrate who they believe I am in their lives. But celebration, the true art of celebrating, surely must include me knowing what I'm here for as well. Convinced this is probably a selfish thought, I look in the mirror to check my makeup and instead I catch my own eyes and dare to look at the woman peering back at me. My hazel eyes flash a mix of emotions and a barrage of requests too numerous to identify, and I look away before I come undone in the presence of that much-unfiltered honesty.

Perhaps celebrating is more challenging than it appears at first glance because almost every ceremonial occasion adds or removes a layer of identity from the person being celebrated. Yippee! I'm a high school graduate. Woohoo! I'm married. Yeehaw! I'm a decade older. The event itself may only last a few hours, but the change that's being celebrated takes much longer to find its way into our bones. And this doesn't take into account that inherent in most celebrations is a layer of loss. Graduation means the end of many friendships that were held together by proximity. A wedding means that I am no longer single. A new decade means accepting that the last one is forever over with no comforting proof that the next one will be better.

As I make my way back to the party, I scan the room and observe my current life, animated through the people I've known for a long time but don't see very often alongside those I interact with regularly due to circumstances. Their presence helps track my story, at least the observable part of it, and I am grateful they all came. In the same breath, I wonder how my story is going to continue from here. Fifty seems a lifetime away, and no matter how hard I try to imagine my life in ten years, it's a dimly lit wall of blank canvases. As my mind wanders into that future white space, I feel something lurch inside me, demanding my attention. I sense that my life is going to get more interesting but also bumpier. I have no idea what will happen, but I know that something needs to change because I cannot keep this version of life going for much longer. The scaffolding required to keep this smile in place is getting dangerously unsteady.

As anticipated, with only a few abandoned crumbs of birthday cake remaining on plates scattered around the tables, all eyes are on me to say something to end the evening. The rest of the pub is overflowing with regular patrons as music thumps through the speakers hung in every corner, and I realize there's no way I'm going to be able to express any deep birthday thoughts over the noise.

"Thank you all for coming to celebrate the start of a new decade today," I proclaim to those gathered, my hands cupped around my mouth like a megaphone. "I'm going to send you all an email with some of my birthday thoughts, but as a teaser, I've boiled it down to three words."

The guests have crowded in closer, some standing on their chairs so they can hear what I'm saying. I'm overwhelmed by the support as I survey the chorus of familiar faces gifting me with their smiling presence. I remind myself to absorb this feeling more fully later when I replay the whole scene multiple times in my memory.

"I have a feeling that things are going to get a bit wild from here on out." I pause and wonder why I'm saying this out loud, but now that I've begun, I have to finish. "So my mantra to kick off my new decade is: BUCKLE UP, BABY."

I say it in a joking voice, and everyone laughs and claps in response, but I already suspect that whatever is down this road isn't going to be a laughing matter.

NOT-SO-FUNNY BONE

"Oh no, here it comes! Wake up. WAKE UP!" The part of me that's stirring awake is pleading with the part that is still asleep. I feel a chain of involuntary muscle contractions starting at my feet and, like a row of falling dominoes, slinking its way up my body. I can only assume that my muscles are doing a dry run, checking that all my synapses are firing and ready to go. Has this chain reaction happened every morning of my life or is this a new protocol since the accident? Is it the pain medication or the trauma to a limb that makes me feel like my body is being operated from a war room command centre? Ever since the accident a week ago, I have awoken to the sound of my own groggy moaning as the arc of pain reaches my arm. It's become my highest priority to intercept the impending wave before my injured arm contracts in agonizing pain.

Today I am able to catch the wave before it hits. The moment I sense consciousness dawning, I yell out through the dense fog, insisting that all available focus be directed toward relaxing the muscles of the right shoulder before the cascade reaches my arm. Pain is a particularly effective motivator in learning more about the lines of communication within the body.

With my eyes still closed and the pain intercepted, I

congratulate myself on my new superpower. Then I gingerly curl the fingers of my right hand to see how swollen they are this morning. A sharp zing shoots up and down the whole length of my arm, emanating from the elbow. It's going to be a long road back, much longer than the fifty-five centimetres from the top of the exercise ball to the ground—the distance my body travelled to create this damage. Ironically, my activities at the same athletic club where the accident occurred—specifically, the yoga classes I was teaching—are probably responsible for my newfound effectiveness at communicating instructions within my body.

The first time I snuck into the back row of a yoga class offered at my local community centre, still sweaty after thirty minutes on the elliptical machine, I was nervous about whether yoga conflicted with my conservative Christian upbringing. Since the yoga class was taught by a fitness instructor I knew and she was using language that was more athletic than religious, my philosophical concerns were quickly overcome.

When I met Jean, a curly-haired single mom a few years younger than me and a new face in the pews at the Mennonite church where I was a member, we quickly discovered our mutual enthusiasm for yoga. Before long, she convinced me to sign up for a yoga teacher training course she was taking. She made a good argument that I didn't have to aspire to teach yoga to enrol, proposing that the course would allow me to confidently create my own personal yoga practice. Seeing a parallel to the years I'd spent studying the Bible that had never resulted in my becoming a pastor or teacher, I agreed that taking this course would enhance my life.

My friendship with Jean deepened as we quizzed each other on Sanskrit names and the nuances of each posture between classes. After completing the course, Jean persuaded the owner of a private athletic club where she had just started teaching yoga to hire me on as a reserve teacher. I was initially uncomfortable with Jean opening doors I hadn't considered knocking on myself, but it was also refreshing to spend time with a person who was not raised with the same cultural background and, therefore, thought very differently from anyone else I knew.

After a few months of teaching classes, the owner of the club asked if I would consider assisting with some administrative tasks, which eventually led to my taking on the role of acting manager when the owner was away. This was my first paid job after years as a full-time mother and volunteer in my community. I felt a sense of purpose in this new, fast-paced environment. I enjoyed easy banter with other staff members, and it made my day to see the calm, smiling faces of the yoga students at the end of my classes. An added benefit of working at the club was free use of all of the gym's amenities, including complimentary access to all group fitness classes.

Taking full advantage of this perk, I attended a challenging spin class twice a week and decided to try out a new class on the group fitness schedule—one that used a stability ball. Years earlier, at my local community centre, I had enjoyed learning how to stretch and strengthen my body using this large, inflatable exercise ball as a tool. I enjoyed the challenge of being able to target specific muscles that are only engaged when balancing on a ball. The first time I managed to come to a full standing position on the ball, I could hardly contain my rush of excitement. I felt especially alive and alert. The trifecta of balance, concentration, and courage seemed in perfect harmony for achieving a stronger connection between my body, mind, and heart. I had a hunch that it required balancing all three to be truly successful at anything in life for any length of time—and I loved how this tool helped me work on that balance, both literally and figuratively.

I seemed to be in a constant battle to find balance in the competing components of my life. If I had time, I wouldn't have energy. If I had energy, I didn't have the finances. If I had dreams, they were usually outweighed by the needs of my family. I felt off-kilter most of the time. Like a cat on a hot tin roof, I could feel my life heating up under my feet. Some days this feeling expressed itself in a low growl of irritation; other days the pressure boiled over, spewing its hot contents on those closest to me. Lately, I'd noticed sparks of desperation launching like boomerangs, doing damage on their way out and on the way back, covered in a slick of consuming guilt over the fact that I felt so uncomfortable in my comfortable, middle-class life.

"Alright, ten more leg lifts, everyone!" bellows Nicole, the instructor of the ball class, bringing my thoughts crashing back into the present moment. As I consider how her voice is so much deeper than her compact frame would suggest, I grip the ball tighter between my knees and feel my thighs start to shake. Then my abdominal muscles join the shimmy as I lower my feet to the floor, still squeezing the ball. Laughter interrupts the concentrated effort when someone's ball squirts free from captivity and sends its owner running to retrieve it as it rolls the length of the room.

"Okay, that completes the floor work!" yells Nicole, her voice bouncing around the large studio space. "Today we're going to learn a new game, so gather 'round. I've asked Rita to help demonstrate what we will be working toward."

I feel a flutter of nervousness as I place my ball at my feet. While I've stood on the ball many times over the years, I'd never done it in front of a room of people. Standing on the large ball provides a tangible measure of how balanced I feel, and every day is a little different.

"First, she's going to mount the ball on all fours," says Nicole in a sultry tone, eliciting a snicker from everyone in the room, including me. I position my knees on either side of the ball, just behind where my hands grip the top front of the ball, using my core muscles to keep the ball stable. "And now, the trickiest part," explains Nicole, her voice low and intense, like she's narrating the behaviour of an animal in the wild. "Watch how she transfers her feet to where her knees are." I slowly, then quickly, work one foot into place and then the other, ensuring my feet are spaced wide enough apart to keep the ball steady.

"Now, she's going to push against the ball with her feet and straighten into a standing position." I am already standing by the time Nicole finishes her instruction, keeping my eyes trained on the ground. "Although Rita makes it look easy, you've only got a few inches of unstable ball in contact with the floor so you have to use your proprioception," she cautions, "which means knowing where your body is in the space. Keeping your eyes on a fixed spot means that you'll see, often before you feel, if you're off balance, giving you enough time to jump off safely."

I'd jumped off the ball many times while learning how to stand. It usually felt cat-like as I pushed against the ball, creating enough bounce to be able to pounce safely to the floor. I've just turned forty years old a few months ago, and I am proud of my ability to learn new things and take new risks. My body feels capable and fit, in noticeable opposition to the way I feel about my life in general.

"Alright, now for the fun part!" exclaims Nicole, giving me a mischievous look. Apparently, she has something more in mind than what we discussed before class. "I think Rita is ready to learn how to play catch while standing on the ball." I assume this must be a metaphor and am attempting to figure out what she means as I glimpse, in my peripheral vision, the sight of her picking up her ball and preparing to bounce it in the space between us.

Riding the wave of adrenaline at having all eyes on me, I can't tell the difference between feeling nervous and potential danger sending out warning signals inside me. I put my hands out to show her I'm ready and am startled and delighted when I catch the incoming ball. The motion forces me to make quick, small adjustments to stay upright as the class cheers me on.

With my heart clanging like a bell throughout my body, I jump down off the ball and receive a high five from Nicole. "Okay, listen up!" she shouts. "We're going to start with baby steps by playing catch in small groups. Everyone grab your ball and straddle it with your knees like you're riding a horse." Playing the game on my knees feels more challenging than what I've just done standing. After a few wobbly attempts, I ask my group of four if I could play along while standing on my ball instead.

I fail to take into account that playing catch in a circle means the ball will come toward me from the side instead of straight on like in the demonstration. When it's my turn to catch, I take my eyes off the fixed spot on the ground for just a second to better anticipate the angle of the ball's arrival. A moment is all it takes to put me dangerously off balance. By the time I realize that I am falling backwards, I'm already hopelessly past the point where I can safely bounce off. In fact, my reflexive pushing motion forces the ball to roll away from me even more quickly.

The movies have it right. Time claims a new cadence, and you can live an entire lifetime in a split second, where every thought and action blurs into slurred, flickering motion. And just as suddenly, time accelerates to warp speed, and the next thing I know, I'm hitting the floor hard. There's not even enough time to fully extend my arm in an attempt to break my fall. The entire weight of my careening body lands squarely on my right elbow.

I hear it and feel it at the same time. Instinctively I grab my elbow. If there's any doubt about how much damage I have just done, it's confirmed when my left hand can't figure out why there's a hole where my right elbow should be. I quickly conclude, as a wave of nausea sweeps over me, that this isn't something a little elbow sling is going to fix. As my body drifts sideways into shock, I see faces come into view attempting to assess the damage.

I lie on my back, feeling embarrassed and confused as the pain crescendos. How had the soft pleasure of working toward a fit body lead to such a hard fall? Had I been showing off and suffered the consequence of excessive pride, as so many church sermons had warned? So far I'd only ever experienced a crushed ego if I tried to shine too brightly. Now I'm clutching a shattered elbow.

How could I have gone from feeling so strong one moment to riding in an ambulance the next, with every bump and dip along the route to the hospital causing me to cry out in spite of the laughing gas they're pumping into the mask on my face? When we reach the hospital, my fitted workout top has to be cut off before I'm wheeled away to have scans taken of my arm, a task only manageable because they've administered some very strong pain medication upon my arrival.

It is evening before a surgeon finally comes to explain that not only have I severely dislocated my elbow (hence the donut hole where my funny bone should have been), but I've also managed to break bones in multiple places along the arm. I require immediate surgery to mitigate the danger of losing circulation to my hand. The extent of the damage won't be known until he gets a closer look, but first we have to wait for the arrival of some artificial parts the surgeon may need to cobble it all back together. Through a cloud of pain medication, I joke with him about my transformation into a bionic woman.

Just after midnight, I'm finally rolled into the surgery room. Many hours later, I wake to the strong scent of a man's aftershave, which has the effect of smelling salts, forcing me to consciousness despite a thick haze of lingering anaesthetic.

"Well, I used some nails and wire to put you back together, but I didn't make you bionic," says the voice as I try to force my eyes open. "You're in a removable half cast for a couple weeks so you don't make any sudden moves while things settle into place, but you'll need to start moving that joint within two weeks if you hope to regain any range of motion." By the waves of aftershave that are assaulting my sense of smell, I suspect he is moving his arms around to demonstrate his point.

"Thanks for taking the night shift, doc," I blink, trying to make eye contact, but the greater demand for more sleep makes everything blurry. It dawns on me that he likely hasn't slept at all, so I forgive him for the aftershave, hoping against hope as I drift off again that I didn't actually say that last part out loud.

When I'm home again (after three exceedingly uncomfortable days in the hospital) and the bandages have been removed, my youngest daughter counts the staples that run like a curved railway line down the outer part of my arm. "Thirty-nine!" she shouts confidently, having counted it twice. One more and it would have matched my age, I muse, perhaps a cautionary reminder that no one over forty should attempt to stand on a fitness ball.

As the weeks pass, I am confronted by just how much this injury affects my daily life, especially since it is my dominant right arm that I've injured. I have to learn how to wield a knife, blow dry my hair, type, and clothe myself using only my left hand. I can't open jars or tie my shoes, let alone fasten my own bra. While I have no trouble holding cutlery in my left hand to transfer food to my mouth, I can't seem to taste the food I am eating. The first time I awkwardly spoon soup to my lips using my shaky right arm and can finally taste the broth, I gasp in relief. It is like finally coming home again in my body when I am able to taste flavours delivered by the familiar limb.

I spend months allowing a physiotherapist to push and turn and pull on my arm as tears stream down my face. She hands me tissues as she stretches the scar tissue forming around my joints, reminding me that pain now will ensure the fullest range of motion later. The first time I play a simple song on the piano, able to rotate my right hand enough to greet the keys again, I know the pain during recovery has been worth it.

After a second surgery to remove the hardware that's been in my arm for eight months, I repeatedly thank the operating nurse who took the time to save the hardware for me to keep as a memento. I glue both three-inch titanium nails, the stabilizing wire bent into a figure eight, and some of the staples into the frame of a shadow box. Then I trim the x-ray image that shows all these foreign objects inside my arm to fit the see-through back wall of the frame. Holding my creation (which I dub "injury art") up to the light, I am reminded how a single moment can change the course of one's life.

As my limb continues to heal, I notice my mind attempting to elbow its way through dense emotional fog and scratchy underbrush in search of meaning and truth. However, no matter how much discomfort I feel or how strongly the winds of change howl inside of me, I am terrified by the thought of making any other huge changes in my life. I've seen how vulnerable, even helpless, I am with just one limb out of commission, and so I cling to the life I know with my other hand.

While my physical injury taught me to wake up just before the pain hit every morning, I still can't tell if I'm sleeping through the rest of my life. There are many different kinds of pain—from a broken body to a wounded heart and a restless, distorted mind—and I notice how tempting it is to focus on one kind of pain to avoid dealing with the others.

The event of smashing something to pieces is often labelled a disaster or an accident, or both, but sometimes it takes a life-altering jolt to show us how far we have drifted from ourselves. I have seen how pain teaches, but when fear makes it difficult to open our eyes wide enough, it preaches: "Wake up. Here it comes! Find the door! WAKE UP!"

KERRIE ON

I hear my name break through the buzzing thoughts in my mind. I look around and then follow the sound up to see an outline of Kerrie's lean, muscular frame and curly hair calling to me from the second-floor bedroom of her townhouse. Her front door is about twenty feet from the gate that leads into my enclosed backyard. Our daughters have worn a giddy path along those twenty feet, running from one home into the other with ease and delight over the years. They had taken to calling one another's mothers the honorary titles of "Mother Kerrie" and "Mother Klassen" (the latter more for its alliteration than for the formality of using my married last name). It was the title "mother" that made for a seamless transition of care regardless of which roof they were playing under on a given day.

The sun is climbing higher in the summer sky, and I can feel sweat begin to form along my hairline. Framed by the shadow of her dark room in stark contrast to the bright sun outside, Kerrie is standing in her open window stroking her cat as it wanders from one side of the sill to the other.

"I'm on my way to the pool. Do you want to join me?" I ask, sensing by her tone that she's having a challenging day. Kerrie's daughters, only a year apart and on the cusp of becoming teenagers, are currently in Japan visiting their father. He and Kerrie had met when she worked in Japan for a few years; when their relationship ended, she came back to Canada but maintained a strong bond with the girls' father, who came for regular visits. Now that the girls are old enough, Kerrie drops them at the airport in Vancouver and they find their dad waiting for them on the other side of the Pacific Ocean.

Trying to decipher the expression on Kerrie's face, I add, "I find the cool water really clears my head." She doesn't resist the suggestion, but she also doesn't seem convinced. The majority of the people at the pool on a Friday afternoon will be other moms with their children. By mid-July, the daily rhythm of neighbourhood moms and kids gathering around the pool on a hot afternoon is well established. But without her girls, who won't be returning from Japan for another week, I know it's a long shot that Kerrie will join me today.

I adjust the towel under my arm, scrambling to come up with another way to support my friend, my neighbour, my daughter's other mother. Kerrie and her girls moved into the neighbourhood about six years ago. I met Kerrie's mom first when she knocked on my door, asking if she could borrow a measuring tape. She was helping Kerrie and her girls move in and invited me over to meet them. I felt an instant ease with Kerrie as she shuffled boxes around the room, taking measurements while she chatted with me. Kerrie appeared skillful and fearless. As a single working mom, she seemed content—even excited—with how life was unfolding for her and her daughters.

Our townhouse complex is a great mix of families of every description, many of whom hail from exotic parts of the world. I was pregnant, holding the hand of my three-year-old daughter, Laura, as a real estate agent walked me around Glenacres Village the first time. I could easily imagine my children marching off to the elementary school that was located right next door to this complex. When I saw the large pool and playground at the centre of a web of walking paths that connected all 141 units within the village, I knew I had found a perfect home for our growing family.

There were always lots of kids in the neighbourhood to play

with, but when Kerrie moved in next door, my daughter, Sara, had an instant best friend in Shasta, Kerrie's older daughter, who was also in the first grade. Shasta and Sara escorted each other to school and played together after school anytime they didn't have sports practices or lessons to attend. They shared an adoration, bordering on obsession, for Polly Pockets and cooed over the miniature plastic dolls that could be purchased with every imaginable accessory. They played for hours at a time, huddled over their latest imaginary Polly world until one of them let out a squeal at the other's suggestion to see who might be playing on the swings or drawing a hopscotch in colourful chalk on the walkways between the homes. They thrived in each other's company and negotiated their playtime so effortlessly that neither mother minded having them in their home or coming along on family trips.

Kerrie was a trained massage therapist, and I made appointments to receive a few deep tissue massages over the years if I pushed myself too hard on long bicycle rides. We felt comfortable asking each other for favours and would always take time to catch up anytime we saw each other coming and going. Most of our visits happened spontaneously, leaned up against each other's doorways as we tried, and usually failed, to extract the daughter who was supposed to come home to sleep in her own bed on the other side of the pathway.

By the time the girls' ages reached double digits, Kerrie simply stood at her front door, placed her fingers to her mouth and blasted her distinctive whistle. The sound carried to the far corners of the large complex and even to the schoolyard next door, and the girls knew it was time to return home from wherever they were playing.

"You sure you don't want to join me at the pool?" I press Kerrie one more time. I've only seen her a few times in the last six months, as I've been adjusting to a new rhythm after my debilitating elbow injury. Just managing to dress myself and keep the household going between running to my physiotherapy appointments and doing all the daily exercises required for rehabilitation seems to take up all my time. It feels like half a year has passed me by while life went on outside my walls. Looking up at her now, I can't help but feel a bit guilty, like I've let her down when she needed a friend, despite the fact that I was barely coming up for air myself. I prided myself on being a friend who would drop everything to listen if someone needed to talk.

"I would love some company as I do my arm exercises in the water. Or we could just sit and put our feet in the pool to cool off," I try again, angling for a suggestion she might bite at. Kerrie continues to stroke her cat but doesn't say anything. She seems distracted and distant.

Attempting to close the space I feel separating us, I gush, "Kerrie, I hope you know how much our friendship means to me. Please know I'm here if you need me—but you probably know by now I'm not the type of friend who will bang your door down." I want her to know that I respect her privacy and will never pressure her. Even so, it feels like a strange disclaimer as it comes out of my mouth.

This is the last time I see Kerrie alive.

The weekend passes in a flurry of family activities. My husband, Tom, works long hours during the week, and we reserve summer weekends for family fun. Although it is threatening to rain, we follow through with our plans to attend a Lantern Festival on Saturday evening. The free event, put on by local artists, welcomes all who attend to snake their way around a small man-made lake carrying any kind of homemade light. Cheese graters fashioned into lanterns make the event accessible for less artsy types, and it gets impressively more creative from there. As the darkness settles in, the crowd thickens and we sit on a blanket to watch the magical parade of light. We vow to create our own lantern and join the parade next year.

After attending our regular Sunday morning church service the following day, we spend the rest of the day at a friend's place and finally tumble into bed when the air has cooled again by the gentle breeze off the Pacific Ocean.

On Monday morning, I spy the parking lot through my kitchen window. The lot is a large square, and the townhomes all look out at the parked cars. In one glance, I can see who is home since I know who parks in each designated space. Kerrie's space is in front of our window and our spot is beside hers, in a direct line to our front door. I notice that the distinctive angle of her tires, an unusual way for her to park, hasn't changed from last week. I dial her number but it goes directly to voicemail. When the recorded message claims her voicemail is full, it occurs to me that she may be in worse shape than I thought if she isn't even picking up her messages. With an uneasy feeling swirling in my gut, I decide to wander over.

As I approach Kerrie's place, I see that her screen door is closed but the front door is wide open. I call out to her through the screen. When I don't hear a response, my mind tries to rationalize: Maybe she's just napping in her bedroom upstairs. I feel uncomfortable entering her place without an invitation, afraid of startling her, so I stand there a little longer, aware of a growing list of competing thoughts in my head. I call out one more time and then slowly back away from her doorway and return home. Like the first notes of eerie music in a scary movie, something just feels off. However, considering that my whole life feels off and has for some time already, I chastise myself for letting my imagination run wild, already anticipating how silly I'll feel when I see Kerrie next and hear her logical explanation.

I decide I'll bring over a container of the food I plan on making for dinner, which will give me a good reason to go back and check on her. I begin to chop vegetables for the curry, knowing I only have a few minutes before the muscles in my right arm begin to cramp and any wrong move will cause pain to shoot along the length of my arm. Everything still takes longer and hurts more. I recall that Kerrie has had a challenging year as well. She arrived home from a visit to her father's side of the family a few provinces over with stitches from where a dog had attacked her face. I could tell it was an unnerving experience when she told me about it. The physical attack seemed to unearth discomfort in other areas of her life. I hadn't put it together at the time, but it wasn't long after that that Kerrie began to call me on the phone, which wasn't how we normally communicated. She was uncharacteristically uncertain about where Shasta would get the best high school education the following year, and she seemed nervous about life in general. I had never known her to be indecisive or worried about being a good mom before this, and so I invited her to go for a walk so we could talk in person.

On that walk, I noticed Kerrie's usual easy smile had been replaced with tired eyes that darted around as she spoke. Her laugh tittered with a nervousness that hadn't been there before. She confided that she was seeing a therapist and had recently filled a prescription for medication. I was taken aback by how different she seemed and realized that I hadn't seen her very often since my fortieth birthday party this past winter.

With the curry finally ready, I dial Kerrie's number again and get the same message about her full voicemail. Just then, Tom returns home from work and I share my uneasiness with him. We hatch a plan to go over together after we finish dinner—and in case Kerrie is in a state of undress, we decide I will go in first to avoid possible embarrassment.

Kerrie's door is still open as we arrive, so I call out to her again—and again get no response. This time I open the screen door and walk in. The sensation that spent the afternoon swirling in my gut now swells into my chest. I notice that I'm holding my breath, causing me to gasp as I continue to call her name. After checking for her on the main floor, I head toward the stairs. Her meowing cats, who seem to be trying to communicate something, keep walking between my legs, and I have to watch to avoid stepping on their paws. As I approach the second landing, I spy an open book and a picture beside it. My mind concocts the logical story that she had been reading on this landing and simply abandoned the open book there. On closer inspection, the book is an encyclopedia, open to the letter S. The picture beside the book is a blurry black-and-white image of a young girl. There are other pictures hanging on the walls of the stairwell, and I reason that the picture must have fallen off the wall.

The pulsing sensation in my body has now invaded my head, making it hard to think. My legs are moving, but my breath is coming out in short spurts. Despite a fierce desire to turn back, I feel an equally strong need to go toward my friend, who might need me more than ever.

I step over the book. I call her name. I make the final turn on the stairway. I look up. I stop. I can't make out what I am seeing. My eyes trace the shape hanging through the access hatch to the attic. It looks like a piñata. Overstuffed legs. Toes painted red. Kerrie must be around the corner in her bedroom. What is this obstacle in my path to her?

I feel like I am watching an old Western, filmed in low-quality black and white, and as the picture flickers and zooms in on the hanging object, it appears to be swaying in the wind. In the next instant, or possibly many flickers later, all devoid of any additional oxygen, it becomes crushingly clear what I am seeing.

Fear, like a cold blast of arctic wind, rips through my body and threatens to knock me down. I turn to retreat, but my legs aren't working properly, and I struggle to navigate the stairs. I attempt to call out to my husband, who is waiting at the front door, but like in most nightmares, my voice doesn't work. I try again more forcefully and a sound escapes, more like wailing than words, as I lunge towards the front door.

Tom doesn't wait to ask what I've just witnessed as he rushes past me, taking the stairs two at a time. He knows something terrible has happened by the sound he heard coming out of me. An eternity passes as I stand just outside the front door, waiting for him to return. I feel frozen in place and can't think up a single idea of what to do next.

As a truck driver, Tom has learned how to switch into crisis mode from years of coming upon horrific accidents in the middle of the night. He dials 911 and says words into his phone as I stand there wondering why my brain isn't syncing up to what is happening in real time. The shock of seeing something I couldn't possibly have prepared myself to see is forcing my body to pump out chemicals that alternatively numb and then heighten the sights and sounds around me. My eyes burn as if I haven't slept in days, and my throat is parched.

Sirens scream their way into our quiet parking lot. The entire square fills up with a snaking line of emergency vehicles, their flashing lights bouncing off the white exterior of the townhomes in a dizzying lightshow. Neighbours venture out of their homes and stand in small groups talking in low voices, trying to make sense of what is happening in their sleepy suburb.

Suddenly, my daughter Sara is standing beside me, breathless from having run from the playground to see what all the noise is about. Through the dense fog in my mind and nausea churning in my stomach, I search frantically for a way to explain the situation without unduly traumatizing her. The news that Kerrie, her Mother Kerrie, is no longer alive doubles Sara over. Between sobs, she claws at me to know how and why. I haven't had time to think, and I stare at her blankly as she keeps pleading for answers. I cannot fathom ever saying out loud how Kerrie died, and I have no idea why she's gone.

A police officer approaches me to confirm that I am the person who discovered the body. He requires a statement from me, and as he closes the passenger door of his car, it creates a wall of protection from the chaos outside. He types my answers to his questions into a computer that's attached to the centre console of the vehicle. His novice-level typing skills allow time for my breathing to calm as I wait for the next question. His tone is even, and he seems to understand how to address a witness who has a hard enough time remembering her own name under the circumstances, let alone answer questions that have no answers.

Did you suspect that she was suicidal? "No," I answer, wincing at the s word. But in my mind I begin to wonder: *Did she seem any more suicidal than the times I have allowed myself to imagine ending the pain that gnaws at me?*

I look out the window of the police car and see Kerrie's car still parked in its usual spot. Her pain was obviously insurmountable, but I didn't understand that when I tried to get her to come to the pool a few days ago. My mind tries to build a bridge between what I just saw and what that means. I can't imagine my world without Kerrie and her girls. There must have been something I could have done differently or said better. Now it's too late. The only conclusion I am able to reach at the moment is that I must be a bad neighbour and a selfish friend.

"Does she usually leave her front door open?" the cop interrupts my inner tirade with his next question.

"I'm not sure," I respond. "Probably in the summer for air flow when it's hot. That's what I do." Again, thoughts follow in my head that I don't say out loud: *Or did she leave it open because I told her that I wouldn't bang her door down? Did she leave her door open for me? Was I supposed to find her?!*

By the time I finish answering questions, the coroner has arrived as well as a team of trauma response volunteers. My home becomes the central gathering location. Kerrie's mom arrives some time later and is ushered onto my couch, where the trauma specialists share what they can about what has happened. Tea is made and water is offered to those of us in varying states of shock. I'm not sure from moment to moment what my role is, especially since everyone is in my home. My body needs to sit, but my mind wants something to do other than replaying the horrific scene over and over in my mind.

Just after midnight, before everyone leaves, I arrange for a member of the trauma team to come back to my place the following week to chat with the neighbourhood kids who knew Kerrie and are friends with her daughters. I cross my fingers that this specialist will be able to help cage the monsters that these twelve-year-olds are facing from this experience.

Death is part of life, but the manner in which a loved one exits can make the grief process more tumultuous. The shock and surprise of finding Kerrie is undeniably traumatic. The images haunt me at night and quiver inside my body during the day. In an instant, the world has become a frightening place. It seems like, at any moment, gruesome death or unnecessary destruction may cross my path again. When I do sleep, I have nightmares of being assaulted and worse. I can't watch TV shows that contain violence of any kind. The first time I watch a movie where a hanging body is displayed without warning, I almost throw up. Finding Kerrie felt like a brutal beating, and although the bruising doesn't show on my skin, it has invaded every corner of my being.

A recurring thought taunts me on my darker days. The coroner's report confirms that while I was talking to Kerrie at her bedroom window, she already had all the equipment she would need to end the pain of living that night. If I couldn't see how much pain she was in, could I trust where my current distress might lead me?

Between my debilitating elbow and this devastating loss only six months apart, I don't have any reserve left in my spirit. I struggle to anchor my racing thoughts and eventually accept an offer to attend a counselling session with a trauma specialist. Losing a friend is one thing; discovering a friend's body as you're losing her is quite another. I need help. The set of beliefs I grew up with regarding life and death doesn't seem to extend into this dark terrain.

After some time, I find ways to pin this traumatic event against a larger story: I met a woman named Kerrie when she moved in next door. She loved her daughters. She loved my daughter. She laughed with me. She massaged my sore body. She was fearless and yet overwhelmed by life. She was skillful at living and at planning her exit. She could whistle louder than anyone I'd ever met and couldn't make enough noise to call for help. And in one culminating discovery, her end became indelibly imprinted into my ongoing story.

The finality of her decision has left a lasting impression. I have seen how things could go. And I know, with even more urgency, that aspects of my life need to change if I don't want to find myself in a similar position one day. Kerrie has become a consuming cautionary tale, whether I wanted one or not.

When summer comes to an end, the neighbourhood is still trying to come to grips with the fear and sadness of Kerrie's loss. Along with a group of other moms within the community, I wrestle with how to move forward and restore some hope alongside the confusion for ourselves and our children. Kerrie's family is ready to put her townhouse on the market, and I worry that it will become known as a "haunted house" if we don't figure out a way to bring it back into the light.

Recalling the Lantern Festival I attended on the weekend I last saw Kerrie, I shiver at the realization that even as I was watching the parade of lights miles away, Kerrie's spirit was no longer in her body back at her home. We decide to hold a Celebration of Light in Kerrie's honour at her house. Although I struggle to imagine how I will rally to celebrate, I also understand that those of us who are still alive are now charged with finding a way to do justice to the memory of this dynamic woman.

Invitations go out to everyone we can think of who was impacted by her loss. As friends and family, teachers and residents from the complex arrive at the front door of Kerrie's home, they are given instructions along with a waxed paper bag, a tealight, and some crayons to use. Each person is encouraged to write a note or draw a picture on their bag that helps them say goodbye to Kerrie. Then the bag is filled with sand and the candle is lit inside it.

The pathway to her front door is soon lined with rows of glowing bags. Eventually, there are enough bags to line the side of her house, which is also the pathway to the elementary school, where every child from the complex will soon pass on their walk to school. Kerrie's family—including her daughters, who have returned from Japan—welcome everyone who wants to come into the house. The mourners wish them well as they embark on the next part of their journey without their mom, their sister, their daughter. The colourful bags filled with light and the enduring spirit of those who have come that day help reclaim Kerrie's home and reintegrate it into the community.

Some time later, I linger over the pictures I took of the lights that lined the path to Kerrie's door. The door that my daughter ran through, bursting at the seams to share her latest treasure with Shasta. The door that opened into the world of a woman who lived well until she could live no more. The door that changed my life, the door that I wouldn't bang down and so she left it open. She couldn't have known I'd be the one to find her, but I think she knew I would come. It was a horror of the worst kind and an honour of the highest order.

HAPPY HUSBAND

A loaded semi-truck always takes more time than you'd think to rev the engine high enough to slide it into the next gear. One can easily review a year of your life between first and second gear. After that, it speeds up exponentially. Grinding through the gears, as the truckers call it, without damaging the engine is the difference between a seasoned trucker and, well, the trucker's version of "the other guy"—language a trucker can use but a nice girl shouldn't repeat.

My husband is a seasoned truck driver with a lean body, kempt appearance, and lack of foul language squarely at odds with the image of a typical trucker. Over the years, I've joined him on countless "nightruns," which are basically backhaul night shifts. The loaded rig leaves the warehouse at the end of the day, and then trailers are exchanged in the middle of the night with a driver coming down from his warehouse in the north, and they each return to their respective yards in time to unload the following morning. When the girls were young, I'd drop them at my parents' house, an hour inland, and Tom would pick me up on his way through. It felt like a combination of a date night, an impromptu road trip we didn't have to pay for, and a much-needed break from parenting all wrapped into one. In many ways, I preferred this time with my husband over having dinner in a fancy restaurant. The fact that I could put my feet up on the extra-large dash and enjoy the ever-changing scenery meant I was more comfortable here than trying to make small talk on wobbly restaurant chairs (and it was also easier on the budget, especially after you added in the cost of a babysitter). Once the girls got a little older, they were invited to go along on runs with their dad as well and would eventually crawl into the sleeper berth when they got tired. They always came home brimming with stories of deer in the headlights (one time with a tragic ending) and all the special late-night snacks they had shared with their dad.

On this particular ride-along, only half a year since I fell off the ball, I position my foot onto the grated step, grab the bar with my good arm, and hoist my body sideways into the passenger's side of the truck. I had to think through how I was going to climb up today, as my slowly healing elbow isn't nearly ready to grab anything, let alone pull me into the cab. Tom stands behind me and assists with a gentle push. Chivalry is one defining aspect of his character, and he regularly supports anyone who crosses his path, regardless of their gender or station in life. I just happen to have had more opportunities to receive his kind attention because we've been married for more than twenty years.

Tom hops with ease into the driver's side of the truck and adjusts his seat, the last in a long list of safety and comfort protocols he follows. His smile, even bigger than the one that is readily available for anyone he meets, affirms how happy he is that I'm coming along on this run up the canyon. My presence means that it feels less like work because he's not away from his family, and it also breaks up the monotony of doing the same route five nights a week. Having a rider along helps him stay alert over the long miles, most of them in the dark. He leaves the city around suppertime and arrives home in the wee hours of the morning, sleeping while the girls are in school. It's a schedule and an income that have worked well enough for our family for many years.

I push my head against my headrest so it's out of the way as I watch Tom's eyes dart from mirror to mirror on both sides of the cab as he makes the first sweeping turn out of the yard. The long, loaded trailer follows at an angle that takes years to execute precisely—and even then, things can happen between the tractor rolling by and the last trailer tires making their pass. Turns that start well can still end badly. But Tom is vigilant and takes the responsibility of driving a big rig seriously. He is the same in every other aspect of his life.

The engine roars loudly between gears, so the volume of our conversation must rise to match—but I feel too tired to yell. Once the engine hums along at highway speed, it will be easier to modulate my voice. I don't mind sitting quietly, watching the world fly by from this vantage point. The height of the truck affords me an expansive sightline through the picture-window windshield. Life feels more manageable at this height with time to see what's coming down the road, but in an emergency, it takes longer to bring a truck to a complete stop because of its size and weight. Can I see far enough down my own road to make timely decisions after forty years of life? With no obvious answers flashing like the neon signs that dot the cityscape we're moving through, I release a heavy sigh that no one hears in the noisy cab, not even me. I adjust my seat and settle in for a long ride into the night with my happy husband at the wheel.

It reminds me of a time when we were still teenagers, before we started dating, when I sat beside him on the bench seat of a large older-model car, stuffed full with mutual friends from Bible school. Tom agreed to drive to a Christmas party, and I was only offered the front seat because of my tendency to feel carsick in the back. It was a blustery night, and in typical West Coast fashion, the snow falling was heavy and wet as the temperature hovered around freezing. When the car's defrosting system couldn't keep up with the snow accumulating on the windshield, Tom pulled over and got out to beat snow off the wipers. As I watched the cold wind whip snow into his face, I noticed how safe I felt being in a car with him at the helm, not only because of his skillful driving but also because of the way he saw what needed to be done and was willing to do it without complaint. Watching him through the windshield, I could easily imagine an entire life with this easy-going guy who was willing to be uncomfortable for the safety and comfort of his passengers. A month after that snowy drive, he became my boyfriend.

Tonight, as the truck barrels through the Fraser Valley and the sun sets behind us, green stalks laden with cobs of corn sway in the breeze on the side of the highway. This valley is where he and I met, dated, and lived when we were first married—the same valley where I was born and grew up.

"Do you want to listen to the audiobook I brought along or chat for a while?" I ask, knowing that we have many hours together and there is no hurry to do either.

"Let's start the book, unless you feel like chatting." His answer completes the circle, leaving the same options open. Things are generally easy between us because he is exceptionally flexible, to the point of sometimes feeling spongy to the touch. Tom is the proverbial soft place to land, but this feature makes it difficult to get a firm answer out of him most of the time. As I've aged, I notice that I am drawn to people one might equate to a good french fry. When you bite into them, they confidently reveal their soft interior, while their exterior has the satisfying crunch of a defined personality.

I extract the first cassette tape in the series from its plastic case. I signed out this audiobook from the library earlier in the week, knowing I'd be coming along on a nightrun. Tom has listened to most of the audiobook selections available at our local library over the years. It's a great way to pass time on the road. He prefers stories that involve action or mystery to stimulate his senses and keep him awake. Today, I sold him on this one because the book had been recommended by one of our friends. It's a true story of an English couple who move to France, sharing all the foibles and fascinations of this new country.

"A Year In Provence," announces the voice at the start of the tape as I turn the volume higher to account for the drone of the engine. I'm hoping to be transported to a place I've never been and can't imagine I'll ever end up seeing in my lifetime.

Early on in our marriage, Tom and I chatted about taking a trip to Europe to celebrate our upcoming graduation from theological college, but a couple weeks later, we discovered I was pregnant with our first child. A European trip was never discussed again. Navigating countries with different foods and strange cultures had felt a bit unnerving to me anyway. Having been raised in a conservative-minded faith community, we didn't always understand the customs of our own country, let alone how to behave on the other side of the world.

On our honeymoon to Vancouver Island, a short ferry ride from our home, I had gushed to our waiter that we were newly married, and he had taken that as an opportunity to make the night special for us. Halfway through dinner, the man in charge of the music announced that there were newlyweds in the house and invited us up to the dance floor. Tom glared at me, then looked down at his food, hoping that if we didn't move or make eye contact, the man would stop calling on us. Neither of us knew how to dance, let alone how to slow-dance in front of people. In fact, growing up in Mennonite churches, we had been forbidden from dancing. We made it through the meal but left without ordering dessert. As we walked back to our hotel, Tom made me promise not to tell anyone else that we were on our honeymoon so we wouldn't find ourselves in another awkward situation. While I may have secretly longed to be with a man who could swirl me around a dance floor with confidence, I could hardly blame Tom for his request of me. We were both barely twenty years old and inexperienced in the ways of the world, and neither of us had learned how to navigate the larger world with confidence or sophistication. We were in this together, and with little impetus to veer too far from our traditional roots, we began to build a world that felt familiar.

When the first tape in the audiobook clicks to the end, the author's dry English humour as he describes their foray into French cuisine makes us hungry for more. As the truck starts to climb the first of many hills, I realize that Tom and I are twice as old as when we first married. We have learned how to adapt to a lot of things, but never on the other side of the globe.

"Do you ever wonder what our life would have been like if we would have chosen a wildly different path and gone to Europe instead of starting a family when we did?" I ask, having a hard time envisioning a life path that doesn't involve our teen-aged daughters sleeping over at their friends' tonight as dusk makes its descent and the truck's headlights cut through the dying light.

Ever practical and seemingly happy with what life offers instead of longing for something different, Tom just shrugs. We are so similar in many ways, with our common heritage and the way we both prioritize relationships over accumulating possessions. Neither of us requires grand adventures or expensive stuff. Where we differ greatly, however, is in our happiness quotient. Tom appears happy to follow rules, make the best of a situation, and work hard to provide for his family. In comparison to him, I often feel lazy, selfish, and ungrateful. I try to view the world through his eyes, and while I can go through the motions, it feels like I'm following a well-written script instead of something true inside of me. I watch him for hints that perhaps he's pretending too, even once in a while, but he genuinely appears happy with life.

I was initially drawn to Tom because he seemed undaunted by the things that weigh down most people. If challenges arise, he just works harder and longer and smiles faster and wider. He isn't superhuman, but his superpower is that he always seems to be able to rally. He'll fall asleep exhausted and wake up revived and ready to meet the next day. While I respect the infinite positivity, instead of being inspired by it, I'm growing to resent it.

The next cassette tape clicks over to its second side, the couple in France still desperate to unlock the secret of how to communicate effectively with local tradespeople to ensure the insufficient plumbing in their house will finally be fixed. They are realizing that simply knowing how to speak French phrases isn't enough and that they need to understand the nuance and cultural innuendo behind the words exchanged.

I grew up in a church where the literal translation of a scriptural text was valued above all. This literal translation was funnelled through the minds and hearts of immigrants who had literally lived through war and lost their homeland. My childhood was indelibly shaped by how this traumatized community viewed women, marriage, and life's purpose. My family operated under the principle that one's words, not feelings, were taken as truth. This made it easy to understand and regurgitate the rules but exceptionally difficult to translate one's own burgeoning thoughts and internal reactions to the rules. Tom and I both value digging deeper and talking through the complexities of life, but where we differ is in what we believe it means. He seems content with what he finds upon initial inspection. I continue to pry open an idea in search of another layer that feels closer to what my gut suspects might be a fuller truth. My antsy mind runs around in circles looking for answers from all available angles. I come away looking discontent in part because I live with someone who seems so perfectly content. It isn't anyone's fault, but it is beginning to create a faultline in our relationship.

I can't recall a time when I didn't question everything, and much of this took place in secret. This was even true on our wedding night. Entrenched in our religious upbringing, we had agreed to wait until we were officially married before engaging in intercourse. When the wedding night finally arrived, we were too exhausted to figure out why it wasn't easier to complete our union. We were a tumble of limbs and desire, but also a fatigue so deep that our bodies just gave up. The next morning, there was renewed determination to consummate our nuptials. Later, in the shower, a nagging thought I didn't know how to quiet kept asking whether that experience was worth waiting for. We had had countless nights before this where it felt nearly impossible to resist the magnetic urgency between us, where my guilt-ridden pleas to halt further exploration of each other's bodies kept us from completing the final act. Although Tom claimed to take our commitment to wait seriously, he seemed comfortable letting me pump the brakes, knowing how tightly I clung to the code that it is ultimately the woman's responsibility to maintain her virginal purity.

Throughout our honeymoon, I continued to wonder if our union would have felt more satisfying, more celebratory, if we'd have ridden the natural wave of desire to its fullest expression instead of waiting for a staged night of permission. Were the rules we'd agreed to follow in opposition to a more natural wisdom? I now felt something itchy layered into the sheets of our new marriage bed. It took me a bit to realize it was the feeling of obligation. Overnight, the yearning for sexual exploration flipped over into the expectation to have sex. It was my duty now. I had secretly hoped that marriage would be a way to finally have independence. This fresh layer of obligation, in addition to my lack of experience and knowledge about my own body, made it feel like I had even less say over my life.

"How's it going over there?" My voice calls him back from the enchanting French countryside.

Tom chuckles, as he routinely does. It's his way with everyone, whether in person or on the phone. It's a soft chuckle accompanied by that easy smile of his, the one that immediately endears him to people. The chuckle also buys him a few more seconds to gather his thoughts before he has to say any words.

"All good here," he responds to my question. I could have placed a bet on that being his response.

His consistency provides a sense of safety. There's a formidable stability in the certainty he provides. But it also enhances the feeling that we're onstage. While I appreciate the kindness he proffers through his demeanour, as the years go by, part of me wonders if it may also be a highly polished veneer. I sniff a quiet desperation beneath the layers of his good intention, but I truly cannot be certain I'm right about that. The fact that I'm not sure is slowly picking at the seams of my trust in myself. And this pervasive doubt turns up the volume on just how unkind and pathetic I feel much of the time. Ironically, the less happy I feel, the more happy Tom appears. It's almost like we maintain our balance as a couple by holding each other's wedding-ringed hands while leaning outwards into the extreme edges of ourselves as we spin around. Some might see that as impressive teamwork, but after playing one role for too long, I slowly cannot recognize the rest of myself anymore. I begin to believe I truly am this less happy version, committed to this swirling vortex for the rest of my life.

Our trailer is fully loaded but pretty light on the way out tonight. We easily pass another semi going up a long hill. He's pulling a flatbed trailer, and I can see through my window that he's carrying a massive piece of machinery. From years of observation, even when the trailer is enclosed, I've learned to notice the weight of a load by listening to how hard the engine is working, especially on the hills. And I've seen the tragic result of what can happen if a load shifts because it wasn't secured or positioned properly over the wheels.

Even when we can see what people are going through or hear the pain in their voices, we can still only guess at what it's really like to be behind the wheel of their life. Sometimes our lives are fully loaded and we have a lot on our plate; other times we carry weighty responsibilities that aren't actually ours, putting us in danger of skidding off the road. I hear myself tell and retell my stories to close friends, grinding through a lengthy list of my struggles, attempting to convince others and myself that my feelings of confusion and heavy-heartedness regarding my relationship are justified. I surmise that my load must have shifted over the years because it takes far too much effort to get up in the morning. It's not that I doubt that I married a good man, but I'm increasingly sure that I'm not good at being his wife.

I crunch on a carrot as the truckers complete the switch of their trailers. It's pitch dark outside, and Tom has shrugged on greasy overalls and donned his forehead flashlight in order to unhook the rig from the trailer we just hauled up the canyon. As he backs up the tractor to hook up with the new trailer, there's always a distinct resistance as the engine revs in reverse to force the truck's fifth wheel to clamp around the trailer's pin. It's called coupling, but no one even buys the new trailer a drink first.

Over the course of our marriage, Tom has been a thoughtful, patient husband. He recently admitted that for every ten invitations for sexual intimacy—invitations delivered through words or a touch or a look—he calculated he would get one favourable response from me. He reasoned all he had to do was complete nine invitations to be granted access to my body. His enthusiasm and persistence were impressive, but the approaches he used often left me feeling pestered or handled. I wasn't doing math ratios in my head, but I also had a sense of when my excuses to put him off had run thin. I struggled to find ways to get ahead of the requests, to prepare myself so that my participation wasn't fueled only by obligation. I didn't mind doing household chores because they simply needed to get done, but it pained me to feel that way about my sex life.

Tom says that for him, touch is an easy way to confirm the love he feels for me. But when I receive his touch, my first instinct is to swat his hand away like a mosquito. Knowing that will hurt his feelings, I regularly freeze my response in order to allow the interaction. But then I remain frozen, unable to feel the connection. It wasn't always that way. Over the years there were many times our lovemaking found its way to a well of passion despite my initial resistance. I wish I could find my way back to that well these days. I had hoped that if I could ignite my own individual passions and interests, then we could be happy enough together. But that approach seems to have gone cold as well.

While Tom exchanges paperwork with the other driver, I amuse myself with the thought of the rather one-sided relationship between trucks and trailers. Arguably, they're a perfect couple. There would be no point in owning a rig, or tractor as it's often called, if you don't plan on hauling something somewhere. However, a trailer can be used in many other ways that don't involve being pulled all over God's green earth. Some trailers are used for storage, and lately they are also being transformed into modular homes. Most people seem happy to "couple up." It only seems natural, and I had no reason to think I wasn't one of them. But I'm beginning to wonder if I'm more of a stationary trailer at heart.

Tom climbs back into the cab, and I feel the subtle shift in his energy. He always appears at ease, but once the trailer switch is complete he relaxes into his seat more deeply. The rest of the night is all about getting back home. As our marriage continues into the end of its second decade, no matter what is happening in our life together and no matter how upsetting it is, Tom just whistles more. It seems like the heavier I feel, the softer he walks and the more he whistles—and the lighter his gait, the faster my world spins. I reach out, hoping to grab onto something solid in an attempt to make genuine contact with the guy behind the whistling face. But many times, my arm feels like it continues through his body and out the other side of him with no perceivable change in his smile. I'm beginning to feel like I am living with a perfectly programmed holographic husband.

It sounds pleasant enough, I suppose, but it also has the effect of leaving me constantly guessing. If he's pretending even half of the time in order to protect me, which half of him can I actually trust is real? Was I the one who programmed him?! And since I seem incapable of knowing which way is up within this dynamic, have I lost access to my own true instincts as well?

Static from his radio squawks into the dark cab. He lifts the receiver and rambles off a string of words (because truckers don't just say "Hello?" like you would when a phone rings). His finger releases the button on the mic, and almost immediately a voice mumbles something back. Tom lets the other trucker, who is looking for conversation to beat back the boredom, know that he's got a rider in the truck and inserts the mic back into its metal cradle without looking. It's the type of movement that takes time and repetition to create that kind of seamless muscle memory. I wonder if marriage eventually develops muscle memory so that habits turn into a reflex that overrides what the heart really wants to say.

I tilt my head, looking out my side window at a patch of night sky. The moon slowly appears from behind the edge of the mountain and sprays light onto the other side of the valley. This stretch of canyon highway snakes its way along a river where steep rock cliffs line one side of the road and it drops straight down to the water on the other side. There's virtually no room for error in a big truck, and Tom anticipates each curve in the road with the ease and the precision of someone who could almost do it with his eyes closed but wouldn't be foolish enough to ever attempt that.

Is it possible that navigating through marriage can be as treacherous as this road but that everyday mundane tasks put us into a trance? That peck on the cheek when arriving home, that familiar debate about who last took out the garbage—do all these micro-moments of daily life melt into numbing repetition? In the beginning, it's all new and every moment is a fresh opportunity to think about what kind of life you want to create. But as the miles on a marriage click on, like the treads on a truck's tires, is the health of a marriage actually in increasing danger? When I think about adding another twenty years to the ones Tom and I have already been together, something deep inside me shudders and balks.

I look up at the almost-full moon, inhale a steadying breath and exhale it against the window, causing it to fog up in the shape of a teardrop. There are no towns at least half an hour's drive in either direction, so besides the small focused beam from the truck's headlights, it's the ageless, brilliant moon that is lighting up the full length of the canyon. She highlights the dapple on the river and the jagged crags on the surrounding mountains. This heavenly orb appears to be holding court. I feel small within this dramatic moment and also honoured to witness this haunting beauty.

Tom must have noticed me staring at the moon because the next moment the truck's headlights flick off. The contrast of the breathtaking display intensifies, and I let out a gasp. I'm no longer aware of being in a truck with my husband. I am an interconnected part of the whole universe and its timelessness. My heartbeat slows as I drift amidst a widening chasm of wonder and awe and some other sensations I cannot immediately identify.

By the light of the moon, this expansive feeling brings hope, but that's not a new feeling. It's not even a new approach. I've followed hope in an attempt to find the trailhead of happiness many other times. I've painted my walls. I've done yoga. I've taught yoga. I've joined groups. I've gone to counselling. I've gone to more counselling. I've tried to be of service to others. I've read books. I've written songs. I've talked with people I trust. I've exchanged lengthy emails with people who ignite my creativity. I've worked out. I've organized my house. I've cheered my kids on at their multiple sporting events. I've changed my hair. I've purchased bedsheets with a higher thread count. I've tried new recipes. I've made a meal plan. I've gone for long walks. I've balanced our budget. I've learned how to rollerblade. I've watched funny movies. I've listened with grace to other people's problems. I've volunteered regularly at my girls' school. I've bicycled along the river. I've lost weight. I've worked hard to find meaning. I've worked even harder to come up with new solutions when none of these things seemed to work for long.

The headlights come on and pull me back into the dark truck. I look over at Tom, who is smiling as he gears down in time for the next turn, and express my thanks. Then I pull on my shoulder strap as a feeling of hopelessness makes the seat belt feel suffocatingly tight against my neck. I'm in a familiar thought loop. It's a tunnel with no end. The moon's illuminating presence fades against my new focus on the yellow line that runs down the middle of the highway. You can go one way or the exact opposite way, there are no turnarounds on this stretch of road. The direction I am currently going leads to my home. My home, stocked with quality sheets and a calendar scribbled full of things to do, a home that houses two beautiful daughters about whom I care deeply. It is everything I would think anyone would need for a happy life. Why am I dreading my impending return home so much? There's a hollowness at the base of my heart that no amount of talking, biking, thinking, or cleaning seems to fill. Like putting lipstick on a pig, trying to change my world in small ways seems to be having the opposite effect of what I desire.

An hour from home, Tom pulls into a fueling station built exclusively for trucks. He hops out, and while the large tanks fill, he cleans the windshield. The layer of bugs that have made their final stop on the glass takes considerable effort to remove. He scrubs hard with the soapy brush to nudge away the pervasive smears. Seeing him through the windshield, doing his part so willingly, reminds me of the life I dreamed into existence so many years ago. It was all so perfectly and permanently decided when he asked me to marry him. I said yes (or I nodded up and down excitedly; I don't remember which). He was kneeling beside his older-model white MGB convertible that he had driven past the barns and into the tall grass in the back field of my family's farm. It was a simple and effective engagement. We had window shopped for my ring a few weeks earlier. The proposal wasn't really a surprise; it was an inevitability. It was exactly the narrative that I had been raised to agree with, to foster, to want. I truly believed my life was unfolding as God had intended.

Anyone who knows him agrees that Tom is a loving husband and an amazing father. If coupling up with a man like this leaves me feeling alone and sad, then something must be inherently wrong with me or with how I view life. It's a conclusion that leaves me feeling increasingly distant from him and disconnected from myself. Although he is clearly a good husband, this entire situation is far from good for me. And if both those things can be true—though admittedly it's hard to see through the splatter of thoughts this late at night—then I must be the one to make the impossible decision. Every time he looks at me, I see in his eyes that he can keep going like this indefinitely. He's as committed as anyone I've ever seen or met or imagined I could meet. He's completely committed to the commitment he made. For better or worse, and all the rest of it too.

Another rig pulls up to the pumps, and the driver blinks a few times, adjusting to the fluorescent lighting. Then he looks over at me, sitting at the same height one truck over, and gives me a slight nod. He has kind but weary eyes. He opens his door and slowly makes his descent from the cab. When both feet reach the ground, his back doesn't fully straighten, but he starts to walk anyway. His hunched posture painfully announces that he's been sitting in his truck too long, and not just today. I want him to stretch out, to bring his head up so he can look up at the stars, not just down at the dusty pavement dotted with oil stains and litter. As he makes his way around the front of his truck and disappears, I look upward for him, but my view is blocked by a high roof overhead. I wonder if the heavens beyond the roof actually know anything anyway. I have prayed and I have pleaded with God about my marriage. I have cried, and lately I have stopped crying.

There must be a way for me to see my life differently. Or there must be a way for me to be different. I can feel myself bending over a little more every day. My back is strong and flexible from yoga, but my spirit is drooping more all the time. I imagine myself jumping out of my truck and hopping into the passenger side of the other trucker's rig. We would drive in the opposite direction from my home, and he would tell me about how much his back hurts but why he can't quit this job. I would tell him how much my spirit hurts but why I can't quit my marriage. I know it wouldn't make my life any better to run away, but it might be a better match for my heart than the way I'm currently living. I think it's the mismatch—how things appear to others in contrast to how they feel inside—that makes me feel especially crazy.

Tom opens the door and climbs back inside one more time for the final stretch of road that leads us back to the yard, his ease of movement so different from the trucker I just saw. I'm aware that he and I haven't really talked the entire trip. We've shared a few observations along the way and listened to an entire audiobook, but haven't made a meaningful connection through our conversation. I've noticed when we're driving anywhere together in the car the last few years that we rarely talk. On the way to an event, it's like my mouth won't work, but when we arrive at our destination, I'm joking and chatting with everyone. The moment I buckle up in our vehicle to go home, my voice leaves me again. I can't think of anything to say. I suspect it may be because I have exactly one thing that I really need to say to Tom, and I cannot bear the thought of saying it. I cannot imagine my life once I say it. I do not want to say it. I wish I could think of another way, so I didn't have to say it. I'm pretty sure I'd rather die than say it. Till death do us part. I push back against the thought that it might come down to that if I don't say something soon.

I made a lifelong promise to the really great guy sitting on the other side of this cab, and all I can think about these days is breaking that promise. We're almost back to our house, but I'm nowhere near anywhere that feels like home. Although I've always felt safe with Tom's hands on the steering wheel, I'm going to have to figure out how to get behind the wheel of my own life. At the moment, however, with no home in sight, I'm at an absolute loss about how I can possibly do that.

HANGING IN
THE BALANCE

Fall leaves crunch underfoot as the girls make their way back to school, and while the world has a familiar rhythm, I feel hobbled by grief, physical pain, and my ongoing ache about my marriage. I feel alternatively raw to the touch or calloused over depending upon which part of my life I am observing.

Besides daily walks that calm my spirit, I long for support in this turbulent time. My church community has been a place of solace for many people over the years, and I hope it can be that for me now. Many members of my congregation have become close friends, and I feel genuine concern in their embrace. Some of the ideas offered during Sunday worship services move like healing salve through my deformed body and confused heart. Other times, all I can hear from my seat in the pew is a haunting duet from the sadness in my heart and the ache in my arm.

It is difficult to sort through some of the sentiments church members offer up as consolation for Kerrie's death. I know they mean well, but repeated offers for prayer make me nervous considering the circumstances. The thought that they feel the right to be "judge and jury" over where Kerrie's spirit goes after taking her own life leaves me skeptical of their offer. Even in happy times, it's difficult to know what people mean by "It's in God's hands," but when you've recently walked into a horror scene, phrases like "Things happen for a reason" can feel more like a threat than encouragement.

I was raised in a Mennonite Anabaptist faith, where culture and belief are two sides of the same coin. My parents were both born in the same Mennonite village in what is now Ukraine but was then under Russian rule, and both were children when World War II broke out and they were forced to flee for their lives (along with their entire community). Many of these families eventually started a new life in the southwest corner of Canada, where the dirt smelled familiar and they had the freedom to practise their faith without the fear of religious persecution.

In the old country, their community had revolved around the church, with laws made based on the Bible and punishment meted out from the same book. Now in Canada, they abided by the rules of this new country but dutifully maintained that the Bible remained the ultimate authority over their lives.

My upbringing operated under the assumption that I would become a member of the church as a young adult, follow its beliefs, and seamlessly accept its culture as my own. Language was one way to ensure the continuity of the culture. Since the church services, business meetings, and conversations around my family dinner table were all conducted in German when I was a child, my siblings and I were sent to German school on Saturdays to learn to read and write the language. Once my older brother and I began to attend our local public school, more and more English was peppered into the exchanges at home. Eventually, the church had to address the next generation's strong preference for English from the pulpit but not without a battle that caused a split in the church.

Meals at home and at church followed the diet from the old country, a cuisine referred to as "Russian Mennonite." As I grew up on the hearty meals consisting of meat and potatoes accompanied by home-grown vegetables and followed by a decadent homemade dessert, calling them all by their traditional names, the culture naturally folded into my identity without anyone having to tell me where I belonged. When the waft of a large pot of borscht from the basement kitchen of the church combined with words about faith from the pulpit, the stomach, the head, and the heart were all getting the same message. We prayed and sang and ate together, and the underlying message was: These are my people. If there was any doubt whether the message was clear, every single decision that was made at the family level was based on the assumption that church attendance and adherence to this faith were non-negotiable. Any whiff of participation in the "English" lifestyle in this new English-speaking country, from competing beliefs to wearing makeup, was met with great suspicion and dismissed out of hand.

While there's no way I could have voiced my own personal values as a child, I sure could feel it when even my preferences were summarily dismissed. It showed up first as a weekly interaction with my mother over my choice of what to wear to church on Sunday morning. If I had pulled on tights that felt less scratchy but appeared stretched out or shoes that felt better on my feet but showed their age, I was swiftly overridden by a disapproving "What will people say?" This often ended the discussion but not my frustration. Wearing one's Sunday best, even for farming folk—perhaps especially for farm families—seemed an important expectation within the community. When I got older and wanted to wear my newest jeans, I got the same reprimand. Armed with some theological knowledge by then, I would pompously remind my mom that the phrase "Sunday best" meant donning one's best for God, not for fellow mortals. There were always people, apparently, who held opposing views on what I preferred. I absorbed the understanding and, rather dangerously so, that what others could observe was up for discussion and judgment, but what they couldn't see or guess at could remain within my private domain. But when it came to God, things were different.

We were taught that God could hear and see everything. God knew what was in my heart and on my mind. And the kicker, presented with cookies and juice during Sunday school lessons, was that if God didn't approve of what was going on in my heart or mind, then I wouldn't be going to heaven with the rest of my family. There was a terrible place for people who sinned against

God. Hell was described as a lake of fire, a place where you would be in constant pain and forever separated from God and loved ones. And to make it even more terrifying, God was preparing to do a sneak attack. No one knew when God was coming back to gather the faithful and leave everyone else behind.

I hold a generous assumption that those who presented these "truths" to my young mind in the early seventies didn't understand its dramatic effect on my sensitive psyche. While they believed they were planting biblical truth that would grow into a strong faith, for me these beliefs grew into my own private hell on earth. The fear of thinking the wrong thing, mixed with the shame that spilled like used oil into my naturally curious mind, created a slippery slope inside of me. I had no choice but to separate myself from myself. I hid my gut instinct (which was uncomfortable with what I was being taught) from my heart (which felt afraid most of the time) and from my mind (which suspected there must be bigger answers to life's questions). These three parts of me were instructed not to speak to each other so that I had some chance of getting to heaven. But many nights, all three parts came together, huddled under my bright pink bed covers, wrestling with life's regular challenges alongside the threat of being left behind on Judgment Day. I had recurring nightmares. I would have welcomed dreams filled with relatively benign characters like the bogeyman over the eternal damnation I was facing after the lights went out. With groundwork like that, it's not surprising that my thoughts about ending my marriage all those years later brought on the fear not just of condemnation from my church community but of eternal damnation.

If I count up all the Sunday school lessons, years of biblical training culminating in a bachelor's degree in theology, and the sermons I sat through for forty years, Christian teaching accounts for the bulk of my education. At the epicentre of all that training is the Bible—a combination of oral traditions, stories, firsthand accounts, and letters that can be used to shame and blame as well as guide and support, depending upon who happens to be wielding the leather-bound book in their hands.

I was reminded on a regular basis that I was born sinful—

inherently bad in my natural human state—so it's no surprise I found it nearly impossible to hear my own voice clearly. My human thoughts apparently were not to be trusted. Even when I did have a nagging sense that what I was learning couldn't be the whole story, it was far too risky to turn my back on the only framework I'd ever known. After all, eternity was on the line. As I matured and participated in the secular world around me, I was constantly caught in a sticky spiritual web as I tried to sort through what was right, let alone what was right for me. And so I did what most people who find themselves fractured do: I lived for the external approval of those who claimed to hold the keys to heaven and sorted through my darkness behind closed doors.

In addition to regularly attending a Mennonite church, I became an official member at the age of sixteen when I was baptized. Of all the countless volunteer positions I held in church over the years, my favourite was the ten years I spent playing the piano for the worship service every other Sunday. Seated at the piano, I had eye contact with the rest of the music team, who sang and played various instruments as they looked out at the congregation. Even with my back to the pews, I could feel how the worship experience was going by the energy in my body. I felt a tingling sensation swirling around me when I could sense the congregation was emotionally engaged. I played mostly by ear, using guitar chords scribbled above traditional musical notation as my guide. Not being tied to prescribed notes meant that I could easily adjust how I accompanied based on what I was sensing in the room. If the final verse of a song called for a more reflective tone, I might play an octave higher to soften the sound. If the song demanded a more victorious ending, I would pound harder and faster on the low bass notes to add a percussive rhythm. Playing the piano like a guitar meant I had the freedom to create the feeling and flow that my spirit was picking up in the moment.

This avenue to express myself and the regular encouragement from members who appreciated my musical contribution were significant motivators in my ongoing attendance. Any Sundays our team wasn't in charge of the music, I noticed how simply sitting in the pews held less and less interest for me. I'm not able to play the piano for almost a year after breaking my elbow; during that time, as I grapple with my feelings about Kerrie's death, attending church feels like little more than a lifelong habit.

One day, the church sends around a pastoral evaluation form for each member to fill out, requesting honest feedback in various areas. Pastoring is undoubtedly a challenging job, for it comes front-loaded with high expectations and requires the discipline of strict confidentiality. I give our pastor high marks in most areas on the form, but in one area I express concern over how he dealt with a specific sensitive situation and recommend that he be supported with mentorship from other pastors to ensure vulnerable members are protected.

Things go off the rails so quickly I don't even see the train coming. When the pastor hears there are concerns from a handful of members, he insists the committee in charge of the evaluation process allow him to read the comments. I promptly get a call from the pastor, who wants to meet with me to discuss my specific concern. Our meeting ends up being a platform for him to defend his actions and reiterate his right to know exactly what was written on those forms. While it was a clear breach of confidentiality by the committee to hand the pastor the evaluation forms that identified members by name, these committee members, many of whom are people I consider close friends, vehemently defend their actions and express anger at me for speaking up in the first place.

Over the next few Sundays, I find myself unable to look up when the pastor is standing at the pulpit. The irony is that the way he's handled this situation is precisely what I addressed on the form. It seems like a lot of things are breaking of late—first my elbow, then my neighbour, now my trust in a person who, by his very role, should be trustworthy.

Ultimately, it's not the pastor's actions that leave a lasting scar; it's the fact that I am now seen as an adversary by my friends. How could it take so little to lose so many friendship? I know from growing up in the Mennonite community that any criticism may be seen as an attack and can result in a person being shunned, even if just socially. Still, it stuns me how easily I am cast out after so many years of faithful participation. In quiet moments, I wonder if I actually understood this in my bones and was testing it as part of an unconscious exit strategy? All I know for sure is that something needed to give or go, and it turned out that it was me.

"I'm so hurt and confused by church right now," I sob in frustration to Tom, who hands me a tissue. He lowers his head; this hasn't been easy on him either. "Hey!" I brighten as an idea starts to form. "How about we take a break from all the church politics for a few months and attend a variety of other worship services at local churches? A fresh perspective could be just what we need after the year we've had."

Tom's face remains heavy. I see fatigue etched into the lines on his face and remind myself how much extra has fallen on him this past year. For many months he took on more of the household chores in addition to his long work week when I only had one working arm, and he suffered the trauma of Kerrie's death as well.

He begins to speak but doesn't look at me. "I agree the pastor evaluation wasn't handled right, but this is my church, Rita, and these are my best friends. I need my faith community *more than ever* right now." The emphasis on those words makes it sound like a proclamation.

Feeling like I'm drifting off in a boat while Tom is standing on the shore, I speak more quickly and raise my voice to fill the space. "I'm not asking you to leave the church forever. Just take a break—like going on a trip—so we can get a taste of how people worship outside of our Mennonite heritage. This could be such a great thing for us—and the girls too," I add, struck by the thought that changing up this part of our life might be the change that shifts our marriage into a better place. It's a powerful, giddy thought. A desperate idea.

Without what appears to be any real consideration, Tom looks up and declares, "You can do what you want, but I will be going to our church this coming Sunday, and the girls will be coming along with me."

In stark contrast to his easy-going character and usual willingness to discuss decisions at length, his words end the conversation. With that, something that's been gnawing at me for a long time regarding our marriage rips open. I can hardly blame him for not wanting to wander a spiritual desert with me, but it's more than that. For the first time in our marriage, I feel like I've tripped over an invisible line in the sand. His commitment to our marriage suddenly seems inextricably bound to the life of faith into which we were both born and to which we pledged our lives. My proposal to leave the church has snapped that line like a guitar string under tension. It's not that he wants our marriage to end, but now I know where he stands if I don't ultimately join him in church—and it isn't by my side.

As Tom and the girls drive off to church without me on Sunday, I lace up my walking shoes and pull up the hood of my raincoat the moment I step outside. It is almost winter, and the clouds appear to be brimming with expectation. I draw in a deep breath and wonder how I can use this time alone to fill me up, as recent emotional storms have left me dangerously depleted.

I feel a heaviness in my shoulders, and yet as I lift my eyes to the darkening sky, I know exactly what I want this morning to be. Instead of walking the well-worn trails of my mind, I desire to tune in to something deeper. I decide I will go on a "spirit walk." Even giving it this name softens something inside that has felt hard for some time. I can feel my spirit—the part of me that feels trapped in this broken, exhausted body but is not limited to it—begin to stir.

Having planned countless worship services while on the music team, I know the standard outline of a service without thinking. A church service has a similar format to a coffee date with a friend, but in this scenario, I'm sitting across the table from the Divine. First, there's the welcome, akin to a warm exchange of greetings. The congregation singing creates the feeling of communal intimacy while we check in with each other by asking, "How are you?" and allow time for it to deepen into, "How are you really?"

Coffee-date conversation typically settles onto a topic of shared interest, often sprinkled with kindly advice—not unlike a sermon. As things wind to a close, plans are often made for the next coffee date, along with other reminders and announcements ("So you'll come to the party I'm having this weekend?"). Finally, there is a heartfelt farewell, which in the church service takes the form of a final song or a spoken benediction.

It strikes me as a little strange to follow the outline of a church service when I'm choosing not to be in church, but I remind myself that my experience today is on my own terms and I can structure it however I desire. My overwhelmed, flickering mind craves calming familiarity, and I smile when I realize I am walking in the direction of my favourite local coffee shop. Coffee is always served directly after the service at church. Why miss out on the best part?

I choose a route with minimal traffic and begin my "service" with a welcome and a few songs. I don't analyze or plan; I just flow with whatever comes into my mind. The oddest old songs bubble up. I realize that as an accompanist, the songs I love to play aren't always the songs I most enjoy singing. Sometimes a song's tune is better than the lyrics, and sometimes it's the other way around. I tighten the toggles on my hood against the wind, making my voice sound like it's in an echo chamber, giving it an ethereal quality. I sing softly and watch my breath dance with the cold air.

Mennonites are known for their impressive four-part harmony singing. Singing is as important as any sermon to most members. Through choir practice and the use of songbooks that include music notes, everyone eventually learns how to find the part that matches their voice best. The fact that it requires all the voices in a congregation to create such a melodic, rich sound is a weekly reminder to church members how important community is for worship (and also historically for survival).

My lone voice on the side of the road strikes me as a fitting image for where I stand if I don't return to church. The songs I sing today aren't backed up by instruments or other voices, but they are an honest expression of my heart. Growing up in a community means you don't have to do it all yourself, but it also means you don't always know your own voice very well. I spent many years playing and arranging songs that I knew people in the congregation would enjoy. If they were happy with the service, I would be happy. It's high time I stop calibrating my decisions for the approval of others and figure out what brings me joy.

As I walk past a long row of houses, I move on to the next part of the service: the Prayer of Confession and Thanksgiving. This is an opportunity to let go of the past week's missteps and remember there is forgiveness available when we ask for it. I consider what I need to confess—and not just from the past week. I feel like I've spent a lifetime saying sorry to God just for being human. Today instead of requesting forgiveness from God, I opt to forgive myself instead—specifically for all the ways I have abandoned my own heart in an attempt to scrub myself clean for the church community.

I half expect my internal apology to cause a tsunami of anger toward those who told me what I was supposed to think and what I was supposed to do. Instead, I feel something soften as I direct my attention inward instead of looking outside myself for affirmation. My heart opens as I set aside blame in all its forms, and before I know it, gratitude unlatches a gate and floods in. It flows to the parts of my mind and body that work well and to my elbow that is healing a little more every day. I am thankful for friends and members of my family who are pillars I can rely on when the world feels shaky. Gratitude multiplies with every face that comes to mind. I feel my heart expanding after being closed and defensive for so long.

Next in the service comes the children's story. Youngsters in the congregation are invited to come to the front of the church to sit together for a story that interprets the theme of the sermon in a more age-appropriate way. It is an open secret that people of all ages listen more intently to the children's story and take its lesson more to heart than the actual sermon.

As I start to think about a topic for today's children's story, suddenly one presents itself: With no warning in the forecast, snowflakes begin to fall. I laugh out loud. The first snowfall of the season always brings squeals of delight from my daughters, even now in their teen years. I imagine the look on their faces when they exit the church building to view the fresh blanket of snow that wasn't there when they walked in. Taking my cue from their animated joy in my mind's eye, I lean my head back and feel the snow land and melt on my face. My ability to feel joy throughout my body seems to happen so easily after opening my heart with gratitude. As I watch the snow lay down a clean white carpet for me to walk on, I wonder if gratitude is one of the lesser-known keys to the doorway to joy.

Now for the sermon. With my spirit feeling free, I grab the first question that pops into my mind as my sermon title: "Where is God?" Is God at church with my family? Is God here with me on the side of this snowy road? Was God with Kerrie in those final moments, invited by her or not?

I follow this theme and notice it's not so much a question of whether God is expansive enough to be everywhere at once but, rather, whether those who drove to church this Sunday have a more direct line than those who walk a different road. Does God prefer to hang out with folks who live a neatly ordered life? Does God stay close to people who can't live with themselves anymore? Where is God? In my head, my heart, my gut? All of them? None of them?

This would be the time when the pastor giving the sermon would turn to the Bible for the answers. I know a lot of verses, many of them even committed to memory. But instead of trying to wrap it up with someone else's words, I decide to trust that the answer is in the question. I don't need the final answer to where God is. All I need to know for now is that God *is*.

I come out of the coffee shop with an extra hot pumpkin spice latte and renewed energy to walk back home. I hold the drink in my gloved left hand and return my right hand to my warm jacket pocket. Once I could walk comfortably without a sling, I found supporting my right arm in a pocket kept the injured joint happy longer. Sometimes as parts of us are healing and other parts are formulating a new way of being, a little extra support can go a long way in creating moments of relief. I already know

I will be doing this Spirit Walk again next Sunday. And with that thought, the announcements and sharing portions of the service are checked off the list.

I have the whole walk home for the closing hymn and the benediction. I imagine how anyone driving by would likely take me for a happy person, smiling to myself as I tip my head to take tasty sips from my steaming cup. It feels good to see myself as happy and moving forward.

One of my favourite songs to end a service, and a fun one to play on the piano, is a rousing tune with lyrics taken from the Old Testament:

> You shall go out with joy
> And be led forth with peace,
> The mountains and hills
> Will break forth before you.
> There'll be shouts of joy
> And all the trees of the fields
> Will clap, will clap their hands.

It's timely that the trees clapping their hands in this song are in reference to the wind, as I feel it swirl around me. I recall from my theological studies that the wind in this song is from the Hebrew *ru-ah*, a word that encapsulates both the breath in our human body and the spirit of God moving in us. *Ruah*, our breath, our spirit's wind, is the first action we take when we come into the world and the last thing we release when we die. It bookends our entire human experience, and it flows through every breath we take while we're alive. This Hebrew word stuck in my memory because *ruah* is also the feminine aspect of God, a fact that was never highlighted from the pulpit in all the years I attended church. Everyone realizes that an infinite God isn't relegated to a gender, and yet the authoritative masculine version is the default in many religions around the world. There are so many things that have informed my belief system over the years, but it's no surprise that the earliest image, a bearded fatherly God, requires ongoing effort to reform.

I feel my energy flow constrict, so I tell theology and church politics to take a backseat so I can continue to follow where my spirit is leading me. With trees still gently clapping and feminine energy guiding my hips forward, my singing stops short as I hear myself say out loud, "Kerrie, you're going to be okay."

I am instantly transported back to her house, to the day I found her. A coldness sweeps over me. Since that horrible day, anytime Kerrie comes to mind, I attempt to stop the final image of her from developing further to keep myself from being swept into a strong riptide of despair. Even though I understand this is a normal reaction to a traumatic event, it still has the power to unleash a vortex of dread inside the walls of my chest. As time passes, the assault is slightly less intense, but it has by no means completely subsided.

But today, something inside me decides not to turn away. The snow has intensified and huge flakes are starting to decorate the trees as snow falls faster than the wind can usher them away. I sense that all I need to do is stay in the scene that is playing out, so instead of running away from the image of Kerrie hanging in front of me, I approach her. Her toes hang at the level of my waist. My heart feels like it is going to beat out of my chest as I lean in and slowly wrap my arms around her legs.

The image feels so real that I have stopped walking in order to keep my balance. Tears spill onto my cheeks and leave a warm trail on their way to the ground. Out of nowhere, an image of the dead body of Jesus hanging on a cross appears. In flashes, my mind alternates between the image of me embracing Kerrie and the one of Christ. I stand there blinking away tears and willing my lungs to keep working. Everything is quiet except for the sound of my jagged breath softening to match the slowing beats of my heart.

The next words to flow from my mouth are, "You're going to be okay." These words, I am surprised to realize, are for me.

I swallow hard on the stunning truth I've just experienced. It's not that I think Kerrie is my saviour. But at the same time, moving bravely toward the most terrifying thing I have ever experienced has opened a new door inside of me. While I'm unsure where this door leads, I know that if I can face this pain—even embrace it—I will eventually find a way to save myself.

OUTSIDE THE LINES

The room is dim. My thoughts are darker. I am hiding behind the closed door of my bedroom in the middle of the day. I'm not sure anymore what I might say to my girls if I open my mouth to speak. A flurry of angry words, like squawking birds, might escape in response to whatever pricks my thin skin at that moment. Even worse, what might come out of my mouth may be the truth.

The truth is that instead of finding peace and momentum, I have created a deep hole by spinning my tires. I am stuck and I have no idea what I might do next. Taking the wheel of my life hasn't been as easy as I'd hoped. It isn't as simple as swapping out one life for another. In the confusion, I'm starting to wonder if I'm actually further down the same road that Kerrie travelled last summer. The notion that she doesn't have to fight with her own thoughts anymore or make any more tough decisions is beginning to sound, well, restful. Like finally getting off a nauseating ride at the fair, it seems like a definitive way to just make it all stop. I am aware that if I don't do something soon, take some kind of concrete action, I may lose my sense of direction completely, a thought that raises the hair on the back of my neck.

There is a soft knock on my bedroom door. I don't say anything, but I sit up in bed. I still desperately want to be, if not a good mom, at least a mom who doesn't disappear completely. My younger daughter, Sara, is at the door. As she leans her body into the room, she clings to the doorknob, unsure of what she is walking into. She swipes her long silky hair from her face, and then her mouth moves as she says words that sound very far away to my ears. I strain to hear, but I'm distracted by the louder conversation going on in my own head. If I open my mouth to speak, will I make things worse? I have no excuse to be in bed in the middle of the day. How did it come to this?!

Sara asks me a question and I don't, I can't, seem to answer back with anything more than a monosyllabic grunt. Then, as if she is applying the paddles that restart a dying person's heart, she looks at me and in a quiet voice simply says, "I love you." I can feel the jolt deep inside, and I want to respond in kind. I try to force myself to say something, anything. I look at her searching face, and my heart collapses in on itself as I blurt out, "That's nice."

For her sake and mine, I wish I could say "I love you," but at the moment love feels like such a foreign, inaccessible concept that I don't feel I have the right to use that word. We've all seen the movies where one person says "I love you" and is crushed when the other person responds with "Thank you" or "That's nice." It's a cop-out, a way to avoid feeling too much—but is it worse than saying words your heart can't back?

Sara stares at me for a little longer and then closes the door behind her as she leaves. I know she is hurt and confused. I might as well have been drunk or high on a drug for all the damage my inability to engage with her at that moment has likely done. She reached out to me, and I was too emotionally immobilized to reach back. This is a new level of disconnection. I feel myself being carried downstream by something greater than my own will, and I can no longer muster the energy to swim.

I roll over sideways and curl my body into a ball. I feel encased in a lifeless shell, but somewhere deeper in my body, hot magma advances in thick, slow swirls. My breath is uneven and shallow, and for now, all I can do is lie here, hoping I don't erupt and wishing I could erupt. My eyes dart around searching for somewhere to land. I fixate on a square-foot portion of my bedroom wall.

I painted the whole room a burnt orange colour years earlier, which made it appear as if the sun was setting any time of the day—perfect for a space meant for sleep. I had heard that orange was the colour of celebration, and as I painted the walls, I crossed my fingers that it would infuse my marriage bed with warmth, at minimum, if celebration was aiming too high.

I have always enjoyed painting walls. Two gallons of paint and some green painter's tape and I could transform any room. If the girls were going to be away for at least a few days, at summer camp or visiting their grandparents on the farm, I would plot another painting project in the house. Paint was the least expensive way to make a significant visual impact. After a while, I got more creative by taping off part of the wall to design a pattern. My favourite was the picket fence effect I painted around the girls' room when they were young. That project gave me the confidence to try my hand at applying texture to the wall of a bedroom that became a playroom when the girls were a little older. After applying a coat of clean white paint, I taped off the lower half of the room and applied a splatter technique I had read about. I flung red paint at the wall and, before it dried, quickly dobbed it with a moist sponge. I liked the concept behind this plan—that a chair bumping the wall or a splash of errant paint or playdough would easily be obscured. I hadn't anticipated how much it would appear like a blood-spattered crime scene once it dried.

A few years later, the girls pleaded for their own bedrooms, and so the playroom became the master bedroom. Tucked away from the noisy parking lot, the former playroom actually worked better for Tom's need to sleep during the day after long nights on the road. It was during this room swap that I painted the room orange. I had forgotten just how much blood-red paint I had previously hurled at the wall but hoped three coats of orange paint would free me from the arduous task of sanding the entire room. The furniture pushed up against the walls mostly hid the raised textured pattern.

Today my eye goes straight to the offending blobs of paint that catch the shadow created by my bedside lamp, appearing like sins from my past that cannot be painted over. I can't imagine having the energy or desire to ever paint again, let alone undo the evidence of poor decisions splayed across the walls of my life. I see how I have slowly painted myself into a corner, and now I am stuck, my back against the wall, running out of room to even breathe. These are my walls, my colour choices, my decisions, my carefully curated life. How have I not noticed that I've been slowly trapping myself with no reasonable way out?

I must take the next step—a heartbreaking, messy step I have tried everything to avoid. If I don't get out of bed and leave, I could die here. I will have to track my fear and transgressions across the lives of everyone I care about if I ever hope to breathe, let alone paint, again.

Jean, my yoga friend, calls me later in the day. As soon as she hears my voice, she knows this is an urgent situation. We've had many conversations about my options over the last few months. Unlike my friends who were raised like me, with the belief that ending a marriage is a sin to be avoided, Jean has a way of painting outside the lines. I can say anything to her and not worry about shocking her. In fact, she seems to thrive on situations that skirt life's edges. She has become my closest ally, and while some of her suggestions feel more drastic than I am comfortable imagining, I realize now that I'm in desperate territory and have to consider all the options.

Jean insists that it's time I look for a place to rent. The thought of actually packing a bag and leaving my children and the life I know causes a massive wave of anxiety to crash against my body, threatening to pull me under. She also insists that I call my doctor to discuss taking medication that can help during the transition. Sensing how frozen I am with fear, she makes the doctor's appointment herself and drives me there. I allow my mind to go limp under Jean's care and follow the step-by-step directions of someone who has walked this path herself.

As I sit in the brightly lit office, I cannot imagine how I am going to say the words out loud to my doctor of twenty years when she walks in the door. She is Tom's doctor too, and now she is going to find out about my plan to leave my marriage before he does. My heart feels too big, or maybe too small, inside my body.

My breath can't keep up. I stand up and pace around the room to avoid imploding or exploding. I want to run and keep running until maybe I can wake up from this nightmare that distorts my perspective like funhouse mirrors at the fair.

Jean sees that I am coming undone and opens the door of the examination room to flag down a nurse, saying I am not doing well and need to see the doctor immediately. I have never had a panic attack before, and I don't know how to stop the feeling that I am at active war within myself. My body and my mind are scrambling to retreat, but in opposite directions, and I feel pulled to the point of tearing open at the seams.

With one glance, my doctor sees my distress. She asks me a few questions in a calm, low voice that makes it hard for me to hear against the noise inside of my head, so Jean helps answer many of the questions. After the appointment, with inner voices still screaming at me to just shake it off, I walk into the pharmacy to fill my prescription. I usually avoid taking prescription medication, but if these tiny blue pills will help ease the desperation that threatens to punch its way through my chest cavity, I am willing to try them for a little while.

The next day, Jean calls to say that she saw a furnished rental in the paper that morning and has already called the landlady to confirm it is still available. I remind her that I can't move too far away from my girls. With no mental energy to do my own research, I agree to look at the rental she's found about a mile from my home. Things are moving very quickly now. Like balancing on a large, unstable ball, if I don't keep making small movements, I fear I will fall off. This time, I'm certain it will be more than my elbow that will break. I am prepared to endure pain and disorientation now in order to see what the world feels like on the other side of this massive life decision. If it's no different or worse, so be it. At the moment it's too hard to think straight as I bounce around in the jarring discomfort of going off-road instead of staying on the straight and narrow path I was raised to follow.

The moment I meet the landlady, I feel calmer. She has renovated her two-car garage into a furnished space. It's the width of two queen beds and a little more than two beds long.

There is a tiny kitchen along one wall with a sink, a stove, and a mini-bar fridge. A table with two compact chairs sits on a Persian carpet a few feet from the end of the bed and in the kitchen at the same time. It is the perfect size to unpack a few belongings but not enough space to unload all the baggage from my past. It reminds me of a beaver's lodge—a space I can escape into while the world howls its disapproval outside.

A few months later, my Iranian landlady will share that just before I arrived, she sat cross-legged on the Persian rug and prayed about who might come live under her roof. As a newly divorced woman with grown children herself, she understood the dangers and advantages of renting out a space in your home. The moment she met me, she felt her prayers were answered, which is why she agreed to my request for a six-month commitment instead of the minimum of a year she had put in the paper.

My prayers, although I doubt they deserve to be heard, have been answered as well. Until I could imagine an actual space and the real people who would surround me in this strange new world, it all felt insurmountable. With a plan and a place and the friendly face of my new landlady in front of me, I possess some of the tools I need to make my uphill climb. A tingle of hope I haven't felt in a long time worms its way through the darkness. I'm such a long way from feeling good, but I know taking this step is worth acknowledging. The sensation lasts exactly one breath, and while I wouldn't call it a moment of celebration, I enjoy the microscopic rise in my emotional elevation.

If there's a list of really hard conversations to have in life, the one I have with Tom later that day is near the top of that list. How did "I do" turn into "I don't anymore"? There was no exit clause in the commitment I made in front of my family and God at the age of twenty that permits me to break this contract. I am going against all the values I have ever been taught and ascribed to for most of my life when I open my mouth to speak words that will make all of this glaringly real.

I tell Tom I need six months in my own place so I can see what part of this is me and what is our relationship. I am not asking his permission, and he knows it. And with the same gentle, pragmatic spirit he has displayed since I first met him, he sits with me on the living room floor, in a circle with our teenage girls, as we tell them what is about to happen. I cry through most of it, so Tom ends up doing more of the talking. I cling to a tiny piece of hope, scrunched inside the tissue that wipes my tears, that I will be able to explain things better to everyone, including myself, sometime down the road.

The timing of this massive transition coincides perfectly with a Fearless Living retreat I registered for some time ago. One of my former yoga students, Katherine, convinced me months ago to join her on this retreat organized by one of the coaches from Starting Over, a TV show we both love. On the show, a group of women work with trained life coaches who help them turn their lives around. It seems very appropriate that the same day I move out, I embark on the six-hour drive to Portland, Oregon, with Katherine, a gentle, caring woman with an infectious laugh. This retreat feels like a bridge of support into my new life that will give me a chance to secure my lifeboat to a steady dock.

On the retreat, I learn a practice I'll continue using long after I return: taking note of ten moments every day—five acknowledgments of moments I have control over to move me in the direction I desire to go (either things I do or say or things I don't do or don't say) and five things I'm grateful for. Although it is much easier for me to list my gratitudes, it is the focus on where I make small, wise choices that lays an increasingly solid foundation under my feet. These daily acknowledgements show me the difference between a reaction and a decision. With practice, I learn to spot more quickly where I'm still following the rules from my past and where I grant myself the freedom to choose the best course of action for myself.

I acknowledge myself for feeling helplessness in the face of my daughter's anger and having the courage to walk through it with her anyway is one acknowledgement I capture in the first pages of the green journal where I write them down.

Having a way to record all these new decisions at the end of the day, together with the little blue pill, allows my mind to relax long enough so I can fall asleep. I have traded a life I knew inside out for a new world order where most of my days are strange and unfamiliar. But at the centre of the fatigue and confusion is another feeling. As I make more and more decisions for myself, there is a growing sense of sure-footedness, where each step I take feels authentic because it is stamped with my heart's approval at the end of every day.

FAIRY-TALE FAMILY

Despite my courageous strides forward, I regularly feel pulled back, as if I'm at the mercy of the tides, flailing to stay afloat in a sea of change. My body doesn't always know what it wants or needs. Watching television or listening to music feels overly amplified to my spirit in my small garage apartment. I seem to have lost the ability to feel hunger, but I force myself to eat because otherwise my hands start to shake and my legs feel weak. A small bowl of cereal or half a can of soup is the extent of what I can spoon into my mouth before I feel like I'm going to burst. I am surprised to realize that the thought of chocolate or alcohol, both things I thoroughly enjoyed in my former life, turns my stomach these days. Weight drops off, and after three months, I have unintentionally lost over thirty pounds.

Like a young adult leaving home for the first time, I have left with just a few personal items and some cash in my pocket—enough to pay the deposit and first month's rent and a meagre allowance for food and gas. Since I'm moving into a furnished space, I don't need much—and this means I can leave the family home looking mostly intact for the girls.

Because of my guilt over leaving the marriage, I've walked a wide berth around any financial conversations with Tom. Money feels tied to worthiness, and when my new bank informs me that I have no personal credit and they can only authorize the same credit card limit they offer a college student starting out, it feels like the whole world agrees that I have little to no value on my own. Although I've always insisted on having my name on our mortgage and vehicle ownership papers, the seemingly innocuous decision to simply add my name to Tom's credit card when we first got married put me on a tenuous financial path. Unbeknownst to me, with every purchase from that moment onward, I wasn't building my own personal credit. The bank manager hands me a tissue as I allow the reality of this new information to sink in at the age of forty-one. To help me over my immediate financial hurdle, my sister generously loans me some money, but I know it's imperative that I get a job.

Considering my fragile state of mind and body, I can't imagine what I can do for work, let alone where to start looking. I had spent most of my adult life as a full-time mom, clocking countless hours in volunteer positions that hardly make for a robust resumé. Although I was employed at the athletic club until my accident, I won't be able to teach yoga anytime soon with an elbow I can't even straighten, let alone support my body weight in order to demonstrate postures for students.

My friend Jennifer encourages me to apply where she works, with a company that hires temporary employees for all sorts of jobs. At the end of my interview, I am told that my typing score is as impressive as my people skills, both of which are in high demand in administrative work. I gratefully sign up with the company when they assure me that I will have the ultimate say on where and how often I work. I view the temp job as a great way to be a fly on the wall of a wide assortment of industries and organizations. It's a front-row seat to observe how the working world operates and a good way to get a feel for what I might be good at long-term. The temp job also allows me to regulate my wildly fluctuating energy levels. Some days I feel keen to see what the day will reveal; other days my body and mind shimmy with anxiety and fatigue, like a car going too fast on bald, unbalanced tires. I trust that my stamina for work and life will increase if I ramp up slowly because losing control and crashing is not an option I care to imagine. If I manage to work a few days a week, I calculate I'll have enough to cover my rent, groceries, and the gas to get to jobs. Every purchase I make, including which brand of deodorant to buy, is metered against my available energy to make the equivalent amount of money. It's a simple approach to finances that doesn't account for the future but reminds me every day that if I want a future, balancing my time, money, and energy—all versions of currency—is how I will get there.

On the first day of my first temp job, I'm already in a full sweat before I sit down in the chair assigned to me in the reception area. Finding the location, figuring out all-day parking, and navigating the rapid-fire orientation feels akin to being told to run across a busy highway, dodging honking vehicles while maintaining a professional smile. Every time the phone rings at this temporary desk of mine, my hands get clammy as I try to sound competent while attempting to determine what the caller wants so I can direct the call to the right recipient through this complicated phone system.

At the end of the first day, I sit in my tiny kitchen, a few feet from the end of my bed, half a bowl of lentil soup cooling on the table in front of me, wondering how I will possibly manage it all again tomorrow. *I acknowledge myself for rising to the challenge of learning new things despite the panic lodged in my chest all day,* I write in my journal. *I am grateful for Jennifer, who knew I could do this job when I didn't.*

I begin to enjoy the variety of tasks and the interesting people I meet, building more confidence every time I am welcomed through the front door of another temporary workplace. After the first month or two, when I only accepted jobs that required a two- or three-day commitment, I slowly began to accept contracts that would last a few weeks. I noticed how much of the job is discovering what the company actually needs from the temp, even when they don't quite know themselves. I am there because their regular employee isn't available for some reason, so things are often in upheaval. I notice I'm good at interpreting what people need—which in many cases is just a moment to talk through what they need. I have done a version of this my whole life, but now I am getting paid for it.

Some days, if I don't look too closely at the deepening lines etched around my eyes, I can imagine that I'm fresh out of college, new to adult life, slowly building my own credit and merging into a world that values my natural skills and personality. But in reality, I'm twice that age, having lived a whole other life already. It is hard to know sometimes if I am brave or just pathetic, waking up at five in the morning to hustle to a near-minimum-wage job, with few friends to call on the weekends. It's probably a little of both, depending on whether I'm looking out from my heart or seeing my current reality through the eyes of former friends from my old life.

While I'm still a mother, and legally still a wife, most of my time outside of work is spent alone, sharpening my inclinations as a single person as I squint toward a horizon that has no recognizable shape yet. Considering the alternative, I am grateful to have a chance to experience this new life and its fresh perspective. There is a simplicity and an order to my days, while all the loose ends of my former life still wait in the wings to be dealt with.

A few months after I leave, Tom requests that we do counselling together. He is hopeful there is still a way to save our relationship, and his unwavering commitment to the marriage demands that he do everything possible to bring us back together under the same roof. For the sake of our ongoing relationship as co-parents to our daughters, regardless of the final outcome of our marriage, I agree to see a therapist with Tom. As I listen to his responses to the therapist's questions, I receive weekly confirmation that the world of faith and values my husband lives in—a world I was raised in and agreed to participate in for forty years—is a world I have no interest in returning to.

As I walk to my vehicle at the end of every counselling session, I shake my head in amazement at just how much I don't actually know about this man whom I have essentially grown up with over the last twenty years. I wonder, are his answers different now that we're living apart or are they just more honest now? Are my own blinders regarding myself slowly coming off too? He and I started dating when we were teenagers. We couldn't even legally drink or vote yet when we decided to weave our lives together. I get the sense we are like a two-person horse costume with one person making the head and front legs and the other forming the body and hind legs, blindly putting full trust in the one leading—but I honestly can't figure out which one of us has been leading.

Tom and I met during our senior year of high school when he moved to Canada from California because his father had taken on a pastorship in my hometown. Tom played the trumpet, enjoyed sports, and had a lilting tenor voice that landed him a lead role in the school's musical. He seemed to integrate well into the culture of our small, private Mennonite school where many of his cousins also attended—some of whom I knew better than he did since I'd grown up with them. He asked me to be his date for graduation, and I easily agreed, feeling safe and comfortable in his presence. The bonus was that, unlike many of the other guys I had sat beside in school desks since the first grade, he didn't feel like a brother to me. Tom rarely expressed frustration, let alone anger, and he didn't seem to crave the spotlight. As we chatted on our first date, which was an early-morning bicycle ride along country roads near my home, there was an easy balance in our exchanges. He didn't swallow me up with his agenda, and he seemed genuinely interested in what I had to say.

When we both ended up at the same theological school after graduation, it didn't take long to make our relationship official. I could tell him anything and trust he'd keep my deeply held childhood secrets—ones I hadn't even entrusted to my best friend. He was an upstanding guy, a hard worker, and a gentle spirit, and we had been raised under a common faith. These were enough—more than enough—reasons to imagine a life together. We were married around the same time as all my closest friends. I was right on track. My life was on the same approved trajectory as everyone else I knew.

And now I am separated, not only from my spouse but also the life path that seemed so clearly marked out twenty years ago. As more people in my neighbourhood and church find out about my decision to leave my marriage, public places are suddenly fraught with potential landmines. Until recently, if I bumped into someone I knew at the grocery store, there was always a cordial, if not exuberant, greeting. I was welcome anywhere I went and felt respected by everyone who knew me. Since the separation, people turn their cart away the moment they see me in an attempt to pretend they didn't see me. I catch them shaking their heads disapprovingly as they walk away. It is gut-wrenching to see a flicker of recognition turn into a visible scowl because seeing my face now elicits judgment instead of joy. For the first time in my life, I feel like a social outcast.

Although I often imagine moving far away, if I am going to keep my promise of remaining close to my girls until they've graduated from high school, this is my new reality. I survive running errands in my neighbourhood by remaining expressionless and avoiding eye contact. Once I am back in the safety of my car and out of the parking lot, I release my breath and sob, the tears coming so fast I must wipe them repeatedly, like windshield wipers clearing my eyes so I can see the road as I drive home.

The few neighbours who will still talk to me confirm that Tom and I were considered the least likely couple to split up. Tom is now the poor guy whose wife "just up and left." And although I know I left a million times in my mind and I paced the dark halls of my heart a million more trying to find a way to stay, our current marital status is a genuine shock for many. Our community had put us on a pedestal, and we willingly stood there. Over time, we had accepted our role as the hard-working, church-going, big-hearted fairy-tale family, smiling and waving from the top of our well-designed life. It was a long, hard fall from that height, and the disparaging looks on people's faces are a daily reminder that I smashed a lot of expectations when I left the marriage. Since it's usually more comfortable to be angry than sad when a person is disappointed, I became an easy target for a torrent of unflattering labels.

I find solace in going for long walks. As I follow the undulating path through a local park one day, I recognize a couple from my former church coming my way. They served as leaders for many years and were not shy about stating their opinions on issues at our church meetings. I am instantly nervous about how they will react when they see me and find myself searching for an escape route. But fleeing means walking across tall, sodden grass and abandoning the dignity I've worked hard to build up—so instead I search inside myself and find an idea that has recently crossed my path. I utter the quote under my breath, "It's none of my business what anyone thinks of me." Then I repeat it, locating a small corner within myself that agrees to abandon a lifetime of letting others' opinions and judgments dictate my behaviour.

It's none of my business what others think of me. It's not even my business to try to imagine what they think of me, I tell myself as the couple gets closer.

The couple looks up, and we offer a nod of recognition to each other as we pass. Instead of looking for further evidence of disapproval on their faces and allowing my insecurity to fester for hours, I look ahead to where I'm going. Once they've passed by, I let the temptation to linger on them pass too. And then I smile. Broadly. Not because of anything they did or didn't do but because I have managed to beautifully stay in my own business. And not only have I stayed steady and gracious within myself but I have also test-driven a new way of being in the world. My only business is to be mindful of my business. Staying in my own lane, not trying to change or judge others, has opened up a surprisingly peaceful path inside of me. I look up at the clear blue sky and feel like popping the cork on some champagne to celebrate the stunning fact that it is within my control to create this feeling of effervescence anytime I choose!

As the warm days of July approach, so does the first anniversary of Kerrie's death. I smell it coming like a summer storm brewing in the distance as I stare at the open door of my empty mini-fridge. On the counter above, a container of milk and a bottle of juice bookend a row of contents from the disembowelled fridge. A block of ice had formed at the back of the appliance, and I knew if I didn't defrost it, there soon won't be room for anything inside.

Water drips off the block of ice, and with increasing frequency, I have to empty the container that I've positioned to catch the drips. I consider where my own inner frost, the cold numbing of emotions required in order to make it through some of the tough times this past year, is beginning to thaw as well. The chaos of breaking my elbow, finding Kerrie, and leaving the church and my marriage was too much trauma to feel all at once, and gratefully, our minds are set up to protect us from feeling too much too quickly. But as I begin to thaw, those frozen feelings thaw as well.

The anniversary of Kerrie's death has pushed a load of complex emotions back onto my path. For all the hope I am finding in unexpected places and for the accomplishments I am able to list, there is also a foreboding shadow of grief ready to pounce at any moment. With no way to wrestle a shadow, hopelessness descends instead. I had always assumed that hopelessness was simply the absence of hope and, therefore, devoid of feeling, but as I imagine nothing ever feeling better than this, a chunk of hopelessness breaks off and lands at my feet with a startling thud. Thick tentacles of hopelessness, very much alive and rife with feeling, slither toward my neck threatening to choke me in their own time. I try not to panic as a shiver runs the length of my spine and sweat beads against the back of my shirt. If there is any way out of this clammy chokehold, it has to be by continuing to defrost. I must be willing to be increasingly vulnerable—not only with others but especially with myself.

The icy determination I have built up over years to protect myself from pain will need to keep thawing. This isn't just about my marriage or Kerrie anymore; the orderly walls of my entire belief system will have to continue melting if I desire to have a healthy, authentic life. I will need to check the expiry date of every belief, every adopted value from my upbringing, then toss it out or put it back into the fridge. It's not because everything I was taught was wrong—it's because it isn't yet mine.

CARTWHEELS

I stopped after my sister called out, "Four hundred!" I could have kept going, but she seemed tired of counting for me, and I had now wholly proven to myself that I was a master at cartwheeling.

My young body was the perfect balance of weight, length, and strength, and even after doing so many cartwheels in a row, I didn't feel dizzy when I stopped. I had worked up to it. Without a doubt, it took much longer to learn how to do my first full cartwheel than it did to complete four hundred in one go. Some things you can learn in a summer; other things take a lifetime.

It was early in my summer break from elementary school, and the days, like my limbs, seemed to stretch on forever. I always had chores to do in the late afternoon and random requests that my mom would yell out if I didn't manage to scatter from earshot fast enough. But since she was usually looking down, stirring something on the stove or weeding the flowerbeds, vanishing from her sightline was all about timing. When I got it right, I gained the freedom to do whatever I could dream up for a few hours.

It was the early seventies, and children roamed their neighbourhoods freely until the street lights came on. Growing up in a rural farming community, however, there weren't many streetlights or many other kids who lived along our stretch of road. I was fortunate to have Darla, a classmate who lived two properties over. My parents didn't like it if I spent too much time at her house, as she was the youngest in her large family, and most of her siblings were already driving cars fitted with loud engines that rumbled home well after my bedtime. It didn't help that they always smelled of smoke and yelled words at each other that I'd never heard before. Outside of public school, all the rest of my close contacts were from my church, where the language and lifestyle fit squarely into the Christian model that matched my family's values. Darla's family offered a close-up peek into another way to live.

With an entire summer to fill, I clung to my friendship with Darla despite our differences, as she was my most accessible playmate. Wandering around the back fields of our farms, she and I made up games and compared notes on life. One summer, she and I burrowed our way into a massive pile of abandoned wood from a torn-down building on their property and created a secret hideout where she showed me pictures of women in various states of undress in a magazine she had found in her brother's room.

There was never an organized plan for what skill or game we might spend hours attempting to perfect. Our days were as organic as the vegetables growing in my mother's massive garden behind our house. "Hey, can you do this?" was how a lot of our best summer days began. Sometimes the skill was already in place, ready to be demonstrated; other times the question introduced us to another hill waiting to be climbed.

One sunny afternoon, while loitering under a large tree on Darla's front lawn, it was easily decided that she, my sister, and I would learn how to do a cartwheel. My sister was almost three years younger but was regularly permitted to tag along, since, if I was looking after her, it meant my mom was less likely to ask me to do other tasks. My sister learned early on that following my instructions and not saying too much meant she had a better chance of being allowed to join again the next time.

None of us had ever done a cartwheel before, but I had seen

someone on a playground spin their body around recently. The sheer physicality of the movement made it an agreeable quest for us all. Sequestering a chorus of muscles to accomplish a new skill was an indelible trademark of my childhood. I liked doing things with my body, testing its limits and noticing how it changed from season to season. The beginning of summer always felt like a fresh start. I already knew from previous summers that it would take at least a few weeks to toughen up the soles of my feet, and then running barefoot over our rocky driveway would no longer cause me to flinch. Clothes from the previous summer usually still fit around my body but were inches too short. Now that I was in the double digits but not yet a teenager, every year I noticed that I could run faster, jump higher, and think deeper thoughts.

The first thing we all learned about cartwheeling was that it's best to first look down at the grass where one's hands are going to land. Unlike our grass, Darla's lawn was full of various weeds, and nothing stops the fun faster than a handful of prickles—which my sister learned the hard way.

Once we'd committed to a spot for planting our hands, things got animated. Arms reached to the sky as one knee bent high, in preparation for the arms to make contact with the ground—but an impressive reach didn't nearly guarantee a completed cartwheel. It was still a mystery how to ensure our legs would follow in the right time and place to catapult us back into a standing position. We would hurl our bodies in the direction we wanted to go, but our arms would collapse before our legs completed the rotation. Time after time that afternoon, we crumpled into the grass, landing awkwardly on our heads and shoulders. Observing someone else make an attempt gave you some clues—mostly for what not to do. Once our arms got tired and our faces glowed red from the time spent upside down, we rolled around on the grass for a while teasing each other. We were not used to supporting our body's weight with our gangly arms for any length of time, but we never stopped trying, occasionally yelling instructions to the others if we noticed any small successes in our own progress.

After a while, we determined that the main hurdle was creating enough thrust to carry the torso around in order to land on our feet. It wasn't something you could just think hard enough about. You had to activate all the body parts at just the right time. We experimented by grabbing hold of each other's legs as they came around to assist the rotation, but that didn't help at all. This conversation was between you and your own body.

The subsequent ease of accomplishing a full rotation was surprising once our bodies showed us where to focus our energy. Magically, the straining ebbed and our bodies moved through the steps fluidly. Once we had this embodied "knowing," it wasn't long before we were flying effortlessly, arms outstretched and legs akimbo, then returning to a standing position with beaming faces.

By the time the sun had somersaulted its own course through the sky that day, all three of us had figured out how to do a complete cartwheel. But the celebration didn't last long: Someone proposed that we attempt two cartwheels in a row, and we were off on a new challenge.

There was a dizzying effect as we completed the first rotation, followed by a slight pause to set up for the next one. But the second one consistently failed. We'd land with a thud and lie on the grass for a while, looking up at the blue sky and wondering why it wasn't working. It took many more attempts to realize it was the pause that was the problem. Instead, if you anticipated the subsequent cartwheel in your body while you were still doing the first one, then you could create enough momentum to continue into the next one—prickles be damned. Like the most successful plans in life, cartwheels weren't single entities strung together; they were energy in motion linked by common intention.

Once you could do two, you could do three, and before long, my neighbour rounded off her twenty-fifth cartwheel without stopping. We had fallen into an effective tag-team approach where one person would be cartwheeling while the others sat nearby and counted out loud and cheered for whatever number had been successfully completed. Then you rested, waiting for your head to clear and arms to recover as you counted in unison for the next person's limbs to levitate the length of the lawn. It was a memorable day of accomplishment and camaraderie.

When we realized how late it had gotten, my sister and I ran home through the field, under the barbed wire fence, and across the newly cut grass to report on our adventure. We asked Mom if she had learned how to ride bikes and do cartwheels and make forts when she was young, but her curt response made for a short conversation.

"We didn't have time for those kinds of things," she blurted in response. "We had other things we had to do."

When I was older and able to bend time enough to imagine my mother when she was my age, I learned that those "other things" that didn't leave time for cartwheels weren't just more chores, although there were a lot of those in her young life. My mom grew up in a small Mennonite village in the fertile "breadbasket" of modern-day Ukraine, where her family had lived for many generations. As more Mennonites immigrated to the area, a series of tight-knit villages cropped up on either side of the Dnieper River. All the villages grew their own food, which included watermelons so sweet and large that they often made a summer meal of them, accompanied by *rollkuchen*, a delicious deep-fried dough. Their yield was bountiful enough to last through the long winters, with canned fruits and vegetables and sausage they made themselves sustaining the community. Each village worshipped together and socialized exclusively with each other and other nearby Mennonite villages. Their goal was to be self-sufficient and autonomous so they could live a peaceful life anchored in the Christian Bible. They became known as *"die Stille im Lande,"* the quiet in the land, but ultimately that didn't save them from an incursion of Communist rule that threatened their way of life.

Over the centuries, Mennonite communities had been uprooted many times. Their faith didn't allow them, under any circumstances, to take the life of another person, which meant they refused to enlist in the military. Pacifism was a core belief, and they stuck by it even when persecuted for their faith.

By the time my mother was born, after an idyllic era spent in this corner of Eastern Europe, the colonies were again coming under pressure to adapt to the revised laws under the new Russian regime. Most of my father's uncles were taken behind the barn and executed by local bandits who took matters into their own hands because they were suspicious of these cloistered Mennonite colonies that were thriving due to their communal and agricultural way of life. The women and children were at the mercy and whims of soldiers who raided the villages. Despite Catherine the Great's promise a century earlier that their religious freedom would be protected, Mennonite men of eligible age were forced to take on jobs for the war effort under Stalin's rule in the early 1940s. Some ended up in supporting roles as cooks and cleaners and others were sent to the frontlines, where they acted as medics. Instead of carrying guns, they ran in pairs carrying stretchers to retrieve injured bodies as bullets rained down on them. On these bloody battlefields, they found themselves in the horrifying position of having to choose which body to retrieve based on who had the best chance of survival as dying soldiers cried out to them for assistance.

My Opa, my mother's father, received a less grievous war assignment: He was sent to Italy to guard Mussolini, who had heard that Mennonites had a religious obligation not to take another's life. It was rumoured that Mussolini didn't trust his own people's motivation, so he surrounded himself with these pacifist foreigners.

As law and order eroded and most families were separated by war, most Mennonites decided to flee for their lives—and many of the men who stayed were eventually sent to work camps in Siberia. The conditions in the gulag were as chilling as the weather. Most never made it back to their families, including my dad's father.

My mother was eight years old when she and her mother, accompanied by the rest of her siblings and an aunt, fled from their home and headed out on foot in the direction of the ship they hoped to board. They walked west toward Germany for almost three months, finding what food they could (often through the kindness of farmers along their way) and sleeping when and where it was safe.

My mother remembers the fatigue and the constant fear. As the second-oldest daughter, she had to keep up the best she could, while her mother and aunt focused on the needs of her younger siblings. They would stop for short periods to rest and share what meagre food they had for the day. My mom's young feet were so sore and blistered she didn't think she could take another step. When it was time to start walking again, if she didn't make a move to get up immediately, her mother would turn around and, out of sheer desperation to keep her family alive and moving, would hiss at my mom, "Do you want the soldiers to get you?"

When Opa was finally released from his wartime duties and joined his family in Germany, they spent two years in refugee camps jumping through bureaucratic hoops to secure their travel to Canada. It was a jubilant day when they finally set sail. After they made it across the ocean, they travelled the length of this new land by train to reach their final destination: the West Coast of British Columbia.

Within a short time, the town of Abbotsford—which they still call home today—sported long, straight rows of raspberry fields and chicken barns behind modest houses graced by well-manicured flower beds. One could identify the orderly arrangement of a Mennonite farm in one glance. As their numbers grew, they built churches where all their social and religious needs would be met, just like in the old country. They quickly worked off their travel debts and continued to purchase land through hard work, communal support, and disciplined living.

The day I was born—the second child in my family, just like my mom—a new Sunday school wing was under construction at the church my parents attended. Upon hearing my arrival was imminent, my father dropped his hammer so he could drive my mom to the hospital.

The few black-and-white pictures taken of my childhood captured me in hand-sewn dresses, all made by my mother. A few years later, my sister and I were photographed side by side wearing matching outfits, ready to attend a special Christmas or

Easter service held at our church.

Mennonite wives cooked, cleaned, gardened, sewed, canned foods, worked the fields alongside their husbands, and raised the children. This matched the life they had left behind. They didn't leave because they wanted to escape their way of life; they left because it was a matter of life and death. In their minds, recreating the same rituals and routines they'd known before the war was a recipe for success—for them and the next generation.

All the traditions and practices from the old country were staunchly entrenched in every decision they made in this new country. So were the rules. No dancing. No drinking. No smoking. No swearing. Pray before you eat. Attend church every Sunday. Accept Jesus as your saviour. Share your conversion experience. Wear your Sunday best to church. Learn German. Get baptized. Get married. (Implied: Stay married.) Bear children. Love your neighbour (but don't be like them if they aren't from the same faith). Work hard. Be modest. Be humble. Did I mention work hard? Don't discuss your private life with others (if they're from outside the community, but especially if they're within your church community). Don't take another's life (and therefore do not join the police force or the military). Be responsible with your belongings. Tithe faithfully. Do not covet. Do not gossip. Do not overindulge (and to be on the safe side, stay clear of pleasure when possible). Love the Lord your God with all your heart, soul, and mind.

As a basic framework, those rules can create an upstanding community—that is, when the bulk of the community members are emotionally and spiritually healthy. But when an entire community is uprooted and transported to another country because of the brutality of war, there will be some breakage and spillage. Things don't heal well when there is an unspoken consensus that being grateful to God for the new opportunity means no one should discuss the terrible things that happened before they got here. Under these conditions, rot can set in. Simply making the outside appear tidy doesn't mean the inside is functioning well. When outward appearances are prioritized through rules that can be enforced and measured, an individual's pain is often held captive. When innocence is lost long before a child is able to mature naturally, other things get lost as well. And when a new baby slides into the world through a birth canal dotted with grief, trauma gets passed along, requiring emotional shovel work for the next generation. Damage from unspeakable trauma almost always shows up in unexpected places later in life.

I am not thinking about my ancestors' traumatic trek to a new world as I sit at the edge of my bed trying to drum up the courage to dial my parents' number. I have to tell them I am leaving my marriage. If telling Tom and the girls was the hardest, this conversation is a close second.

I know what they'll think. I know what this means about their status as parents within their church community. In their world order, a daughter who is leaving her perfectly decent husband has no justifiable excuse. They may even be forced to turn their backs and shun their own child in order to preserve their beliefs.

My stomach is in knots and my heart is beating into my throat as I dial their number and wait for them to pick up. I am having a hard enough time trying to explain how tremulous my life feels to me, so instead of requesting their understanding, I plead for their grace. They have noticed how unhappy I seem but had no reason to think it had anything to do with my marriage. It does and it doesn't—and this is what I need to figure out, I explain to them as my body slumps forward so I can rest the weight of my head against the flat of my palm. The phone feels like a brick in my other hand.

As I listen to the ensuing protest, I'm not surprised that it all feels like failure with no chance of redemption. My mom clambers to locate a lifeline in what I'm saying so she will have an explanation when people ask. My father is quieter, waiting for what I've just said to sink in. In the weight of waiting to hear my dad's thoughts, my mom trills on about my girls and how bad divorce is for the children. She prods her husband, demanding that he speak up, hoping that he will draw a line in the sand or make a statement that will change my mind. To my Mom's disappointment and my surprise, he simply says that while this news is shocking, he loves me and will continue to love me, regardless of what happens.

The phone line is quiet. Tears are streaming down my face, and my voice doesn't work. My father has said his piece, and he doesn't qualify it with how heartbroken he feels or what my decision will cost him in arguments with his wife later. He opts to express love to a person in pain instead of berating them with biblical mandates and community rules. My father somehow manages to stand in the gap, leaning in with his heart. This is not something I imagined I could dare hope for. I can't tell if I'm crying because I just received what I didn't think was possible under the circumstances or because now that I've told the two people who have known me the longest in life, this is really real. There's no turning back; there's only crawling forward.

Like in the game Jenga, I have pulled out the one block that up until now has kept all the other pieces, even some secret ones, together. Leaving my marriage, being such a public act, forces everything to come crashing down. All the pieces of my life lie scattered around me, making it difficult to move in any direction. I am in a Cold War of my own, chaos and destruction as far as the eye can see, the enemy not immediately in view. In my new home, with my head sleeping on a new bed, I am also in a new country of sorts.

One thing I know for sure is that in this new world, nothing is off the table for discussion. In fact, things that haven't been dealt with in the past, in my life and the generations that came before me, need to be brought to the table. How am I going to create a better life if I keep doing the same thing? What worked well enough for previous generations will not be the default template for me.

Since that day on my parents' lawn, I've never again done four hundred cartwheels in a row, but these days I regularly feel myself turning, twisting, and spinning myself around as I summon the wisdom of my body. I ask my arms to point me in the right direction. I ask my hips to reveal their intuition. I ask my legs to take me on adventures. And I invite all this information to make its way through my heart first so I can know what is true and what is façade. When I fall, I lie searching for evidence of blue skies on the horizon, even if the forecast calls for clouds.

My life isn't a singular entity; it's strung together with what came before me and what comes next. However, my foremost responsibility is to follow the energy that's in motion inside of me now. There are prickles. There are successes. And every time I land upright, back on my feet, I am grateful for another rotation around this planet.

HARD CANDY

While intercourse may be how I lost my virginity on my wedding night, I lost my innocence long before that. The way life dragged me across that wobbly bridge jaded my perspective from then on. As I was coming of age, two men I should have been able to trust plucked my innocence to feather the nest of their own pain.

The first was my grandfather.

Opa had seen his fair share of a world gone mad during wartime, yet still maintained a rare sense of optimism in his older years. For as long as I could remember, I was always invited to climb up into his lap. Most times this would initiate a round of "*Huppa, huppa reiter*," in which he would bounce me in rhythm to the poem's words, which he would say-sing in his mother's tongue. The song always ended with me squealing in delight as his legs would part and he'd catch me, his oldest granddaughter, before I fell through to the ground.

Opa loved to hand out hard candy to all the grandchildren, but it was only the granddaughters who were invited to play the game where the candy was passed back and forth from his mouth to yours and then back again. He sat in his overstuffed chair, pushed against the wall of their living room so there was room for all the gathered relatives to visit in a large circle. The candy game with Opa was played on full display of the extended family and deemed a cute exchange.

He had fathered seven children—two sons and five daughters—and survived a war he didn't sign up to fight, but under their roof, it was his wife, Oma, who was in charge of their lives. When our family arrived at their house for Easter or Christmas holidays, the aroma of roasting chicken or turkey greeted us before we opened the door. We spilled into the house and yelled our hellos. We only ever saw Oma's back at that stage of the event, as she vigorously stirred gravy at the stove. A tight bun captured her long, grey hair (which I never saw loose), while her full-body apron kept her homemade dress safe from stains. She barked orders at her eldest daughter and her older sister, neither of whom had married and consequently lived with Oma and Opa. As children, we knew that it was best not to enter the kitchen close to mealtime (or anytime, for that matter).

It was always Opa who came to greet us as we stripped off our shoes and piled our jackets on the growing heap in the laundry room. You knew the order in which you'd arrived by the height of the pile already begun by the other relatives.

When the call was sounded to begin the meal, each of the adult women grabbed a steaming bowl to carry down the stairs into the large multipurpose room that had been set up ahead of time. There were long benches for the cousins to squish onto to maximize space in this growing family. From a young age, I felt the tension and urgency of keeping the food hot while everyone jostled for seats. No one was allowed to touch the food until grace was said, so a crescendo of raised voices, most especially my Oma's, was how the meal would always begin. The women did all the cooking and cleaning, but traditionally, the male "head of the household" had to bless the food. Oma seemed disappointed in Opa at these times, and the contempt in her voice as she snarled at him usually landed just as the room had finally quieted. Any attempt by him to plead his case was met with a swift rebuff in their common language. It was a public window into their private relationship that I didn't understand. He always seemed to disappoint her, and I couldn't imagine it was just the fact that he hadn't said grace in a timely fashion.

As I doused my mashed potatoes with rich, buttery gravy, I wondered if hot food was truly more important than how people felt around the table of this large extended family. These thoughts didn't last long because there were always enough cousins around to distract me with the latest crafts they'd learned. As the women were doing dishes by hand upstairs, the men returned to the living room to rest their full bellies over easy conversation, and the kids had free rein over the rest of the house.

During any large gatherings that spanned the better part of the day, I'd eventually need a break from people of any age, and I'd wander around the house alone. With increasing frequency, my Opa would find me at these times. He seemed to magically be around when I was coming out of the bathroom on the far side of the house or in the laundry room rooting through my bag for a book I had brought from home. I had no reason to feel cautious in his presence; in fact, he was the one adult who seemed to care what I was up to. But as I reached my pre-teen years, the way he approached me and wanted to hug and kiss me felt uncomfortable and struck me as odd. My parents never hugged me; it wasn't part of our culture to show affection in that way. He would coo about how much he loved me and what a good girl I was. I would try to make an excuse and brush past him, but he always seemed to be blocking the exit with his large frame. He was speaking so sweetly to me that I felt guilty for not wanting to stick around and reciprocate.

As my legs grew longer and my body began to show the first signs of maturing into a young woman, he kept insisting that I come sit on his lap in order to show me things. I was too big to sit on anyone's lap, but because of our history, it felt familiar. As I sat against his chest, he sometimes slid his hand under my shirt. I had no reason not to believe him when he whispered that this would help my breasts grow as he rolled my budding nipples between his fingers.

There was no place in my life where I was being taught about sexuality or boundaries with the opposite sex, let alone adults. Growing up on the farm, I saw how animals interacted and procreated, but this didn't help me know what was appropriate in my interactions with my Opa. My body didn't understand what he was doing, which made it even more challenging to express my discomfort to him. I plopped my uneasy resistance to his touch onto a growing list of other things I didn't prefer but had no choice about because an adult was in charge. These included going out in the middle of winter to collect the eggs for hours or being forced to eat lumpy porridge that made me gag. Most of my personal preferences weren't under my own jurisdiction.

In my world there was no category for my Opa's behaviour, so when it came time to file these experiences, I didn't have a label for them. My innocent mind didn't make any sexual connections, but my body mounted its own defence. I began to cross my arms over my chest when Opa walked into the room, avoiding eye contact and keeping my distance from him. I tried to carefully plan my trips to the bathroom, but I wasn't always successful at avoiding him. When I refused to sit on Opa's lap when he called me over, I was scolded for my lack of warmth by my parents, who had no reason to suspect anything inappropriate was happening to their eldest daughter. Secrets became my inner armour since boundaries weren't allowed.

Mr. Grimsby was my sixth-grade teacher. In stark contrast to the gentler female teachers I'd had since kindergarten, his explosive, red-faced reaction to anything that angered him made the entire class uneasy. To my twelve-year-old eyes, he appeared tall—and ancient. Stray grey hairs curled out of his nose and ears; long sideburns framed his thin lips, which were always slightly pursed. His beady eyes darted around the room, always seeming ready for a fight.

At the start of each new day, he barked out orders as he marched into the classroom; I kept my mouth shut and sat up straight, hoping to avoid attention. The first time Mr. Grimsby called me out into the hall, I rose slowly from my desk on shaky legs, nearly paralyzed by fear. I prayed I hadn't done anything wrong, because students asked to leave the room were usually in serious trouble. Once I was in the hallway, he smiled and asked me to follow him into the office. He needed me to run off copies on the Gestetner, a machine that duplicated pages long before photocopiers were invented. His voice was soft and he seemed like a completely different man as he showed me where to refill the paper and how to turn the large drums. I watched carefully and hoped I wouldn't forget the steps because I sensed this gentler version of Mr. Grimsby could turn back into a raging bull in an instant if provoked.

That was the first of many tasks and special requests I received from my teacher. He moved my desk to the front of the classroom and positioned it right next to his. I could tell by my classmates' snide comments at recess break that they weren't thrilled with my upgraded status, but I hadn't asked for the extra attention and didn't feel I had any say over it.

Several times a week we were required to hand in our spiral-bound notebooks at the end of the day, and the following day our work would be returned to us marked up with red ink. When Mr. Grimsby placed my notebook on my desk one day, I noticed a paperclip attached to the front cover. When I opened my notebook, I saw that an envelope with my name on it had been clipped to the inside cover; I opened it to find a long, handwritten letter. When everyone was working quietly at their desks, I read what Mr. Grimsby had written to me about his life outside the classroom. He went on to express how he saw me as a close friend in whom he could confide. The letter contained instructions to clip the letter back inside the cover when our notebooks were collected again at the end of the day so it wouldn't fall into the wrong hands. There was no doubt in my mind that this was to be our secret.

My innocence peeled away slowly over the school year as events I didn't understand collided with my developing body. Interactions I filed away without any identifying labels from my interactions with my Opa got lost in my patchy filing system, making me more vulnerable to the overtures of this new man placed in authority over me.

More letters came attached inside my notebook, and the topics became increasingly personal. Mr. Grimsby shared about ongoing challenges he had in his marriage and with his children. He expressed in glowing prose how special I was and how much he appreciated having me in his life. As I read his letters at my desk, I felt increasingly uncertain about what I was supposed to do with this information. I never wrote anything back to him, which made the exchange one-sided. I felt special that he chose to share things with me, but I also suspected this couldn't be appropriate behaviour from a teacher. But since I was raised to obey adults, especially male authority, I continued to do what I was told.

Occasionally Mr. Grimsby sent me to the supply room to retrieve paper for a class project. The supply room was a long, narrow closet with deep shelves on either side that held every kind of art supply for the entire school. I'd walk the length of the school hallway and turn on the supply room light searching for the requested item. Mr. Grimsby would arrive moments later and turn off the light but leave the door open; when I noticed how he would leave the moment he heard footsteps, I understood the door stayed open so he would be able to hear anyone approaching.

One particular day in the supply closet, Mr. Grimsby took a few steps toward me, closing the space between us. "God brought me to this school so we could be together," he said in a soft, gravelly voice. I was taught to always accept God's will, and if an adult male proclaimed to know the will of God, my own thoughts about the situation were to be dismissed out of hand.

I stood still, wishing he would back away. I could feel my heart beating into my neck as his breath flooded my face. Whatever he had for lunch offended my nose, but I didn't dare turn away. *These interactions usually only last a few minutes, so I just have to be patient a little longer.*

"Rita, do you understand how special our relationship is?" He peered at me, and I felt thankful the lights were off so he couldn't examine my face for agreement. "But no one will understand this, so I need you to keep it a secret. It's our secret." He smiled and then continued, with more urgency in his voice, "You have to promise me you'll never tell anyone."

I blinked my yes but that wasn't enough. "Promise me. Say it." His voice escalated and I knew I had to respond.

"No, I, I won't tell," I managed to say. Even if I had wanted to tell someone, I wouldn't have known what to say. *Mr. Grimsby sends me to get supplies and writes me letters and he says nice things to me?* In my twelve-year-old mind, if I spoke up it would result in the same look of disappointment from my parents as when I tattled on my sister. I would be the one who would be punished.

My words seemed to settle Mr. Grimsby's anxieties; satisfied that I'd keep the secret, he wrapped me in a tight hug and then turned to leave.

I knew the drill. I would wait a few more moments before returning to the classroom with whatever paper I chose from the stacks around me. Looking through all the colourful art supplies would soothe my worries and distract me from what had just happened.

In the spring, under Mr. Grimsby's guidance, our sixth-grade class hatched a plan to put on a play. We calculated that the admission fee we would charge would make us enough money to go on a much-desired class field trip at the end of the school year. For the first time that year, there was a sense of optimism in the classroom. The parts in the play were given out by the teacher, and I landed the lead role of the princess. We practised during school hours, but when we were ready to learn the staging at the venue, Mr. Grimsby arranged to come by my house to pick me up for the final rehearsals at a local community centre.

Driving in his car, he grabbed ahold of my hand. I didn't dare remove it. Instead, I sat quietly, my palm clammy, waiting to reach our destination. The inner resistance I felt reminded me of the times my Opa would touch me, and I wondered if this was simply what affection from men felt like.

The night of the dress rehearsal, Mr. Grimsby came by the house and my mom proudly showed off the dress she had sewn for me. He gushed at her skills, also exclaiming over how beautiful I looked in the dress. I could see in his gleaming eyes that I was his princess, and not just for this play. It felt selfishly good to be chosen, picked out of a group, in contrast to my regular life where I was just one of four children vying for attention. But competing with that feeling was my confusion over this special status. *I know I'm not the most beautiful or the smartest girl in class, so why me?*

The following week, Mr. Grimsby insisted I follow him to the back of the library. Once we were out of view, he pulled me to him behind a tall rack of books.

"What's going on?" he asked. "You seem upset about something."

I had tried to distance myself from him since the night of the play. With my escalating confusion over his advances, combined with the fact that now he'd been to my home and I had sat in his car—my worlds felt like they were collapsing into one uncomfortable, endless play.

"I'm not sure," I stammered, uncertain how to put words to any of it. "I don't think this is right," I managed to say, feeling I was walking an impossible tightrope between honesty and not upsetting him.

"But I've told you time after time how special this is and how much I care about you. How can you say that?" His voice was a whisper, but I could hear frustration leaking through in his strained tone. I wasn't going to risk saying more, so I just looked down at my shoes.

He wrapped his arms around me, and I smelled a mix of aftershave, smoke from the teacher's lounge, and something else that reminded me of a dark closet. As I scrambled to figure out a way to get away from him without offending him further, he released the embrace. But instead of stepping back, he swooped in and kissed me. I fought the urge to turn away and wipe my mouth. I didn't like the feel of his lips on mine. Mercifully, he made a hasty exit moments later, probably fearing someone would see us—but little did he know we'd already been spotted.

I hope he'll never do that again, I wrote in my diary before going to sleep that night. I was learning that was the only place I could express my true feelings—especially with all these secrets adults were asking me to keep.

I tried to think of a way to get out of my situation with Mr.

Grimsby but came up empty. Since there was only one sixth-grade class in the school, it wasn't like I could be moved into another classroom. I decided that enduring his rage would be much worse than putting up with his advances for the last couple months of the school year. If I just stayed small and quiet, then it would all be over soon. In some ways, it wasn't so different from attending long weekly church services. *Sit quietly, don't attract attention, and it will all be over soon.*

The next night, after bedtime, my parents came into my room to inform me that I wouldn't be attending school in the morning. Instead, my principal, Mr. Weeble, would be coming to the house to talk to me. I lay awake late into the night, clutching my blanket tightly to protect me from the cold dread that had crawled into bed with me. I couldn't put all the pieces together, but I suspected that somehow the secret was out. The thought that other people knew, and that God saw it all, made me want to run rather than face their looks of accusation. I was sure that I would be punished for my part in those secret encounters with my teacher.

Mr. Weeble sat across from me in our formal living room, which was usually reserved for Sunday guests and special visitors from abroad. My parents sat beside him and all eyes were trained on me. I methodically stroked the raised embroidery of the couch material, my hand tucked behind my leg so nobody else could see how nervous I was as I sat there, hanging on by a thread in this surreal situation. Mr. Weeble held a clipboard on his lap with a pen hovering above it. I could smell his hair cream and shoe polish—the same kind my dad applied on his Sunday shoes before church—from across the room. My parents appeared nervous and unprepared for this kind of conversation as they sat there quietly, wearing neither shoes nor product in their hair.

A sour taste of my betrayal of my teacher began pooling in the corners of my mouth as my principal extracted details about all those private moments while my parents listened. I felt exposed and confused. With Mr. Grimsby, I'd felt like an adult, and now in this room, I suddenly felt like a child again. I'd kept my promise to guard the secret, but now I was being forced to break it. I was more afraid of how Mr. Grimsby would react than any repercussions from the people in this room. And while I hoped this conversation could mean my freedom, I couldn't make sense of the allegiance I felt for my teacher. I ached to close my eyes and my mouth and my mind and go somewhere where I could think it through by myself.

When Mr. Weeble finally shoved his clipboard back into his briefcase, his verdict came in the form of an instruction. "You must not go anywhere alone with Mr. Grimsby again," he stated matter-of-factly as if that would solve everything. With that, he said his goodbyes and left. *Is that it?* I wondered as confusing emotions continued to rumble like a thunderstorm in the distance. I was relieved that I wasn't in trouble, but I couldn't quite believe I was just supposed to return to Mr. Grimsby's class as if this had never happened. It felt to me like shoving a toy back into its packaging but not being able to close the flap.

My parents had no idea what to say to me. I could tell they were disappointed that I had kept this secret from them. I tried to explain that I hadn't wanted this to happen, that I was just doing what my teacher told me to do, but I wasn't used to hearing my voice talk about such adult things out loud, and my parents had little else to say on the topic.

The limited conversations I had with the adults who knew what happened left me feeling that by keeping this secret, I was partly to blame. It felt similar to the time a whole stack of eggs crashed to the floor when my cart caught the edge of a wood post in the barn and I didn't know what to do with the sinking feeling in the pit of my stomach. I was doing my chores as directed, steering the cart the best I could, but now there was a huge mess and my father was upset. I didn't intend for the eggs to break or for my teacher to kiss me—but was I guilty of sinning because they were my eggs and my lips?

When I entered Mr. Grimsby's classroom the next day, I saw that my desk had been moved to the back of the room. I sat with my eyes downcast, but I could sense that he was in a foul mood the moment he strode into the room. Once we were working independently on the practice sheets in front of us, he approached my desk and, in a low growl, demanded I follow him out of the classroom. This time I was absolutely certain I was in trouble, and I had to force my legs to carry me.

As I entered the hallway, each beat of my heart clanged like a warning bell inside my body. He told me to go to the gym, pointing his whole arm down the hall to give his command extra punch. My voice quivering to match my knees, I told him that Mr. Weeble said I wasn't allowed to go anywhere alone with him. Anger flashed across his face, and I might have run in the direction of the principal's office if only my legs would work. Spit gathered in the corner of his mouth and then took flight as he barked at me. Like arrows shot from a bow that I wasn't allowed to dodge, he kept up his rant. He was disappointed. He thought we had something special. I had betrayed him. Why would I jeopardize his career and his family like this?

My body felt limp as tears threatened to flow from a faucet of emotions too complicated to name. When he finally stopped to demand I say something, all I could utter in my defence was that I hadn't told anyone. He didn't believe me, of course, and even as the bell sounded for recess and students came streaming out of classrooms, he kept yelling. Mercifully, the din of the student's excited voices and the smell of peanut butter and apples distorted the voice of a man who had decided I used to be everything and now I was nothing.

The truth didn't matter. My actual allegiance didn't hold up in his eyes. A girl in a man's world has to hope for the best and learn how to tuck and roll in order to survive. I stopped writing in my diary around that time. I had too much noise in my head to simply record the childish observations of normal life and not enough understanding to find words for what had happened.

No one took the time to help me put the pieces together. The agreement between the adults, I learned much later, was that because he hadn't violated my body, this would blow over with the least amount of fallout for everyone if it wasn't submitted for further review up the chain of command. Mr. Grimsby was allowed to finish out the school year to avoid any disruption to the rest of the students, and he would avoid disciplinary action if he promised to leave the school quietly after that.

Innocence evaporates slowly as we learn that the world is filled with people we cannot trust. Innocence is yanked out in fistfuls when an adult in authority over a child breaches sacred boundaries and the rest of the trusted adults in the room remain silent. Although the intent may be to protect the child from a messy world, this approach leaves the child without the necessary tools to navigate a messy future.

I tucked the incidents with my Opa and my teacher somewhere I didn't have to see or feel them very often. I didn't forget; I just didn't think that thinking about it would make my life better. At the time, I was too young to understand any of it, and misplaced guilt took root in the naive soil of my young heart and slowly rotted into shame. Not only had something bad happened, but I decided at some point that this also made me bad. Since I had been taught that I needed to be good or I'd go to hell, I did everything I could in my adult life to convince myself and everyone around me that I was indeed good.

I concluded that I'd been right to keep my situation with my teacher a secret. This exposed version felt much worse. I had questions that no one seemed prepared to answer. As I tried to formulate my own answers, the only resource I had access to was a handful of mislabeled files shoved into the filing cabinet of my twelve-year-old mind.

EMBRACING THE PAST

"We need to talk about what happened with Opa," I say matter-of-factly, wondering why my voice sounds different, higher and thinner, as it comes out of my mouth.

"I don't know what there's possibly left to say," responds my mom, her eyes not venturing anywhere they might have to look into mine.

"What I'd like to discuss," I continue calmly, noticing my pulse speed up the moment I begin the sentence, "is how much I still want you to believe me. It's so hard to heal from what happened with Opa knowing you side with him."

The encounters with my Opa during my childhood might have remained buried in my memories had it not been for another incident at my parents' house many years later.

It was my parents' turn to host the Easter gathering for my mom's side of the family, and Tom, the girls, and I had come for the whole weekend to help prepare. When it looked like relatives were getting ready to make their exit at the end of the evening,

I figured I'd get a jump on lugging our overnight bags upstairs from the basement, where we slept as a family when visiting my parents on the farm. My youngest daughter was only a few months old, and that meant a full arsenal of baby things needed to be packed up. I reminded myself that I'd have to leave room in the trunk for my sister's stuff because Ruth would be returning to the city with us so she could catch the ferry in the morning.

I heard footsteps approaching the bedroom and assumed it was my husband coming to help—but when I looked up, I saw my grandfather's stooped frame instead. Something about the way Opa was standing in the doorway sparked a wave of uneasiness, but I brushed it off.

Opa made small talk in a mix of German and English as I folded my daughter's tiny clothing into the diaper bag. I only saw Opa a couple times a year at family gatherings, and my childhood interactions with him were mostly folded away and stored as well. At that point, he was an old man with bad knees, and I was a married, educated woman with two small children, so there was no reason why we couldn't have a pleasant adult relationship. When he saw my bags were zipped up and ready for transport, he asked me for a goodbye hug. Despite the resistance that flared up instinctively, I opened my arms and went in for a quick embrace to avoid any awkwardness. His right arm circled around my back, but his left hand landed squarely on my right breast.

Feeling as if an elastic band on time had just snapped against my body, I stood immobilized, feeling heavy and weightless at the same time. I instantly felt twelve years old again, transported back to the last time his hands were on my body, powerless to move and without a voice. My brain launched into overdrive, frantically trying to find a way to explain to my body what was happening. The only plausible explanation that emerged was that Opa had mistaken my breast for my shoulder. There is no way he would have the balls to cup the breast of a nursing mother.

The entire scenario was inconceivable to whatever parts of me had not gone numb. The moment he released his grip, I flipped into action, unable to tell if I was embarrassed to be so shocked or shocked to be so embarrassed. Fumbling to grab my bags, I muttered something in departure as I brushed past him and ascended the stairs, two at a time, the bags slamming against my legs as I went.

My husband buckled himself in between our daughters' car seats in the back of the vehicle. The three of them would be asleep in minutes. As my sister arranged herself in the passenger's seat beside me, I could barely make out what she was saying, feeling everything and nothing as I put the car into drive. I interrupted her chatter to offer a monotone description of what just happened in our childhood bedroom.

Blood slowly returned to my limbs as I told her everything, including all my childhood experiences with our Opa. I'd never said anything to her before and was only a little surprised when she in turn confided a few of her experiences as a child. The times she recalled weren't as frequent or exactly the same as mine, but as she spoke, anger crawled up my spine and into my throat, making it difficult to swallow the truth that this most recent incident couldn't be written off as an accident on Opa's part. His inappropriate behaviour wasn't relegated to the distant past, and it didn't just happen to me.

I was furious with myself that I hadn't said something or done something the moment Opa's hand grabbed my breast. I still didn't understand why my body and mind betrayed me as it was happening. The following week, after many sleepless nights, I made an appointment to speak with him alone. The language barrier between us often got in the way of a fluid dialogue during normal conversations, and this topic made it almost impossible to have a frank discussion. I left feeling frustrated but proud that I had finally taken action.

Soon after, I learned that Opa had taken similar "liberties" with other females in my extended family. We shared our experiences with each other and decided it was important to bring the entire extended family together to discuss the situation. My most recent experience with Opa meant that the next generation, my young daughters, may also be at risk.

The shocking consensus of those relatives who spoke up at the extended family meeting was that we were giving our kind-hearted patriarch an unwarranted bad name by labelling a simple misunderstanding of affection as sexual indiscretion. When questioned by his own children, Opa expressed that he loved his granddaughters, and while he never denied his actions, he claimed that it wasn't done with sexual intent, and therefore he had done nothing wrong.

Any follow-up conversation with my relatives was encrusted with the message that if our concerns became public, it would damage our family's honour. This left an especially bad taste in my mouth. The fact that family honour was valued more than the impact of Opa's dishonourable behaviour towards vulnerable minors made it feel like the knife already lodged in my back was now being turned.

Historically, the Mennonite commitment to family and community was a matter of faith and survival for many centuries. There were so many sermons preached about the dangers of the ungodly world outside, but no one was watching their own flock for signs of danger. With no models in place within the church community for how to process these kinds of situations in a healthy way, my family's solution was to minimize the claims of the younger generation, hoping that would put an end to the uncomfortable conversation. Although I was learning this was a common response, repeated in families and communities all over the globe, I was utterly gobsmacked by this blatant dismissal from my own God-fearing family. It was painfully clear that women in a man's world are willing to sell out their own daughters.

Eventually, it mattered less what the rest of my extended family thought—it was my relationship with my mother that I cared about. This was her father, and she found it virtually impossible to believe my account if that meant disagreeing with her siblings and seeing her father as a perpetrator. The idea that my mother so openly sided with her father instead of me, her daughter, was a razor-edged thought that continued to cut every time it crossed my mind. I had explained it all to her countless times and had asked her to read books on the subject. I had been upset with her, I'd cried and pleaded with her, but nothing seemed to shift my mother's position on the topic.

Sitting across the table from me now, my mother looks uncomfortable, the same look of agitation around this topic that she had ten years ago when it all came out. She lets out an audible sigh, interlacing her fingers in preparation for another round of an impossible conversation. Now that I am essentially starting my life over and questioning every belief I've held, it feels important to give this large chip on the shoulder of our relationship another opportunity to be removed. The thought that she might feel vindicated, that the end of my marriage was somehow added proof of the weakness or fault she had suspected in me, makes my heart ache all over again.

"I know this is hard, Mom," I say more softly, "because we're talking about your father. This can't be easy. But you believe me about what happened with my teacher in elementary school, right?"

She looks up with a weary look on her face and says, "I've already told you that I don't remember any of that."

"Not even the principal's visit in our living room?" I prompt, trying to control the disbelief that is creeping into my voice, even though this isn't the first time I'd heard her say that. It didn't seem to matter that after my best friend saw my teacher kiss me, she told her mother, who promptly called my parents and the principal. There are other people who could help fill in the blanks of her memory, but she seems content to claim ignorance on the entire event.

"No. I told you I don't remember," she stammers, looking away.

We sit quietly for a moment, but it is far from quiet inside my head. How can a healing conversation happen if one party doesn't want to participate? I feel a familiar sensation trickle down the length of my spine into my legs. I want to get up, walk away, and never come back. What kind of mother doesn't believe her own child and doesn't want to remember major events in her child's life?

Perhaps a mother who has experienced the brutality of war as a child herself, I remind myself. I've never known true hunger or blistered feet from running for my life. I was raised by parents and grandparents and a whole church full of relatives who had been to hell and back in their lifetime. Against that backdrop, my pain seems small in comparison. Is it possible that the places they've let me down are the exact spots where their own pain hasn't been addressed? Could there be places where their own scars have created a "dead zone" for memory and feelings?

"Mom, is it that you *can't* believe me," I say when I can finally speak again, "or that you *won't*?" It sounds like a trick question. She doesn't respond, so I try a different approach, "Is there a way for you to be my mother for a few minutes, instead of your father's daughter?"

I am asking the world of her. This request could tear a hole in her safety net and rip mine down alongside hers, and I know it.

She looks up at me, her face miserable with confusion and frustration. I sense she doesn't have anything else to say. She still can't give me what I think I need the most—for her to believe me and thereby acknowledge what happened to me.

I feel my heart sputter as I imagine this conversation ending the way all the others have. I fear I will continue to hold this against her forever and therefore be powerless to ever heal this festering wound.

What is it I truly need at this point in my life? I ask myself, trying to keep desperation at bay a little longer. *What might she be able to give me that won't require her to upend everything she counts on to make sense of her life?* I search my mind, but nothing comes into view. Then I take a slow, deep breath and search the acreage of my heart—and that's when I know.

As if she can read my thoughts, she looks me directly in the eyes for a fleeting moment, and in a strained voice, she asks, "What do you want from me?"

I know she needs this to be over too. It gnaws at her mother's heart. She looks like a trapped animal, pacing the cage of her many roles—mother, daughter, sister, wife—with no exit available that won't hurt someone. I feel her panic and her pain.

I suddenly want to free her from it all—and in doing so, I can only hope that I might free myself as well. I see my mother as not only a daughter who cannot betray her father but as a woman who is being asked to narrow her gaze and peer inside the scariest parts of herself.

So instead of asking the impossible, I ask her for one thing.

"Mom, will you simply acknowledge that you weren't able to be the mom I needed in this one area of my life?" I say gently. Not the areas where she loved me by spending the better part of the day baking fresh bread and making a huge pot of borscht, or by reading a mountain of books to my young daughters, or by sewing the broken seam on my favourite pants. Not in the way she taught me to be tidy without being afraid of getting dirt under my fingernails, or the way she showed me to use the pan drippings in my gravy to make the best chicken dinner, or the way I learned to do tasks efficiently just by being near her.

I cannot ask her to denounce her whole world by judging her father, and I don't want to reject all the goodness she has showered on me over the years. But right now, I need to know she understands that her decision to side with her father has had a massive impact on me. I need to hear that she gets that. I desperately want to forgive her, to allow her to just be a person who is doing her best like everyone else. If she can manage to give me this one key piece, I will find a way to do the rest.

"I'm sorry," she sputters, tears filling her eyes. Then she does something unusual for her upbringing and within our family. She stands up, comes over to me, and opens her arms to me. I am out of my chair to receive her hug by the time she reaches me. It is more than I asked for. It is exactly what I need. Her apology, an acknowledgement that she can't be my mom in this area, allows me to release her from the role I assumed she had to take in order for me to heal.

I accept the baton that my mother hands to me and continue the redemptive race from there. I am now free to nurture myself in the areas that still need care and mothering without waiting for my mother to do it. Not only does this allow me to heal on my own terms, but I believe it makes me a better mother to my daughters. It helps me admit my own limitations as a parent and to know when to apologize to them. I don't need to have all the answers for their lives. I just need to do my part the best I can, try not to fumble my hand-off of the baton to them, and then cheer them on as they run their stretch.

A few years later, in a rare moment alone with my father, he comments on how much better the relationship between my mother and me has become since those hard conversations, even though her perspective remained the same.

"She's still the same person. She hasn't changed." He winks knowingly, having recently celebrated fifty years of marriage with her.

"I know." I smile back. "But I've changed what I need from her. I am able to love her as a person living the human experience alongside me—a person I also call 'Mom.'"

THERE'S A WAY

He asks me to sit down as he reaches for a pen. "Show me your wrists, Rita," he urges with a voice that I've never been able to resist for long. It's not exactly his voice that's particularly sexy; it's the way it lilts so playfully, even as he sounds completely certain about what he's saying. It's the combination that's sexy. He is a salesman, and he has mastered his craft. At times, his approach feels like something out of a 1980s sales training manual ("Lesson One: Even if you're not sure, you must sound and look sure"). Yet, being with him, it's easy to see why these sales techniques are effective. His combination of slick charisma with just the right amount of vulnerability draws me in, even when I can see right through it.

Will has continued to develop his communication skills, and after more than twenty-five years in jobs that all required selling an idea or a product, he is exceptionally good at it. He can read people instantly and then cleverly adjust his volume and eye contact so he never appears desperate. Sales is an instrument he plays better than anyone I've ever met. Even when I know I'm being sold to (and I have peeked behind the curtain a few times over the years to watch him pull the strings) things have a way of working out the way he wants. And the few times they didn't,

I never saw him sweat, which left me wondering if he readjusted so effortlessly that he made it work for him anyway.

As instructed, I stretch out my arms and turn them palms up, resting them on my legs. I would have preferred to curl up into a ball and disappear, but he knows how important this is to me, and he is here to help. He applies his sales savvy to everything in his life, and this time he is using it to sell me on my own future.

He uncaps the pen with his mouth and begins to write something on my skin, just above the last crease on my wrist. On my left arm, he draws an upside-down L, so that if I look down, it's the right way up. On my right wrist, he scrawls an S, which takes him a couple of practice swirls in the air to ensure it won't appear backwards for me.

I suspect I know what he's doing, but I don't say anything. I have no desire to go to my friend's birthday party, where I will likely run into people from my old church, including my estranged husband. I don't trust I have what it takes to keep myself steady under those circumstances for an entire evening. This will be my first large event since leaving my marriage where I'll see all the people I used to hang out with regularly.

Now that he has penned the initials of my two daughters' first names, Will clasps my wrists in his warm hands and holds my gaze for a few moments before he speaks. "You need to go tonight and hold your head high. Know that you're doing this for *them*," he coaxes, giving my arms a gentle shake as he emphasizes the word *them*. "It's a long road, and it's easy to get lost if we try to do it just for ourselves," he continues, "but when it's for them, too, we find the courage. When you forget that tonight, just look down at your wrists to remind yourself that you've got this and you deserve to be there."

Will's marriage ended a couple years earlier, so I know he's speaking from experience. I sat with him in a vehicle at the river's edge the day after he left his house, and we probably had some version of this conversation back then. That feels like a lifetime ago as I inspect my wrists and give him a weak smile.

Will and I have known each other for many years. He knows more about me—what my body responds to, what keeps me up at night, what hurts me and helps me—than anyone else, probably even my own husband. I shared it all with Will in pockets of time that we stole from our regular lives. And now that I'm not living my regular life anymore, I want more than just pockets of understanding. I desperately want to know full joy. I want to feel deep peace. And I need to know whether I am capable of unadulterated love. Am I broken beyond repair after everything that has happened to me and after all the dishonest things I have done? I know I need more help than Will has to offer.

After a couple of lackluster solo sessions with the same male marriage counsellor I was seeing together with Tom, I made an appointment with a female counsellor who received rave reviews from a friend. During the first session, she helped me see how I had effectively created a protective persona, an emotional and physical bodyguard, in the form of a subtle seductress. I rebuffed the idea initially, offended by the word and its ramifications, but I also knew what she was saying probably had some merit—enough that I couldn't be sure which part of me was actually taking the lead in this new solo life. I saw now that while I was married, the seductress felt like an outfit I could put on as needed. She was often braver than I felt and could get things done. Now that I was able to identify her role in my life, I saw where I regularly relied on her. I wanted to build this new life trusting all aspects of me, not hiding behind an act.

It made sense that after what happened with my grandfather and my teacher at a young age, I had formulated a way to protect myself from men who wanted something they had no right to take from me. As I matured I learned how to get a quick read on a man's intentions in order to avoid getting stuck in the same situations I had as a child.

It turned out that I could trust my body to know the difference between who was safe and who was not. Since I already learned by the sixth grade that keeping my mouth shut and avoiding eye contact wasn't effective when I was a target, I developed a more complex system. As I gained social skills and life experience, instead of retreating or avoiding men, I'd engage with the men who entered my orbit. I would get a feel for them; I'd sniff them out. I'd notice the way they moved their eyes and angled their body. Their motives became even more clear through their tone and the way they'd veer off into edgy topics (or not). Like a barometer, I could feel the air change when their agenda did not match mine.

"There were some unforeseen side effects when I engaged the help of the seductress," I admit to the counsellor. "Occasionally, I ended up confusing myself and the innocent men I was interacting with, which definitely created extra drama in my life."

"Of course this had pros and cons," assures the counsellor. "Like a magic trick, when you get everyone to look over there, you're also doing something over here, inside of you," she moves her arms apart to demonstrate the distance, "and if you don't understand what you're up to inside of yourself, you can end up tricking yourself as well."

I confirm how sometimes I would catch the attention of someone who enjoyed the ease with which I, and I guess my seductress, interacted. These men had cleared my safety test, but now they were intrigued—and I was drawn like a moth to their newly ignited interest in me. Somehow in all that protective game-playing, I think I became enchanted by my own skills. The seductress became imperceptibly woven into my personality.

"But who was who?" I purse my lips, beginning to understand more fully how a well-honed craft can become a double-edged sword. While I never seduced men with the intention of getting them into bed, my seduction often resulted in an emotional nakedness that was no less addictive. Who was the hunter and who was the prey?

"So, is this how you first met Will?" asks the counsellor.

"I'm not sure." I squint, looking up at the ceiling for a moment to think back through all those years. "But I always assumed that he was seducing me." It was almost like Will and I received the same script, and we each played our roles perfectly.

When Tom and I were new to the church and joined the Bible study group that met at Will's home, we quickly became family friends with his wife and kids. Over the years of weekly meetings, more interesting conversations were starting to happen after the study over drinks and snacks in the kitchen. Once the main group left, a handful of us would enjoy a soak in their outdoor hot tub. As the steam rose off the water, we discussed more worldly topics that wouldn't have made it onto the formal Bible study agenda. I looked forward to those times and the exhilaration that came from sharing our shadow selves with each other under moonlit skies.

I had never met anyone like Will. His wife was from a Mennonite family, but he had been raised in a more liberal church environment. I was drawn to the ease with which he always invited deeper, provocative conversation. Most of the church boys I had grown up with were the silent, hard-working types. With Will there was no topic that was off-limits, and while initially I assumed he was a harmless sales guy, my radar for potential danger admittedly spiked on occasion.

I make sure my counsellor hears just how slowly everything moved with Will. I notice my desire to assure her, and myself, that I'm not a terrible person. I also know I'm only going to get to the bottom of things if I'm willing to admit when I've done terrible things.

"After knowing each other for a couple of years, one day I got a phone call from him regarding the upcoming week's Bible study that he and I were leading together," I begin. "Like butter on hot toast, it quickly melted into a longer talk about tastier topics. The next day he called to tell me he was going to stop by during the day to discuss our plan for the study." The counsellor raises one eyebrow, indicating she already knows what is probably going to happen next. I roll my eyes, knowing it sounds pathetic, and immediately I feel defensive. "I had absolutely no intention of allowing Will anywhere near my body, but he never actually asked. Like a highly skilled sales technique, his approach was so smooth it was almost hypnotic."

The first kiss was part trance, part fairy tale, part awakening. His kisses were like a key that opened a treasure box inside of me that I'd never had access to before. I knew it was wrong and that it trampled on my marriage vows and every image I ever had about what kind of person I wanted to be.

I was frozen in place by the intensity of the thrumming energy that surged between us. And that secret place inside where I had shoved my feelings about what happened with men in my childhood suddenly had an outlet that was consensual. Part of me desired to investigate the darker side of myself while the rest of me was disgusted by my behaviour and openly resisted. While these times with Will didn't go past kissing, it opened up a whole world of new desires that spilled over when our lips met.

After two weeks, I staged an internal protest, calling on every moral fibre I could locate, and in a gush of embarrassment and agony, I confessed everything to my husband. We had been married for about five years, and he had just been hired to take on a paid leadership role in our church, starting the following week. My actions served to end that job before it started. Tom wasn't about to take on a pastoral role while our marriage was taking on water. The next week, Tom accepted a job as a truck driver instead and insisted that I go to counselling.

I sat in the centre of the chaos I had created with a heart full of shame along with a whiff of secret relief. The role of being the associate pastor's wife had felt cloying before it even began. If my effort of keeping up appearances felt overwhelming as a regular church member, this role would have run roughshod over my desire for privacy and my aversion to endless church events. The unspoken but very real expectation of being a pastor's wife ramped up the pressure to perform beyond what I thought I could handle. I didn't know how to say this without sounding ungrateful and wrong. So I didn't say it with words but fractured it with a forbidden kiss.

"Did I intentionally want to ruin my husband's opportunity to be a pastor by what I did with Will?" I ask the counsellor with downcast eyes.

"What do you think?" she asks back, a frustratingly familiar echo from that side of the room that puts the spotlight back where it needs to be for true insight to happen.

"I'm not certain how clearly I saw the full connection at the time," I say slowly, measuring my words, "but I believe some part of me sent out a 'Hail Mary' at the eleventh hour. And my sessions with a counsellor back then helped me begin to identify some of the threads that connected my actions with my childhood experiences. But ..." I stop for a few moments, paging back through fifteen years of "regular" memories, attempting to catalogue where they intersect with my secret memories. "But then why did I start up again with Will once the pastoral job was off the table?!"

Prodded by shame, I would end my interactions with Will, sometimes for years at a time. But one phone call from him, asking how I was doing with that knowing voice, and a fire I thought had gone out would instantly burst into flame again. My guilt sensor became so overused by the number of times we started and stopped that I began to marvel at how numb I felt about my behaviour with Will. I had separated out parts of my life at such a young age, with files and feelings for my secret parts walled off from the visible aspects of my life. So this secret life with Will slid conveniently into the filing system that was already in place. And just like in my childhood, when I was sworn to secrecy, I told no one about my time with Will.

"Will became like a satellite life," I explain, extending my right arm its full length with my satellite fist hovering just beyond my peripheral vision. "In that life, that hour or two when we'd meet on occasion, it felt like I could step into that part of me I couldn't be in my regular life. By having a space where it was okay to be with the good, bad, and unacceptable parts of me, ironically I felt like a fuller version of myself with him. He introduced me to corners of my body I'd never met and places in my mind I'd never travelled. It was like when you take dance lessons with another beginner and it's awkward, and then the instructor takes you by the hand and whisks you around the room and you feel like you've always known how to dance. Will's hands communicated expertly with my body with no instruction required. I wouldn't have dared to go looking for this on my own, but all I had to do was allow Will in. He became my confessor, my sin, and my lifeline all wrapped into one. I recall wondering if perhaps I'd become addicted to playing in the shadows with him because I knew that at any moment this affair could ruin my whole life, but I did it anyway."

"What else did having access to a secret satellite place give you?" asks the counsellor, her face relaxed, showing no sign of judgment.

I take a few breaths, unsure how words are going to be enough to explain something I've never described to another person before. "I loved that I could go to this satellite world anytime, especially in my mind. When real life felt confusing, I knew I had a special place that was mine, and no one could follow me there. I never felt bored, because I could escape there in the middle of a church service, while I washed dishes, or on a late-night drive home from my parents' place. I don't know when this satellite world was first created, but I remember feeling like I needed a place to put things that didn't belong anywhere else. I'm guessing that started around the time I didn't know what to do with those interactions with my Opa. But it certainly was used a lot when my world cracked into pieces in the sixth grade. I got quieter and opted to spend more time alone after that experience with my teacher." I stop, surprised to realize how long I've had this place, like an inner tree fort that was eventually upgraded to an apartment in the sky that only I had the key to.

I look up, my eyes narrowing as I take in the abstract artwork hanging on the wall, trying to slow my spinning mind. I'm struck by how using language to express my inner world, I'm already beginning to change the shape of it. It's no longer a complete secret, and by choosing words to describe it, I'm inadvertently shining light into new corners of my world that I'd never have thought to look into by myself.

I scramble to collect the thoughts that glimmer in the corners of my mind. "Is it possible that when someone steals our innocence, our world breaks into two—the exterior world and our inner world? Like our brain creates a safe space where we can comfort ourselves?"

The counsellor seems in no hurry to respond, probably guessing that my question is answering itself.

"So, with Will, for example," I continue, sitting back in my chair, looking at where the wall meets the ceiling above the counsellor's head, "was he my satellite world, or was that just the place I processed everything I felt about what he and I did? Keeping our affair a secret made it feel extremely intimate and, I don't know, like, otherwordly at the same time. Was spending time with Will one way to keep my secret world active and interesting ... or was it an attempt to bring my broken worlds together?"

"Say more about *that*," the counsellor interjects before I even finish the sentence.

"Well, for all the rules I broke with him, he also helped me open in the places that were wounded at a young age and consequently on lockdown. For all the areas of my body that were trespassed by men whom I should have been able to trust, Will's welcome touch helped me reclaim those parts of myself. And although I was lying to others to be with Will, my body was telling me the truth. I doubt he knew what he was doing to me—for me—but I've suspected for a while now that this was providing something similar for him, although he and I barely spoke about his past. Is it possible that in addition to breaking our marriage vows, we were two wounded souls sneaking away for a few hours to make a break with our past?"

I stop talking to allow the pieces I just puzzled into place to come into sharper focus. Do these pieces fit, or am I searching for a way to justify bad behaviour? My right shoulder is tired from the number of times I held my arm up as I talked about my alternate, satellite world, and my brain feels fuzzy from sorting through so much history.

I feel extremely exposed. I have allowed someone into a space that wasn't prepared for inspection. I want to slam my satellite's door on the counsellor and suspend further conversation. I need time to wander around my secret place to figure out what to do with all these new thoughts.

The counsellor breaks my silence with a question that flies straight past my brain and lands at the door of my heart. "If Will was here right now, what would you say to him?"

Instantly, I feel an old familiar ache, a longing to escape into his voice on the other end of the phone one more time. I hadn't heard from Will for well over a year before I left my marriage, but two months into my new life, he found out somehow, and after hearing my distressed tone, he came over to give my wrists a pep talk. I saw Will a few times after that, but I already knew that he and I would never make a complete whole. Any temporary shelter I found in our exchanges wasn't a place I actually wanted to live. What he and I had together never walked either of us home through the front door; we always snuck out the back door under the cover of night. It wasn't sustainable or healthy. And now that I'm creating a new world, I desire to bring all these parts of myself together under one roof, into one mind and body, so I can expand into the fullest version of life yet.

"I'd thank him for the time I got to hang out with the unguarded parts of myself, parts that didn't yet fit into my regular world. I'd thank him for all the practice sessions." I laugh, but I know it's also true. And while the comment may have sounded flippant, it was actually a position of great honour and trust. I had grown up in an environment where there was no room to practise and learn from mistakes. There was the right path and there was the "get left behind" one. With Will, I couldn't pretend I was a good girl, and that allowed me to explore a larger swath of my humanity.

"Eventually it all came to a tipping point inside of me," I conclude, my hour with my counsellor in its final minute. "The façade I was struggling to keep in place in my regular life was probably doing as much damage as the secret affair." I see everything more clearly now that I'm able to talk it through. "The divide inside my spirit was so large that I couldn't possibly straddle my inner and outer lives anymore. It forced me to tumble out of both worlds," the inevitability hits me as I am saying it, "and I fell with such force that, like a walnut, I cracked myself open in the process."

"And now," the counsellor leans forward in her chair, preparing to stand, "you have a fresh opportunity to forge a more integrated life."

"Where there's a Will ..." I laugh lightheartedly, allowing the second half of that sentiment to escort me out of the office.

ACCOMPLICES

Even though I can't officially check the *single* box or the *divorced* box on government forms, the reality is that I live like a single person. I alone decide whether I play soft acoustic music while making dinner or turn on the English Premier League soccer game early on a Saturday morning. I have total say over which lights I switch on and when and what I eat. I notice that most often I opt for silence, dim lighting, and simple meals.

Growing up, I shared a bedroom with my sister, and in college I had roommates. Getting married young and adding two children a few years after, I've spent my entire life negotiating my immediate environment with others. While on occasion I went out for dinner by myself or to the theatre to watch a movie alone while I was still married, I've never lived completely on my own before. For the first time, I watch myself discover my own unfiltered preferences inside my living space. Although I feel emotionally pummeled by the separation and financially stretched by starting again from scratch, living alone feels like a healing sanctuary.

Well over a year into my new life, I join a group of girlfriends for a late-summer weekend away in Whistler, a year-round world-class resort a two-hour drive away, surrounded by picturesque mountains. It feels so good to laugh and be swept into the silliness of a gang of girls as we ride the gondola to the top of the hill to throw snowballs at each other while wearing t-shirts and flip-flops.

I feel curiously drawn to Pearl, an occasional backbencher in the Mennonite church I'd attended until recently, who is a member of this new gang. Our paths have never crossed before, even though we have numerous friends in common. Pearl is shorter than me by inches but easily makes up for it with a boisterous personality. She gives off a masculine vibe in how she dresses and speaks, and in the way she insists on making sure everyone's comfortable and their drinks are topped up.

Pearl and I stay up late the first night getting to know each other. I can't quite define what I feel in her presence. She takes charge and, at the same time, is very respectful and attentive. As we exchange intimate details about our lives, I begin to suspect that she has been born into a female body but is a male in all the ways that truly count.

Years before celebrities broke the silence around the gender conversation, I was introduced to the transgender community through a close friend. I understood immediately that it was different than being gay or a cross-dresser. And it was easy for me to see how a person's gender identity doesn't automatically inform their sexual preference. For anyone who hasn't had a reason to question the norm because they, and everyone they know, fit neatly into it, it can be a taxing mental exercise to dig beneath what the eye sees in order to understand all the deeper parts that make us who we are.

While my own gender identity matches the body I was born into, and my sexual orientation leans strongly toward the opposite sex, I have always felt a deep mismatch where my soul's path doesn't sync with my religious upbringing. When a society or one's church or the family you are raised in establishes what's considered normal and acceptable but it chafes you like an ill-fitting outfit, it can take a long time to piece together a version that fits better.

With sleep a low priority for the weekend, Pearl and I go for a walk in the wee hours of the night. As we search for the full moon that is scheduled to present itself from behind one of the snowclad mountains that envelops us, I ask Pearl questions that she hasn't yet dared to ask herself about her identity. She's opted to fly under the radar until now in order to avoid hurtful labels and the painful judgment that would undoubtedly come with them. I share my firsthand experiences of how keeping a secret to appease family and friends could mean the difference between being welcomed and being expelled from one's tribe. My recent loss of most of my church friends is proof positive that I have crossed that line, albeit for other reasons than Pearl's.

Pearl and I slowly test the waters of our deepening affection for each other over the next few months. I ask his permission to call him by the pronoun that matches his identity, and he sheds tears the first time he hears himself addressed in language that matches his true self. He values the safe space between us and trusts me to bear witness as his formerly barricaded feelings spill out from places he hasn't even realized he has stashed them. I am honoured to watch his inner and outer transformation. Where before he had shown subtle masculine traits, he now embraces a fuller version of his masculinity—first with me and then, judiciously, in more arenas of his life. He donates any clothing that is ambiguous and cuts his hair even shorter. I notice a change in his stride as he walks taller, lifted by the core belief that he doesn't have to guard his secret anymore, either from himself or from those he deems ready to hear his story.

PJ, the name Pearl claims for this new phase of life, is a generous man. He loves to serve and delight those around him—a trait that, though not exclusive to men, allowed him to be a "perfect gentleman" long before he identified publicly as a male. He takes every opportunity to shower me with gifts, both tangible and emotional. PJ pours me a glass of wine as I walk through the door after work, eager to hear about my day, and, in turn, shares all the shenanigans that occurred at his workplace. He washes and vacuums my vehicle regularly, and never backs down if he sees an opportunity to defend my honour publicly. While a storm of judgment rages outside, within our world of two, I feel desired, honoured, and protected.

In my wildest dreams, I wouldn't have imagined that my first relationship after my marriage would be with a man who is housed in a female body. And yet, he and I are on such a similar path in all the ways that matter. My world is under major renovation, and so is his—and we are both discovering what we want to be now that we aren't playing by someone else's rules. As he becomes more sure-footed in his identity, he finds the courage to have tough conversations with his family. Some of the family members embrace him, saying this confirms their experience of him; others vow they'll never speak to him again.

My desire to live free of shame and secrets finds its first serious hurdle in how to show up in the world within this new, unconventional relationship. In the beginning, it simply looks like I have a new female friend with whom I'm spending a lot of time. But once people find out it's more than that, the finger-wagging that hasn't yet completely abetted finds renewed fervour from those who feel justified in having an opinion about my life.

My family, still reeling from my recent exit from my marriage and the church, sees my new relationship as a sign that I have truly gone off the deep end. I explain that I am indeed doing deep inner work but that this relationship isn't the end of me. More accurately, it feels like a grand new beginning where I am free from limitations imposed by the church and, now, even society's norms. Despite what it may look like, this relationship doesn't feel like an act of rebellion but rather a decision guided by a brand-new way of responding to what life has to offer.

From our first intimate conversation, I understand who PJ is and I am clear about who I am. I never doubted that I am dating a man. Even when I'm labelled a lesbian by those who don't understand, it has a crystallizing effect on what my head and heart know is actually true. The more others judge the exterior of my life, the more clarity I feel inside me. Like a guitar player who twists the pegs wildly out of tune and then slowly reels them in, playing the string again and again to hear the progress, I may appear to have plunged my life into chaos, but, in fact, I am listening intently to the true tone of my own heart.

After eighteen months of experiencing how love plants a

garden of self-acceptance, PJ and I decide to part ways as a couple but remain friends. Our time of intense learning and support is complete. We huddled under an umbrella together during heavy rains and then, when the clouds cleared, we basked together in the healing sunshine of our supportive connection.

I essentially grew up inside my twenty-year marriage, and now my relationship with PJ has afforded me the opportunity to see that even in a fraction of that time, there are similar dips and turns in the lifespan of a couple. This second time, even with a partner so completely different from my husband's personality, I can see my part more clearly. I notice where I held the same hopes and was poked by the same insecurities and where I still act out of old pain. I have come a long way in a short time, but the nagging question about my capacity and ability to love still plays at the edges of my heart.

I need more practice in the art of loving. I spend time with a few different men I know from high school or meet through work. While I'm initially wooed by their shaved heads or exotic accents, I soon discover that we don't have much in common at a heart level.

My daughters dare me to cast my net wider, so I sign up on a new online dating site that is quickly becoming widely used. Responses to my dating profile fill my inbox, but I cringe at how forward the messages from these men are, their agenda glaringly transparent and their approach painfully unrefined. I'm not certain I would feel safe meeting most of them in person.

After a couple of months on the dating site, I'm almost ready to give up and chalk it up as a failed experiment when I receive a response from one of only two men I had initiated contact with on the site. He explains that he hadn't responded to my message because he was in the middle of courting another potential relationship from the site. Now that he's opted not to pursue things, he's available and interested in connecting with me. I immediately respect his personal code of conduct in this new world of online dating, and after a few more well-written, witty exchanges, we decide to meet in person.

I like his long limbs and full-faced smile right away. He's a graphic designer with two daughters a few years younger than my own. He has me laughing within minutes of our first meeting; this is a man who seems to prioritize heartfelt communication. It's easy to be with him, and he volunteers what's hurt him and what makes him happy with equal ease. Our second date finds us at a craft show in downtown Vancouver. We meander up and down the rows of booths, telling each other what delights and inspires us about each display. I feel new connections to beauty bubble up inside me as my gaze follows where his finger is pointing. He views the world through the lens of a true artist, and it lights a creative spark inside me just being in his presence.

But this expressive man ends up being as tortured as he is creative. The relationship begins to feel like an imbalanced teeter-totter where I'm at his mercy. When he feels good, he is magnetic and engaging; when he is down, I won't hear from him for days. The times when he doesn't respond to my attempts to reach out force me to consider what I truly desire in a relationship. The quieter he gets, the more clearly I hear my own heart speaking to me. His intermittent ability to show up mimics my own self-care over the years, so instead of judging him, I acknowledge where I have been doing this to myself. This relationship helps me see the folly of waiting for someone else to express their love to me so that I can feel lovable. When he and I part amicably after eight months, I know it's crucial I remain single for a while. I desire to learn how to offer and accept love within myself.

While dating, I have intentionally avoided going down any roads that might lead toward marriage. I notice how all my companions have been more like accomplices—a partnership pitted against past crimes against our hearts. Not surprisingly, love shows up dented and often running on empty. I see how often "I love you" is spoken to mask obligation or derail guilt, the true culprits behind so many so-called loving acts between two people. A proclamation of love is routinely slapped onto so many other feelings and situations that try to masquerade as love.

Healthy, real love insists that I ditch a trunkful of handy disguises, get into the trenches, and be willing to get dirty for the cause. I need to sand off years of war paint applied in the name of love and find the courage to peer at the love reflected in my own eyes when I look in the mirror. I am ready to fall in love with love. So instead of another boyfriend, I usher more friendships into my life. I realize that what most people really need is a go-to person—a close friend who cares enough to listen to the mundane events of any given day as they volunteer the same. While the instinct to couple up is strongly encoded in our DNA for good reasons, I prefer to dance to the rhythm of my own heart for now.

I head out on solo adventures on weekends. I walk countless miles in beautiful places and purchase tickets to movies and plays that catch my interest. I allow delight to call to me, and I don't feel sad or pathetic as I figure out not only what I enjoy but what enchants me. I'm not distracting myself—I'm discovering myself.

If I notice an issue niggling at me, I take time to sit with it. Instead of trying to fix the problem the way I used to, looking for someone or something to blame, I gently ask myself one simple question: "What would love look like right now?" As I present this query to my heart again and again, I am humbled to notice that the best answer is the one that makes my eyes go moist.

When asked in a kind and curious way, the question "What would love look like right now?" bypasses my problem-solving brain and knocks gently on my perceptive heart instead. "Keep moving in this direction," it will sometimes respond. Other times, "Turn for home; that's good for today." After an upsetting encounter, I might hear love whisper, "Just let it go; this is not yours to hold right now." My heart knows answers my mind can't even guess at.

When I ask myself "What would love look like right now?" I'm asking for the best answer at this moment; I don't need to know what the answer will be for all time. And it doesn't require a complex solution for every aspect of my life—just the very next step, guided by love. In the past, I regularly tried to out-think love, which made me unwittingly commit crimes against my own heart.

"What would love look like right now?" is a perfect reminder of what I desire most and immediate permission to take action, all rolled into one. And the answer always comes in the form of love, because that's what I am asking my heart to filter for. I'm in awe to discover that love has always been close by, patiently waiting for a simple, heart-felt invitation.

MIND WHERE YOU GO

I scan the atrium for a place to sit. Vancouver's Granville Island Market is brimming with its usual Sunday lunch crowd, a blend of tourists and locals. The food court offers my favourite Indian dishes—comfort food that was already calling to my stomach halfway through this morning's church service.

When I stopped attending my Mennonite church, I went exploring. I walked through the doors of many different faith backgrounds and eventually found myself regularly returning to a non-denominational church located near the market. The pastor has a way of delivering ideas that don't grate against my spirit—until today when I'd looked around at the congregation huddled in prayer and couldn't help but think it was the same game in a different jersey, that theology is essentially the same everywhere. The message from every pulpit is that I'm not enough and that I have a "God-shaped hole" that can only be filled in one way. I've already spent a lifetime shovelling myself into a sweat trying to fill that hole. Viewing my life through religious glasses places the focus on areas my eyes have no desire to search anymore.

The rich scent of my butter chicken is making my stomach growl as I stand with my tray in hand searching for a place to sit. I spy an empty chair at a table occupied by an older couple enjoying their lunch. I normally wouldn't even consider imposing, but after meeting so many new people in my temp job, I am more confident interacting with strangers. I approach the couple, who are focused on the plates in front of them, and ask if I can join them at their table. Their easy smiles, accompanied by an open-handed invitation to sit, turn a potentially awkward encounter into engaging banter. With rain softly falling outside, I didn't hope for more than a dry place to eat, but once I sit down, the conversation bounces from jovial to intimate, and I feel like I'm catching up with old friends.

"So Rita, what do you do for a living?" the gentleman asks after wiping muffin crumbs from his beard as his wife quietly sips her coffee beside him.

I feel the curry's spicy heat on my lips as I tease back saucily without missing a beat: "What's your best guess?"

A sparkle in his eyes gives away his delight at being able to play along. Guessing is fun but can also be dangerous. He seems undaunted by the potential of offending me with his answer as he quickly proffers his first guess. "I think you might be a doctor," he says, a sense of admiration for the profession obvious in his tone.

His guess is way off but in the right field. I was recently asked by a friend if I wanted to work at a pharmacy while a staff member went on extended medical leave. She thought my background as a temp, which included months at various medical facilities, would allow me to learn the position quickly. I was ready for something more permanent and was thrilled that the commute was less than ten minutes from my home.

Before this, I honestly haven't given much thought to what strangers might surmise I do for a living. I assume his guess has been influenced by the fact that I am wearing my best coat, having come directly from church. Clothes really do make a strong first impression, I remind myself. I'm intrigued and can't help but enquire what made him guess "doctor."

"Well, you're well dressed and you seem compassionate— and you're obviously intelligent," he begins, easily explaining his reasoning, then pauses. "But there's something else too. You have an air of hard-won self-possession," he adds with a considered seriousness that makes me stop thinking about how I'll reply so I can focus on what he just said. I know all four words individually, but putting them together in that order—"hard-won self-possession"—they seem to form a sturdy four-sided box, the kind someone could enter and then exit a moment later outfitted with superpowers.

When I tell him I work at a pharmacy, I expect it will puncture his lofty image of me, but he seems pleased with the closeness of his guess. I don't share how it was my work as a lowly temp that ushered me into the dispensary to count pills whose names I couldn't pronounce; I don't have formal training, but perhaps life itself is the ultimate training ground.

Before we part ways, I ask if he would write out those four words for me. He taps his jacket pocket for a pen but comes up empty; I reach into my bag and retrieve the pen attached to the journal that rarely leaves my side. Along with the pen, I pull out the only other piece of scrap paper available, today's church bulletin, and hand it to him. It might seem an odd request, but I feel compelled to capture the magical quality of our exchange, and he seems honoured to have his words documented in his script. As we part, the noise of the market once again bursts through the bubble we had created together; I wish them well and express my gratitude again for allowing me to join them. It strikes me how delightful this exchange was in comparison to conversations I've had before or after church services with those who linger in the foyer.

Outside the sun has come out behind the clouds, and I manage to find an almost-dry bench to enjoy a coffee. I pull out the bulletin and notice how "hard-won self-possession," written exclusively for me in cursive script, stands in stark contrast to the message in the sermon's title, "Giving Yourself to God," typed in Times New Roman for a roomful of people. I'll keep this bulletin, but I know I will not be returning to the church. Whatever comes next in my life, won't be viewed through a church's stained-glass windows for the foreseeable future. I've organized my outlook within a religious template most of my life, and choosing not to do that right now is exactly the balancing perspective I require.

This random but perceptive observation by a bearded stranger allows me to see myself and my next steps with new clarity. Hard-won self-possession. Hard-won speaks to determination and grit in the face of challenges—but it's the part about self-possession that makes the effort worth it. The win isn't based on what I possess in the eyes of others—a good job or a nice coat. The reward is realized when, instead of giving myself away, I gather myself in and welcome my heart home. There is nothing more centering, more anchoring, more self-possessed, than this.

I end up working at the pharmacy for two years, counting pills and fitting joint supports, walking aids, and medical compression stockings. It doesn't take me long to learn that how I present a medical product makes a significant difference in how a customer perceives it. This is never more true than with men who've been prescribed compression stockings, an item associated with pregnancy and old ladies nursing swollen ankles. I regale these men—most of whom initially insist they will never wear stockings—with true stories of other men who felt the same but returned for a second pair, reporting how it improved their golf games or their ability to walk around the block because they felt energized by the support in the stocking. I joke that they're starting a new fashion trend, but what's actually happening is that they're trading old beliefs in for something they want more: to feel better and be active.

Another tough crowd: elderly folks who, under the threat of losing their independence, begrudgingly enter the store clinging to the arm of their son or daughter—and also clinging to the idea that a cane or walker would make them look old. As they try out the device, I invite them to notice what they are feeling in their bodies. Can they stand up with more confidence? Do they notice they can move more quickly supported by the walker? Then I gently remind them that any tool or device that allows a person to be in charge of more of their own decisions usually appears more youthful and maintains more, not less, independence. The conversation almost always helps them get over the mental hurdle because it offers them a way to redefine their identity instead of allowing a device to define them. Their grown children regularly mouth a relieved *thank you* back to me as they escort the parent, walking more confidently with their new support, out the door.

These successful experiences at the pharmacy combine in my mind with what I've learned about the transformative power of coaching from watching the TV show *Starting Over*. A seed is planted in my mind with some encouragement from a lifelong friend, Rudy, and I decide to pursue training as a life coach. After some research, I enrol in an online program with Erickson College. I like the idea of learning from home, and since many coaching conversations happen over the phone, it seems an effective way to train alongside others from all over the world.

At the end of my second day in the course, I feel something snag in my lifelong approach to how I naturally support people. Friends often joke about needing some "Rita time." I know this means they are hoping to talk something through with someone they trust. They desire a listening ear, another opinion, and a safe space to share, and I have felt proud to offer wise counsel on those occasions. But my new Erickson instructor draws a clear line between talking things out with a friend and the role of a coach. Giving advice, she emphasizes, is never done within a coaching session—no matter how much you think you have the perfect answer for them. A powerful question asked by a skilled coach is more empowering for the client and has far better long-term follow-through, she continues. As I allow this to land, I feel my heart sink at the thought that I might need to unravel all my natural instincts on how I help people. Surely there's a place in coaching for offering an outside perspective? The instructor adds that coaching doesn't preclude calling in experts as needed—including therapists, accountants, doctors, and even friends—but deciding why and when to get support from others leaves the client in the director's chair, where they belong.

When the instructor proposes that a coach is to assume each client is okay and has all the resources they need, I feel the rumblings of another internal protest. In my experience, people finally ask for help because they're not okay and they *don't* have what they need. She explains how seeing people as capable and resourceful is actually more accurate because, given a safe, engaging environment, people ultimately *do* know the best direction for their own life. They just might not be aware of it yet.

Just like my recent rethink on matters of faith, I am getting a massive overhaul on how to be of assistance to others. In so many ways, my instructor's words describe where I've arrived in my own life; I just haven't made the shift in what that means in how to be with others.

In my mind's eye I see a parade of people in my life, all carrying their own lanterns, some dim and threatening to go out, others shining brightly. If it's true that people know what they need deep down, then I'm not ultimately responsible to figure it out for them. I don't have to be smarter or wiser or more intuitive in order to help. Most importantly, it's actually not my job to fix anyone. A weight I didn't even know I carried begins to melt and dissolve into my tears of relief.

In the same instant, I realize that if this is true for others, then it must be true for me as well. I have everything I need. I am okay. I've already experienced how powerfully my question, "What would love look like right now?" has helped me know my next step. What if that wasn't a fluke—or the only question with such clarifying power? I've already found a place inside me that knows when to say yes and when to say no. But after so many years of ascribing to other people's versions of right and wrong, every new turn in the road seems to require me to pause to remember what I know to be true *now*.

Recalling my elderly pharmacy customers, I took note of the difference in life-force energy between those who could make the internal adjustment to embrace their reality and those who refused to change their perspective. What part of this was a Jedi mind trick and what part demonstrated the limitations of one's brain?

I knew about my brain at a young age, but not because I was told I was smart. I was having strange episodes inside my head that seemed to come on randomly. I would appear to be daydreaming for a bit and often felt tired and a bit disoriented when I "returned." Because I wanted to get my driver's license when I turned sixteen, my father decided I should see a doctor first. They used an electroencephalogram (EEG), attaching probes to my skull in order to monitor my brain waves. The test resulted in an inconclusive diagnosis, but the irregular electrical activity on the scan suggested that what I was experiencing was likely a form of epilepsy.

The neurologist explained I was having petit mal seizures—or absence seizures, as they're often called due to the vacant expression that comes on while they're occurring—triggered by the "overexcited" brain waves in my left temporal lobe. He assured me that many young people grow out of these. Because I didn't have regular episodes and never lost consciousness, he sent me on my way with instructions on how to avoid typical seizure triggers. To ensure the episodes wouldn't escalate in number or severity, I was encouraged to get adequate sleep, avoid alcohol, and steer clear of stressful situations.

I avoided all alcohol until my mid-thirties and became hyper-aware of my sleep habits, but I didn't have a clue about how to manage stress. Life seemed to be an ongoing series of stressors. I could tell I had crossed the stress threshold when my head started to feel "loose," the closest word I could find to describe my experience. My thoughts were less crisp, my body felt disconnected from my brain, and it felt like I might get lost inside the ocean of my mind and never find my way back.

Over time, I learned to predict which situations or events might be exhausting or overstimulating—but I didn't always guess right. I could feel perfectly normal and clear-headed one moment, but the next a quick turn of my head to laugh at a joke could trigger a slow-motion wave of *déjà vu* through my whole body. Everything slowed down, as if I was being submerged underwater, but I was able to predict exactly what was going to happen next. I knew what a person was going to say the moment they opened their mouth. It felt prophetic and disorienting. It was as if I'd already lived the scene that was playing out in front of me. Anxious feelings would rush in as my stomach began to churn and my brain seemed to flounder. I would sit motionless and wait for it to pass, or lean against a wall if I was standing. The whole event seemed to take infinitely longer than the thirty to sixty seconds cited in the seizure educational materials. I'd swallow hard and often to combat the dryness in my mouth. My mind was desperately trying to catch up to the present moment. After a good night's sleep, I usually felt significantly better, except for the lingering angst over when and where it would happen again.

I learned years later that having a *déjà vu* experience—meaning "already seen" in French—is exactly what it feels like to have an "absence" seizure. One area of my mind is in the moment; another area has misfired like a skipping record and is playing back the part of the scene I have already lived to the part of me that hasn't seen it yet. My brain felt like it had a mind of its own. It was unsettling that I couldn't fully count on my brain to behave itself, which made it difficult to trust myself.

Things escalated when I was past my due date during my second pregnancy. In the middle of the night, I awoke to a room full of first responders. I sat up slowly, the baby inside my belly moving around with such force that it felt like she was attempting to kick her way out. As I tried to blink away the heaviness camped inside my head, I wondered why everyone was looking as if there was an emergency in progress. Tom calmly explained he had been roused from sleep by the grand mal seizure I was having on the bed beside him. I was treated to an ambulance ride to the hospital, where they decided to induce labour.

My body spent the entire next day playing along with the plan to birth the baby, but by the end of the day, I still hadn't dilated enough to deliver. My brain felt sloshy and heavy, and I desperately needed rest. I was given sleeping pills with the intention of starting fresh in the morning. Fortunately, Tom decided to stay, even though the nurses kept encouraging him to go home to get some sleep as well. I woke a few hours later with an urgent need to pee and called out to Tom from the bathroom in dismay when I realized that my water had just broken. I was quickly ushered into the birthing room. Laying on my side with my eyes closed, I struggled to hear the nurses' voices yelling instructions at me through a fog of medication and fatigue. I kept falling asleep, then awakening in a panic to the sound of my own voice moaning as another contraction cascaded through my exhausted body. Gratefully, only thirty minutes later, my second daughter made her debut in the world before a doctor made it onto the scene.

I was put on a strong prescription of antiseizure medication and was told I couldn't operate a vehicle until my abnormal brain activity had stabilized. I was housebound and juggling a three-year-old and a newborn alone through a haze of disorienting medication, as my husband regularly worked sixty hours a week to provide for our family. My relationship with my brain was at an all-time low. The medication was designed to keep my brain's electrical system from short-circuiting, but it's undesirable side effect was that this also slowed other information from travelling along my mind's neurological pathways in a timely manner. I couldn't read a book. I could see the words and I knew what they meant, but by the time I read to the end of the line, I couldn't retain what I had just read. Even more upsetting was how the medication affected my ability to communicate. I would begin a sentence and then realize the rest of the thought had been snatched from my mind as if by a thief in the night.

I became acutely aware that my ability to articulate an idea or follow an inspired thought along its creative path was a crucial part of my identity. I loved nothing more than the anticipation of hearing what I was thinking by listening to myself engage in a conversation. I was now denied access to that part of myself. I couldn't trust my mind to locate words, let alone track the idea that the words wanted to build. My confidence in myself and my contribution within my social circles was shattered. Life felt weighed down and appeared colourless. I struggled to find purpose and meaning in what I was doing. But since I had two young lives under my care, I compensated by making life as simple as possible. If anything was added to my plate, I felt like I was teetering on the edge.

After a few years, with the support of my doctor, I managed to get off the medication and feel more like myself again, but my sense of caution remained. Viewing my brain as my weak link,

I turned down jobs that I thought might prove too stressful. I filtered every decision I made through the lens that if I pushed too hard, I might have to go back on that debilitating drug. I parented and partnered with my husband under the ongoing threat of what my brain might do next. It was a precarious juggling act: living in fear of my mind while trying to use it to make good decisions for my life.

All these years later, training to become a life coach is providing me with a credible guidebook to a whole new relationship with my brain. Unlike my participation in religion and a regular diet of self-help books—all designed to tell me what I should think— life coach training teaches my brain *how* to think. I finally have a way to filter and file information through my mind's very own personalized central operating system.

Not only am I blown away with my brain's processing power, but I learn to utilize this power in transformative ways. A simple question like "What do I want instead?" instantly shifts me from fretting about something out of my control to redirecting my energy into a creative mode where better options present themselves. The mind is wired to look for answers, for solutions, for relief. After overusing my mind in an attempt to fix damage or avoid feelings, I'm finally working with my brain. Instead of a flaky tool that I feared would let me down, my mind is now an invaluable resource. It's like I have a new best friend who is not only always at my side but on my side.

THE STATE OF THINGS

"And now, take another step backward," she instructs in a soothing voice. The moment my foot makes contact with the floor behind me, I feel a sensation flood my lower back and penetrate inward, swirling like a tidal pool around my gut. I'm wondering how I could be feeling such dense emotions since I'm safely standing in a hallway at Erickson College, having decided to take the rest of the coach training in person.

It's early afternoon, but with no windows along the corridor, fluorescent lights are casting a surreal blue hue onto the white walls, and a soft drone of voices hums in the background. We've been instructed to disperse within the building and find a space to work with a partner as we have so many times before in this experiential course. In front of me is a paper that says TRUSTING, written in my own handwriting; behind me is one that says NOT TRUSTING.

To experience this new coaching tool, we've been instructed to decide on polar opposite states of being—states that have an easily identifiable negative and positive version. We've been encouraged to select a state of being that tends to show up most often in its negative version, but one we wish to access more often in its positive version. It didn't take me long to choose, since I'd seen how distrust has guided so many decisions in my life. From walking the long way around relationships when I don't trust myself to denying myself adventures when I can't trust I'll be safe. It's a long list and it's high time to increase my ability to trust. I understand how as a child, hiding under a bed—literally or figuratively—was the best I could do at that time. But this is no longer that time, and I long for healthier ways to trust in myself and, consequently, in the world at large.

Before lunch, I led my classmate, Joy, through the exercise and was surprised at how powerfully this particular tool seemed to impact her. It all happened on a ten-foot piece of industrial-grade carpeted flooring. Together we established an imaginary line down the centre of the hall, with the handwritten papers positioned at each end of this line. The center line between the two papers was designated as neutral space, and anytime we stepped off the imaginary line, it was like walking offstage and out of character so we could discuss what had just happened "on the line." Now it's my turn to be the "client."

"Take another step back," Joy coaxes gently. With her pen poised over a clipboard, she asks me to describe what I'm experiencing. "The heavy sensation is expanding," I explain. "It's moving up my torso, toward my throat. Um, now my chest is pounding harder and my breathing feels different. My hands feel clammy and disconnected," I manage to report.

"Would you like to take one more step back?" she whispers, half out of concern, half in an attempt to follow the instructions we've been given. She reminds me that I don't have to step all the way back onto the paper lying behind me on the floor with the negative state scrawled on it. I recall the instruction, given earlier in the day, that walking backward into the negative state was encouraged in order to soften its impact. At the time it sounded a little silly, but now, even facing away from it, I feel like I'm standing with my back to a chilling wind coming off the paper that contains the words NOT TRUSTING.

Joy is standing near me, facing in the same direction and taking each step along with me. As she matches her breathing to mine, her presence is a constant signal that all is well, even as my body is clearly expressing that it is not. I am curious about what will happen next, and I want to experience this coaching tool fully, so I tell her I'd like to take another step.

"Okay, take another step back into 'not trusting' when you're ready." She speaks with a quiet confidence now that I have agreed. I gulp in air as I step back, and before I even begin to exhale, all the places in my life where trust has been broken flash through my mind like a screeching, fragmented video. I see my grandfather standing in a doorway. My teacher is blocking my exit in a dark storage room. I see Kerrie hanging. I see the glaring looks of disapproval on the faces of the people who used to smile when they saw me. My body jolts as my internal protective wall thickens; my torso suddenly feels clad in uncomfortable armour as images from my life play in rapid, non-sequential succession. My arms feel cold, then numb. My legs are wobbly, and my eyes begin to burn where tears are held back by uncertainty. As my breath quickens, I feel unsafe, like at any moment someone may come at me with a weapon. I want to move, to break the spell, but instead I stand there and focus on my breathing—the one thing I can control—and wait for the feeling of panic to slide down my arms and then slowly drip off my fingers.

My "coach" invites me to lock in the sensations that accompany "not trusting." I rarely let it get this far because, if I have any inkling that trust is going to collapse, long before I have to feel it smash to smithereens against my tender insides, I preemptively erect a wall of protection. I don't even like to brush up against disappointment, a common thorn in the side of trust. In fact, the mere anticipation that disappointment may come my way leads me to reroute using some type of evasive or defensive maneuver.

But people are flawed, imperfect humans who constantly let each other down, so instead of activating the kill switch on every friendship I have, I've found a way to expand the space. On a really good day when it feels like a heartfelt choice, I'd call this grace; when I'm less resourceful, I'd label it "giving people the benefit of the doubt." It's not that I have any doubt that their tardiness or gossiping about me behind my back or not telling me the full truth would feel disappointing to me; it's that I choose to pre-excuse them, knowing there are usually more moving parts involved than I can see. I get ahead of the potential disappointment. The upside to this approach is that when I can offer this to others, I can also give it to myself when I mess up. The downside is that while on the outside I may appear gracious, on the inside I am simply too "chicken" to feel disappointment, fearing it might take me down that slippery slope that ends in broken trust and final goodbyes. Being nice out of fear isn't the same as being generous from a well of love, but I can't always tell which track I'm on at first.

"Okay, now walk into the neutral state at the centre of the line," says Joy, sounding audibly relieved, placing her clipboard under one arm, "so you can shake it out." I happily move away from the place on the imaginary line where I've just had some very real sensations. I swing my limbs and shake my head from side to side with substantial force in order to release the density that's fallen over my whole being with my proximity to "not trusting."

"Whoa!" I exclaim, flicking my hands like I'm trying to shake off excess water, then turning myself completely around. "That was intense!" She laughs and shakes out her hands as well, revealing that she had absorbed some of what I experienced just by standing beside me. Joy invites me to step off the line for a moment to catch my breath and reflect on the experience thus far. In an instant, the negative sensations are gone, almost like it never happened. I feel like I did before I started the exercise fifteen minutes earlier. If this had been the whole exercise, I would have considered it a raging success. The fact that I could drop into a state so intensely and not be overcome by it—that alone was a powerful experience. In fact, stepping so easily into a neutral energy, despite the fact that none of the events of my life had changed, felt like a new superpower, like I too had been granted access to a Jedi mind trick! It was incredible to feel something so deeply and, in the next moment, know I could choose to release the feeling.

"Okay, now for the opposite state," Joy smiles and quickly scans the instructions on her clipboard. "Please step back onto the centre of the line—and this time you're going to face forward and move toward the state you want more of."

I am ready. But I am also a little nervous. I managed to drop into "not trusting" so quickly, but what if entering a state of "trusting" isn't as easy? What if my body doesn't know how to get there? I swallow, lift my chin, and decide to trust the process—a thought that strikes me as perfect irony and, at the same time, a glowing affirmation that I'm on the right track.

"Take your first step toward 'trusting' whenever you're ready, RIta," says Joy. I'm moving before she finishes the sentence. As I stand there, I lift my arms and position them like I'm taking a drive with the windows down on a summer's day, instinctively allowing my palms to dance in the positivity that's flowing by. I feel a lightness replacing gravity—like I've just lost twenty pounds from somewhere, from everywhere. I'm smiling, anticipating, and already completely enchanted with this feeling of peace. Joy urges me to take the next step into "trusting" when I'm ready.

I opted to use the term trusting instead of just trust because somehow the active version of the word felt more accurate and accessible. Almost nothing in life is stagnant; everything is in motion—coming or going, expanding or contracting, living or dying. Trusting feels like an intentional choice from one moment to the next, within ever-changing conditions. Just like this exercise, trusting ebbs and flows in modulated amounts with every step I take.

"My feet feel grounded but not heavy, the top of my head is pulling upward, and I can feel the connection between my feet and my head running like a cord through the entire length of my body. There's no disconnection. All of me is part of the whole." I try to make my descriptions make sense as Joy jots them down. "It's like I'm all here and all is well."

"Are you ready to take the final step all the way into 'trusting'?" Joy's giggle suggests that she thinks her question might be unnecessary—but it isn't. Sometimes pure goodness feels as overwhelming as its opposite. However, I'm not going to let this stop me. I've invested so much in this new life, not only training as a life coach but courageously smashing apart my old life and then rebuilding it one piece at a time. Since I left the marriage almost five years ago, I've been picking up one broken piece from the rubble at a time. I've held each piece, seeing each shape in the form of a belief I've had or a preference I've held or a thought I've clung to, and I've weighed whether the piece is coming with me into my new life. I've asked myself whether each piece I pick up is my own or from someone else's version of life. It's required a lot of trusting to get here to this moment, on this imaginary line, so I am going all the way.

I take the final step, moving directly onto the piece of paper, and close my eyes. I hear the paper crunch under my shoes and the sound draws me inward. Suddenly I hear someone singing softly in the distance, a female voice floating on a soft breeze. Then I make out the sound of a bird off to one side, warbling in chorus with the voice. For a second, my eyes flicker open, and I want to laugh out loud because I know I'm going to sound crazy when I tell Joy what's happening. Instead, I close my eyes again and notice an expanding warming sensation. It's like when the sun comes out on a cool day and chases away the chill. I sense a soft, yellow glow in my mind's eye, emanating from the end of the hallway, slowly getting bigger. It doesn't consume me, but I'm not separate from it either. A spray of wildflowers comes into view, and I sense there is a river nearby. My heart seems to pull my whole body forward, yet I don't feel off balance. I want to live here. Everything is possible here.

I haven't spoken in a few minutes, and Joy's voice breaks the silence. "You can tell me what's happening later if you like," she offers. "Just know that this state is available to you anytime. It's yours. It's what trusting fully and completely feels like to you."

I open my eyes and realize that my cheeks are wet as tears flow from a river deep inside of me and overflow onto the outside. My access to fully trusting feels complete. I don't want to move, but I know there's another step in this exercise.

"When you're ready, please step back to the centre of the state-line," Joy instructs. I wonder if my feet will work but then find there's an ease to my movement as I make my way to the neutral zone. "Lift your arms so they reach to both of the states you've just experienced," says Joy, with a tone of benediction in her voice. "Know that there is a time for trusting and a time for not trusting in life. You have access to both, and you have the ability to decide how you will arrive in each state."

I keep my arms stretched out a little longer and turn my face toward the ceiling. I sense a residual cool air from the "not trusting" side and the warmth from the "trusting" side on each corresponding hand. Just like light and dark, life and death, there is a time for both—including all the variations available on the spectrum between any pair of opposites. All of it is part of the human experience. And I realize I have so much more control and self-agency within my experiences than I ever knew. It's not about never feeling the impact of a negative state; it's about not feeling completely helpless in the presence of it.

I walk off the state-line and keep my arms open wide to embrace Joy. She wraps her arms around me and pulls me in.

"What else do you know after having experienced this state-line?" asks Joy, ready to record my observations.

I enjoy the bright energy still pulsing through me as I sweep together what tumbles out of my mouth. "The sheer volume of chemicals released during the course of the exercise was astounding," I begin. "Our thoughts are powerful. Skillfully directing these thoughts, which determines which chemicals will be released, is a seriously underutilized power!"

"And how does knowing this impact your life today?" Joy asks, brilliantly prompting me to integrate the work we've done together.

I feel a thought coming around a corner, and it's a big thought but I can't quite see its shape yet. It's not the first time I've had this feeling, but it's possibly the first time I wasn't nervous about seeing what it will be. I know that whatever comes will align with this new experience. And I have Joy at my side to walk through it with me.

"I am ready," I say as I watch the outline begin to fill in, "to use this new knowledge to shift where I'm still impacted by my friend's suicide." It has been six years since Kerrie's death, and mostly it feels like I've dealt with it, but occasionally I still have startling images zing through me.

"What would you rather experience?" asks Joy, expertly using our training to direct my focus to the part of all that horror that I have some control over.

"It actually happened the other day on my way to class," I say, rather matter-of-factly. "As I made my way down the stairs of my townhouse and placed my hand on the doorknob that opens into my garage, an image of Kerrie hanging, and other gory images that weren't even part of the actual event, flashed through my mind. It's a quick mental image, and it doesn't even really make me miss a step or catch my breath, but it's annoying—and not exactly an image that makes my day better, that's for sure."

Joy scribbles a few notes on her clipboard. Before she can say anything else, I add, "I assume my brain is doing this because it was traumatized, and like a broken bone that can sense a change in weather years later, this is my brain's way of coping with the uncertainty of change." I allow that statement to sit in the silence for a moment before I continue. "But now that I know I can update my brain's default patterns, I'd really like to do that."

Joy smiles and repeats her earlier question, knowing it's still the best path forward. "So what would you rather experience, based on what you know is available from today's exercise?"

I draw in a long, slow breath, feeling my chest expand till it feels it might burst. As I release the air, I hear myself speak with great emotion woven into every word. "I want to express gratitude to my brain for sticking with me after everything it's been through." I stop for a moment to allow this to land. "I believe my brain is trying to protect me from ever having to walk into something so horrific without warning. Flashing those gruesome images on occasion means that if there's ever something awful waiting around the next corner, my brain is preemptively trying to protect me from experiencing such a terrible shock again. My brain has had my back, but instead of trusting it, I've fought against it. I want to trust my brain." I feel deep emotions flood my head as if my brain is communicating back.

"Why is this important to you, Rita?" continues Joy, using the brilliant coaching model we've been taught.

"It changes everything!" I want to shout but it comes out as an impassioned whisper instead. "It means I can stop dismissing my emotions or fearing what comes next. I get to work with myself

instead of against the parts of me I don't understand. I get to be
... ME!" If I was amazed at the outcome of today's exercise while I
was on the line, I'm shaking my head in jubilant disbelief now. It's
like something has clicked into place that has been trying to link
together my entire life. I feel whole.

I smile broadly when Joy asks, "And what's one way you'd like
to incorporate this new learning into your life right now?"

I know exactly how. "Tomorrow, as I descend the steps to my
garage, I'm going to tell my brain how grateful I am for the way
it attempts to protect me. Then I'm going to bring to mind the
fullest version of trusting I experienced today. The yellow glow,
the birds, the amazing feeling of connection—all of it. I am going
to present that image as an alternative to the gruesome default
one. And by doing this, instead of seeing horrible images in order
to protect me, this new image will remind me that no matter what
may happen down the road—even shocking, difficult things—that
I have amazing resources to get through it."

The last step in any coaching session is called celebration.
Initially, I felt uncomfortable with that word, assuming it meant
something akin to a party. Our trainer assured us that it could
be contained in one sentence, but that it was a very important
part of the process. It's crucial to take a moment to acknowledge
the time and effort that's being invested in these transformative
conversations.

"What's your win from today?" asks Joy, half laughing as she asks
the usual celebration question, knowing just how monumental
this experience has been for me.

"I'm grateful that I can ease up on rehearsing for bad things that
might happen and, instead, trust that envisioning really yummy
things is not only a better way to know when to trust and when
not to trust but also makes for a more delicious life." As I attempt
to sum up my whole experience, I notice for the first time that
perhaps celebration can be as simple as stopping to appreciate
the gift of a new way of being with myself.

I BELIEVE

My daughter has asked to speak with me about some issues that are weighing on her. She was in high school when my departure from my marriage put a significant dent in her experience of family. Now she's just completed her first year at a Christian college, living away from home for the first time, which usually prompts a reevaluation of the pillars holding up one's life.

"Do you even believe in God anymore, Mom?" she implores, landing squarely at ground zero by asking the one question to which she cannot imagine I will answer "no." The exasperation in my daughter's voice seems laced with a hint of desperation. I feel a little like a child being questioned by a parent.

I watch her closely, and as her mother, I'm tempted to tuck away my first response and focus instead on making her feel okay about where this conversation is going. I try to ascertain what my daughter needs from me in this conversation. Just because I'm in my mid-forties and have disassembled my entire life doesn't mean she wants to sit in the rubble with me. But precisely because it took me until my mid-forties to crack the hard shell encasing the only worldview I'd ever known, I feel torn. If I keep my mouth shut to shield either of my daughters from my process in order to protect them, is that the best way for us to navigate our new relationships as adults? But if I prematurely crack their shells by speaking too frankly about my evolving understanding, am I taking them along on a ride that could confound them unnecessarily? Am I selfish if I share my emerging beliefs, or am I selfish if I don't?

"Please answer the question, Mom," she pleads, sensing my hesitation. "Do you still believe in God?" In contrast to what she watched me do every Sunday during her formative years, I haven't attended church in a few years now.

She's still waiting for an answer. I take a breath, and then another one. I'm hoping that a little extra oxygen to my brain will help me form a better answer. I want to grab her by the hand so we can move through this conversation at the same speed. I long for her to understand my choices. I want to explain how the Bible was used to keep me in my place as a woman. I want her to be able to imagine the preachers of my childhood, red-faced as they pound the pulpit with their version of salvation, effectively "scaring people into heaven." I want to demonstrate to her how they twisted scripture to keep the community in line instead of nurturing truth in the hearts of the wounded souls in the pews.

I consider launching into an insufferable exegetical romp through the entire Bible in order to show how scripture was meant to be interpreted and how most believers have made a God-awful mess of it. This is my usual safety maneuver—like pulling the cord on a parachute, I pull a lot of words out of thin air when I'm not sure where I want to land. But this time, I make a different choice.

"Yes and no," I finally say, instinctively scrunching up my face in apology.

"That's not an answer," she pouts. She's right. But I hope she'll see just how accurate my simple answer is once I'm finished explaining—that is if she wants to hear the fuller answer.

She says she does and leans back in her chair to listen to what I have to say. Or is she reloading under the table? Either way, I'm prepared to give this a shot. I want to hear what I have to say too. I want to hear the answer that rises up from my heart, trips on the frayed edges of my instincts as a mother, and flows through my new perspective from my coach training and finally out of my forty-something-year-old mouth. It's a circuitous route and a few things might fall off during sharp turns. But I hope it will be worth the trip.

"When you say *God* and I say *God*, it's a little like two people saying Facebook and assuming they're talking about the same thing," I begin, talking a little too quickly, fearing she will make up her mind before I have a chance to make my point. I watch her left eyebrow rise in hollow disbelief, confirming my fear that this wasn't the best start.

"Stick with me." I realize these words of encouragement are as much for me as they are for her. "When I say *Facebook*, I imagine myself scrolling my newsfeed that's loaded with images of familiar faces and the cool things they post. I see my profile picture and the carefully selected groups I've agreed to belong to. Red notifications pop up that take me to 'likes' and encouraging comments about my latest post. So when people say they're going to quit Facebook because it's so full of negativity and has too many pictures of what people ate for dinner, I understand that they are basing that decision on *their experience* of *their newsfeed* on Facebook. They have no idea about *my* experience and what's on *my* newsfeed. They may never have experienced the amazing articles and encouraging TED talks and stunning pictures that are waiting for me when I sign onto Facebook. They may never have had the opportunity to engage in poignant conversations about issues with friends I respect, many of whom I have never met in person. They may rarely feel inspired or encouraged or connected as they click on their Facebook icon. They say they hate Facebook, but what they hate is their experience on Facebook. Two people can have exact opposite experiences with social media, even though we call it the same thing and consequently assume we're having a common experience."

I'm not doing a very good job. I'm trying to demonstrate how a word isn't just a word, how a concept isn't understood the same way by everyone even when we all think we know what the word means. I'm grasping for a way to demonstrate how this is infinitely more true when we discuss an intangible, surreal entity as confounding as God.

"That's just weird. Facebook? Young people don't even use Facebook anymore." She cuts to the chase. "What's your point, Mom?"

"Exactly!" I sound a little too excited that she's made my point for me. "Facebook isn't a platform you relate to anymore, but that doesn't mean you've given up on connecting with people on other social media platforms, right?!"

She doesn't look like she's making the leap. I coax myself to stop dancing around it and give her a straight answer, "I don't believe in the God I was introduced to as a child. I know people I grew up with had the inspiring Facebook version of God. Mine had far too many disturbing pictures and comments that told me who I better be instead of what I could be—so much so that even using the term God sometimes makes me cringe these days."

I stop, not sure if what she needs right now is more information or a completely different approach.

Then she says slowly, "I get that," her even gaze making it seem she's wondering why that was so hard for me to say. "So which word do you prefer to use?"

This is a great question. And I do not have a great answer—yet. I know things by how I feel them these days, and I'm not certain that claiming a different bundle of potentially limiting words will help. There's an ongoing flow to one's spirituality that no amount of memorization of scripture or proclamations of belief should try to stop in its tracks. Labels and mimicry have done more harm than good in my spiritual life so far.

"You know how some people believe there's always one right answer to questions about the Bible and God?" I wade in, trying to engage her recently lived experiences at theological school instead of the muddy pool I was asking her to jump into.

She easily frames her take on my question. "Well, there's a lot of things that we will never know exactly, but that's why we study and try to understand what God wants for us through prayer."

Thrilled that she's engaging with me on her terms, I respond, "Well, yes. I also recall learning that if I followed the Bible's instructions, I'd have a guidebook for my life and that I'd always know the right path—but in fact, the entire time I was adhering to the rules in the 'good book,' I was feeling confused and disconnected from my heart. I knew people who seemed genuinely at peace with the ideas they were sharing regarding their Christian life. For me, while I knew the right words to say, I just didn't have a corresponding echo of affirmation from my heart or my gut much of the time. I accepted the solutions offered by Sunday school teachers and youth leaders—that I just had to pray harder. When that didn't work, I was told that Satan was playing tricks on me and I just had to believe more. I privately believed that I must be broken because none of my best efforts worked for long."

Then I take a sharp right turn, asking, "Have you heard of the 'fruits of the spirit?'" I'm attempting to redirect the conversation to avoid painting my entire childhood as doom and gloom, which it most certainly wasn't, despite all the insidious religious trap doors.

"Well yeah, of course," she answers. "The fruits of the spirit are love, joy, peace, patience, kindness, goodness, faithfulness, gentleness, and self-control." She rattles them off like song lyrics, in a sing-songy lilt.

"Impressive." I smile, the string of words she just shared so familiar to my ear but sorely lacking in my inner experience growing up. I felt a lot of things, but my list sounded more like: confusion, anger, sadness, frustration, doubt, guilt, panic, and shame.

I take a deep breath and continue. "I recall being taught that if the Spirit of God was alive and well inside of me, those qualities would show up in my life. In other words, if I had a true conversion experience, then the fruit of that relationship would be on display for all to see. So here's the crazy part, kid—the part where I'm still trying to bridge my childhood with my current experience. Back then I couldn't seem to feel these qualities during the time when I would have called myself a believer. But now that I'm not attending church or flying the Christian flag or being anything but who I am, I'm beginning to authentically feel those wonderful qualities sprout inside of me ... for the first time in my life!"

I stop, because my voice is suddenly husky, flooding with

gratitude, and while I don't feel uncomfortable crying in front of my daughter, I want to see if she's tracking what I'm sharing. It feels like there's still something waiting to be revealed in this conversation.

Seeing how raw this explanation is for me, she urges me to continue, so I do. "I guess I'm trying to say that the entire time I was trying to be a good person, it felt like I was failing in my faith. And now that I'm just living—not actively following the rituals and rules the church would consider good or faithful—something big has shifted inside. I feel alive and I marvel at how deeply I can experience love and peace."

"That's great, Mom," she responds. "But being a Christian isn't just about being good. Being good isn't enough, according to the Bible. The only way to access God is through Jesus, and if we truly believe, we are given the Spirit. If you don't go that route, well, then ..." She falters, because both of us know that sentence ends in the pits of hell. And I know exactly where to locate the verses in the Bible to back up her point. I know it all. All the stories, all the cautionary tales, all the scary parts—and I even know all the surprisingly sexy parts in the Bible too. Yet my flesh-and-blood experience of my life doesn't neatly follow the script. I dropped from my mother's womb into a rigid, pre-formed faith, and it took running for the exit to discover a world that felt most similar to what all the Bible verses say life can be.

"Is it possible," I start out, avoiding her unfinished sentence in favour of a more hopeful one, "that for some of us born directly into a faith community, that a true conversion may require leaving to actually choose our life?" I'm test-driving this idea as it comes out of my mouth. "I grew up being told that if I didn't believe, then I would be left behind on Judgment Day. So how can a child's reaction to that threat be a real conversion? Making a decision from fear, especially in the developing mind of a child, is the opposite of having a free choice to love."

I continue, feeling a familiar heat churn in my belly around this topic: "I have a lot of names for that but conversion is not one of them! Has it taken me this long to be free to love because for the first time I've felt free enough to actually choose the shape of what I believe? I'm converting from a system of imposed beliefs to following a flow of love, joy, peace, and all the other fruit that is able to grow in a garden of love. If someone's idea of God means I have to say specific words while jumping through flaming hoops dipped in the lake fires of hell, that's not a faith I choose to participate in."

It seems like a good place to stop until I look into her downcast face. I was sprinting to the finish line of that mini-sermon, my words coming out as quickly as my thoughts were landing, and quite possibly I've insulted important spiritual handholds she clings to at this point in her life. This was exactly what I worried about at the beginning of this conversation; my path isn't hers, nor should it be. I don't have answers for her. She will find her own way, in her own time. There is no "one size fits all" for the soul.

"Honey, please hear me." I shift to a more maternal voice, a soft tone I would have used when applying a bandage to her skinned knee as a child. "I'm telling you all this not because I think I have the answer to anyone else's life, including yours. I share this because I hope you can be happy for me. I want you to know that I'm fine. I'm more than fine. I'm better than I've ever been. I've found my way out of the wilderness. You can use whatever words feel accurate for your experience, and I will listen and be happy for you. If I use different words, it doesn't make them better or worse; it just makes them mine. I believe all paths lead toward the light when we allow our hearts to guide us."

She lowers her gaze, but her entire body relaxes. "I'm just happy you're here and that we can talk, Mom," she manages to say, showing me more in that one sentence than she's ever admitted out loud about her concerns regarding my mental health after Kerrie's death.

"Me too," I answer back, feeling my forehead soften along with the rest of my face. This is a vast understatement. It is exactly the fact that I am able to engage with an honest heart and a free spirit that assures me that I'm going to be okay.

Our talk could end here, but there is still a loose thread flapping in the wind. I don't need to wrap up all the non-answers into a nice bow, but I can sense the idea of eternity tugging at the corner of my spirit. My approach is all well and good for now, but what about when I die—when the time to figure this all out is officially over?! The concept of heaven and hell was drilled into me from such a young age that I still feel the occasional flutter of panic at the base of my gut. The thought of getting this whole thing wrong claws at my survival instincts. The alternative, however— the thought of returning to the life I had finally broken free from, its own version of living hell—is actually scarier. I was taught to fear what comes after life, but I've seen that hell on earth is a painful reality for many.

I resolve to give myself time—time to observe how my inner fruit is doing in my new garden of growing beliefs. I might even decide to transplant some of the ideas from my past, ones that don't feel outdated or smell toxic to my spirit. Because at a heart level, I feel the overarching story in the Bible is actually an evolving love story between a parent and a child, between God and creation. Just like we show love to our children by teaching them not to run into a dangerous street, the beginning—the Old Testament—is all about following rules to stay safe and how to be part of a family. Then, in the New Testament, the story is about how Jesus is the example of a new way to be in relationship with God—just like how I'm adjusting to a new dynamic with my adult daughters. And then through Jesus's death, the old rules transform into a new way of being. We are able to access something more intimate and personal through the Spirit—*in Spiritus*, in Latin, meaning breath and our soul's inspiration. Just like with other guidebooks and instruction manuals, we eventually go "off book" because we embody the wisdom. I'm human, and I'm also imbued with the divine. Not only can I experience love—I AM love. Now *that's* a powerful conversion experience!

"I would like to ask you for a favour," I say, an idea streaking like a shooting star through the sky of my mind as my mouth is forming the request.

She nods twice without speaking, albeit a bit tentatively, as she waits to hear what she's agreeing to.

"I see how strange it is for you to watch me go down this path.

It's probably scary to think that, according to the church you attend, my decisions could mean I'll end up in hell." The final word comes out of my throat sounding thick and sticky. I muster the courage to continue now that I've said it out loud. "I'm sorting through a lifetime of fear and lies that got root-bound in the pot of my beliefs. It's a bit of a mess, I'll admit. But in the meantime"—a deep exhalation illuminates my thoughts like Northern Lights spilling across the dark sky—"in the meantime, can I ask you to just leave off the *therefore*?" I know this must sound confusing. I watch her chin lift, which makes her eyes disappear into slits behind her lids, as I wait to see if she is following.

"Like, don't come to a final conclusion yet?" she tests, her eyes still guarded by her eyelids. I notice the mascara lengthening her thick lashes, more evidence that she's no longer a child.

She has it exactly right. "Yeah!" I say brightly, surprised that she summed it up better than I could have, "Instead of thinking that because I don't use the same words or appear to believe the same things and, therefore, I'm not going to heaven, you don't have to work it all out right now. This way you give me the gift of time, and you give yourself a break from worrying about my final destination. Win-win!" I finish by plopping these two "word cherries" on top of a rather grim topic.

She rolls her eyes at the "win-win," but she's smiling. "So I shouldn't say, 'My mom is such a weirdo; therefore, I must have some weirdo in me too?'" This joke is the highest affirmation that she gets it and is willing to play along.

My heart is soaring. I love this idea of "leaving off the *therefore*" more often. My brain is always searching for the best answer, the final word. This new instruction leaves more space to stay in what *is* without making it conform to what it might be. It means that I can notice what I'm thinking about and then come to a gentle stop before feverishly projecting all its random ramifications into the future. If the last years are any indication, the future is impossible to predict accurately anyway. In the meantime, I can plant ideas and watch them sprout and grow before deciding their fate. Leaving off the therefore isn't avoiding decisions; it's trusting that all will be revealed in its time. It will give my luscious fruit trees of love, joy, and peace—to name a few—time to ripen.

My daughter opens her arms and pulls me into a tight embrace. I have no idea if she'll remember this conversation, but I know I will. Her question has opened a door to a place where my spirit and my mind could meet with hers in a lush garden. Turning the dirt through hard conversations grows strong roots and produces delicious fruit. I allow the image to drip like juice through my fingers and down my chin. Life tastes sweet in this new season.

SLUSHY EMOTIONS

With my parents' support, after years of renting, I purchase a townhouse in a rural town halfway between my childhood home and the city where I raised the girls. I choose warm, colourful paint shades and have new flooring installed throughout, giving the space a vibe that matches my confident and creative outlook. At a time when I could just as easily ignore dirty dishes or put off doing laundry because it doesn't affect anyone else, I'm delighted by how orderly I prefer to keep my surroundings. It dawns on me that my visible environment is simply aligning with my inner experience. I enjoy space to think and room to move without clutter or mess squawking for attention. I find soft pleasure in keeping pace with the daily details of my human existence. People can stop by unannounced without causing me to panic or scramble to quickly tidy up. It feels good to live in a space that isn't waiting but is always ready.

Occasionally, I'm still caught by surprise at how much living alone suits me. I feel a distinct giddiness when I arrive home, lock the door behind me, and have complete say over what happens next. This solitary ease is available in all areas of my life except one. Tom has recently requested that we begin divorce proceedings.

It's a common refrain that there are two areas that tend to

burst the dam during divorce discussions: money and children. It made sense to me the first time I heard it, long before I got to experience it firsthand. Sadness over lost dreams and feelings of rejection are difficult to boil down into negotiable details; it's much easier to focus on things that can be manipulated into spreadsheets and entered on calendars.

Money has always been a slippery currency for me. I stayed home with the girls for most of our marriage, which meant my value on tax returns or in a bank balance was nominal. Sometimes, even back then, I felt the sting of feeling duped by society in my role as a wife and mother—that every meal I made, every sock I didn't lose during laundering, every errand I ran for the family, every social engagement I orchestrated, every wall I painted, every appointment I kept, every tear I wiped, every floor I swept, every school and church event I organized—none of this had value compared to a "real" job. In truth, my role only held the value that my partner and I ascribed to it.

I've felt proud of my contributions over the years, but on the day of reckoning, as I sign papers at the lawyer's office, the reality of my meagre book value slaps me in the face. Tom's assurances over the years that the work I was doing was worth everything now feel like a pat on the head when what I need is money to pay the bills. Then shame sweeps in, reminding me that it was my decision to marry and be a mom, and it was my decision to leave.

Shame has a way of making us feel worthless and small. But at critical times in life, shame can make us small enough to be able to escape through the hole we dig for ourselves. Slipping out in shame is not a noble exit, but sometimes it's a necessary one.

Shame and rage are said to be two sides of a coin. Early in life, I learned never to flip the coin over to rage. As is the pattern in many families, from the time I was young, I was urgently hushed anytime even a hint of anger threatened to show itself. I also learned along the way that I maintained more control of situations by holding my emotions close. When my brother would tickle me, I noticed that if I could avoid squirming or showing any reaction for a good five seconds—an eternity when someone has you pinned down, jabbing their fingers into your ribs—then he would give up and move on. Not showing weakness in the moment by keeping a straight face and still body is a savvy survival tool. Over the years, it also became a way to trick me into thinking I was okay.

But divorce proceedings are not a five-second tickle fest; rather, they are a painful dissolution of a life built together over the course of many years. With our church as well as our families agreeing that my ex has gotten the raw end of the deal, Tom seems to find comfort and support in framing our separation and ensuing divorce as my exit from the family. He considers himself and the girls the nuclear family, and I am now an outsider. Because the girls are teenagers, they arrange time with me when they desire. He doesn't stand in the way of our time together, but he feels no need to negotiate schedules with me—not even when it comes to holidays.

The girls and I always find a way to be together over the holidays, but this year Tom has decided the three of them will be spending the entire week of Christmas in California with his extended family. I hear it first from the girls and feel a distinct jab into my ribs at the thought, but I don't flinch. The fact that Tom feels no need to inform me, let alone try to soften the impact of his unilateral decision, produces a familiar heat in my belly. At worst, it seems like retribution on his part. At best, it's an ongoing dismissal of my role in our girls' lives.

I scramble to see this as more than just a sad Christmas without my girls. I already know that I don't mind being alone; in fact, I'm a bit curious about what it might feel like to spend the holidays all by myself. I'd heard how lonely it can feel, but in my experience, I'd almost always felt the opposite. For me, the Christmas season holds too many events, too many people, and altogether too much hoopla. Perhaps this will be an unexpected opportunity to reinvent the holidays?

In preparation for my solo holiday, I decorate my small, scraggly Charlie Brown tree while Leonard Cohen croons in the background. I found the tree in the discount aisle; it was missing its entire top section. It's a five-foot-tall artificial tree that would have been over six feet tall had it been complete, but what caught my attention in the store was how real the bark on the tree appeared. The meagre branches screwed into the bark looked fake, but the core of the tree appeared solid and authentic. While most people probably wouldn't choose a tree based on its trunk, choosing this tree confirmed a new pattern in my life: following what catches my heart's attention or piques my curiosity makes life feel fuller and more interesting.

When I bought the tree, I was aware it had no climax, no pinnacle on which to place its crowning glory. So in lieu of a tree topper, I hang a sparkling orb from the ceiling by a thin wire, just above the tree. In a darkened room, it gives the illusion that the lit ornament is exactly where the tree topper would rest. I am fascinated by the empty space between the tree's actual top and the hanging orb. The space feels sacred, like the firmament between heaven and earth, and it seems to me to symbolize the way the magic of Christmas holds space for all of the invisible unknowns in life. This spindly, broken tree quickly becomes my favourite decoration for the way its imperfect presence seems infused with the Christmas spirit.

When I wake on the morning of Christmas Eve, I can feel a palpable shift in my anticipation. It's not the kind I had as a child knowing there would be gifts to open that evening after church, but instead it feels like the uneasy excitement of a storm brewing in the distance. For my entire life, Christmas Eve has always included a church service. Even now that I don't attend church, I still typically join my girls for a Christmas Eve service or slide into the pew next to a friend at their church's event. But this year, I decide I'm going to create something special for myself at home. I am ready to experience what Christmas feels like devoid of these familiar rituals.

I locate a large glass jar and place a gold-tipped calligraphy pen and a stack of small slips of paper beside it. Throughout the day, every time I walk by the jar, I stop and record one small thing that evokes gratitude and then fold the paper and place it into the jar. I write all the wonderful events and adventures I've participated in and record exchanges of kindness I have shared with others. My mind travels back to the early months of the year to retrieve moments I'd almost forgotten about. The jar is bursting with paper by the evening.

I open a special bottle of wine as I prepare an exotic dinner with spices that linger in the air and on my tongue. I move my body in rhythm to the music that plays in the background, and I smile at how much richness can be woven into a day bolstered by a little forethought and intention. When it comes time to read the love notes I've spent the day putting into the jar, I'm surprised at the anticipation that fills my chest as I sit cross-legged at the base of my sacred, spindly Christmas tree.

On a whim, I raise the jar and pour out its folded contents over my head. Paper trickles down my shoulders and adorns the floor around me like a bride's veil before the big reveal. I feel draped in love as I pick up each note from the pile that encircles me and read them, one by one, aloud. My tears flow freely as I bask in the bounty of a full year's gracious offerings.

I wake up the next morning still wrapped in the delight of the night before. When my sister-in-law heard at our extended family gathering the week earlier that I didn't have plans and my girls would be away, she insisted that I come over for dinner on Christmas Day. I resisted at first, feeling like I had to stick with my original plan to spend the entire holiday alone, but eventually, without anything specifically planned for the day, I accepted her invitation.

The half-hour drive to their house on empty roads brings on a wave of apprehension. I've been married with children for so long that arriving at an intimate family dinner as a single person on Christmas Day, the quintessential day reserved for family, feels inherently pathetic, and I hear the song "Lonesome Loser" cue up on the imaginary playlist in my head.

My brother, sister-in-law, and nephew are very welcoming, the food is delicious, and the easy banter is a lovely injection of lightness into one of the shortest, darkest days of the year. At the same time, I'm a little surprised at how acutely alone I feel now that I'm surrounded by others. Just as coming inside a warm house accentuates how brisk it was outside, being in the presence of a family unit makes it glaringly obvious that I am truly alone, and not just for the holidays. As I drive home to my dark house, I feel a light go dim inside me.

Is being alone over the holidays definitive proof that I have failed at life? Despite the fact that I can happily fill my time and easily fill my days with people, my spirit demands answers about the present status of my life. Will I always be doomed to feel lonely and obligated when I surround myself with people? Will I ever be able to truly celebrate important events without feeling overwhelmed by all the expectations?

Over the next few days, I watch as my discomfort turns into annoyance, then irritation, and eventually bursts into anger. The flames lick higher, clawing back space and air as they expand. As the heat grows into an unbearable inferno, I rip off my sweater and pin up my hair. My whole being feels hot as I pace around my home, muttering aloud under my breath, seriously wondering if this is the path that leads to a mental breakdown.

The inferno finds an easy target in my ex-husband. Any disappointment I haven't managed to mop up during divorce discussions is now brittle fodder for the fire. His recent comment about how it was actually my decision to stay home with the girls instead of working and, therefore, I didn't deserve any financial compensation, adds a gust of wind that fans the flames into another bright hot blaze. The fact that he arranged to take our girls to another country during the holidays without even giving me the courtesy of a call provides thick logs of hostility that burn through the night.

I wander within the walls of my townhouse in search of light, but there is none to be found. With nothing but time in my open schedule, there is nowhere to hide from a lifetime of avoiding anger and not allowing it to burn in its time. My pacifist upbringing trained me how to chop up my anger into pieces and then relive it in manageable chunks after the fact. Anything not fully felt at the time slowly piled up in the far corner of my being. I regularly turned potential anger into shame, heaping the blame on myself to avoid the destruction that anger would surely invoke if I let it fly. Over the years, shame weakened my spirit, but until now the trade always felt like a fair exchange for maintaining a sense of control and not inflicting more harm. With no distractions or holiday rituals to lean on, I am left alone to wrestle with my anger in the dark of night. The wild animal of my unattended anger has grown fangs in the shape of pointed rage—a progression I've done everything to avoid my entire life.

So I rage. I spit out words at full volume that make my own ears threaten to bleed. I blame and curse and hate and despise every bad thing that has ever happened. I've already torn through my ex-husband in my mind and am now well on my way to ripping through anyone who has hurt or abandoned or betrayed me. I cannot sit still. There is nothing else to do and nowhere else to go. Rage and I are in a cage match with no escape. I don't know how to keep score or what winning even looks like. Over the next few days, as I attempt to find shelter from the fierce winds of rage, I find myself flung back into the howling storm again and again.

Eventually, rage burns its way into the forest of my shame. I have always feared what flames of rage would do if they were allowed the fuel of time and air—and now nothing can hold it back. The fire has been fed for days, and the embers are glowing white-hot. Rage burns up one hillside of my forest and down the next until charred timbers of shame lay smouldering at my feet. As I view the devastation, my internal furnace is stoked again and sends a gust of wild fury into my burned-out forest. In the end, nothing is left but scorched earth. I lie down in the residual warmth of the total devastation and close my eyes to rest.

I sleep all night and most of the next day. I eat what is left in my kitchen, watch a couple of movies, and sleep again. The following day, I awaken to snow on the ground. While my body still feels like it had been pummeled, my heart feels lighter and ready to venture out for a walk. I need groceries.

The West Coast only gets, at most, a couple of snowfalls every winter. It is always a breathtaking scene to see fresh snow clinging to tall evergreens like old friends who haven't seen each other in far too long. The sheer size and quantity of the moist snowflakes always send drivers into a panic. Snowplows appear out of nowhere, working through the night to remove the heavy melting snow before the temperatures dip and create a treacherous layer of ice underneath the snow.

I gingerly make my way back from the store on the snow-covered sidewalk that snakes up the final hill toward my townhouse complex. The snow has turned into a predictable slippery slush. I'm carrying two full bags of groceries that grow heavy in my arms as I walk more slowly than usual to keep from slipping. My injured elbow, unhappy with its current load, acts as a constant reminder of what's at stake if I fall. As I concentrate on staying upright, I'm momentarily distracted by a snowplow that is barreling down the road in my direction at considerable speed. Without slowing down, he lowers his front grader, angled to direct snow to the side of the road, which causes an arc of snow mixed with chunks of ice to shoot high into the air. Before I can react, a wall of snow hits my raincoat with a hard, moist thud. The impact stops me in my tracks. I do a quick body scan to ascertain if I'm physically hurt or if the sensation coursing through my body is just a wave of disbelief peppered with outrage. I turn to look as the massive plow continues down the road and wonder if the driver saw me on the sidewalk. Was it an accident or had he intended to shower me in chunks of slush? Since there is no way to know for sure, I soon realize the only decision I have to make at the moment is how I desire to "file" this incident for my own understanding.

Whether the snowplow operator meant it or not, I can't help but marvel at what an accurate hit it was. I hear myself laugh out loud. I'm not hurt physically, and any anger that I may have initially felt has slid to the ground along with the slush on my jacket. I'm aware that getting shat on by a pigeon is considered a sign of good fortune in some countries; it occurs to me that a slush hit by a passing snowplow could be the Canadian equivalent. I start peeling with laughter and have to stop to catch my breath.

Less than a minute later, there is a man standing on the sidewalk in front of me with his arms outstretched, wearing a brightly coloured Hawaiian shirt but no jacket. It takes me a moment to realize it's the driver of the snowplow, and he's doubled back on a side road.

"Are you alright, ma'am?" he begins, concern in his voice. "I honestly didn't see you until it was too late. I'm so sorry."

I believe him. "I'm fine. It startled me, that's for sure, but no harm done." I swing the bags of groceries in my arms to show him everything still works. "Hey, thanks for coming back to check though. That was classy of you."

With a look of relief clearly evident on his face, he allows the corners of his mouth to curl up in amusement. "But you gotta admit," he tests, searching my face for approval, "if I was going for you, that was pretty impressive."

We're both laughing now. "I had the exact same thought," I admit.

"That was like a Hawaiian wave you could catch a ride on," he adds, his oversized shirt billowing in the breeze as he waves one more time before returning to his steel steed.

Like diving into an ocean of possibilities, this has been a thrilling ride, from outrage all the way to bliss in less than one minute. My initial ignition of anger wasn't wrong, but without the added fuel from piles of rage locked inside me, I was easily able to let it go and catch the best wave of the day instead. It seems that giving myself the time and space to burn my backlog of rage to the ground over the holidays has been a refining fire. The inferno has cleared the way for holy ground where emotions are free to roam and signal an honest response to life's ongoing adventures, without the buildup of past hurts running the show.

As I arrive home and place my groceries down, my arms feel like they're floating up. This lightness matches my spirit as I celebrate the way I'd already transformed the experience by the time the snowplow operator came back to apologize. Independently of anyone else's input, I'd allowed a whole banquet of feelings to make their way through my body. The driver's kindness was gravy to the holiday feast of feelings I'd already laid out for myself.

MY IMAGINARIUM

"Where do you want to be on your forty-ninth birthday?"

The question sounds more like wind than words, but I understand it perfectly because it dances on the breeze of my Imaginarium. This is my name for that place between sleep and wakefulness that is only accessible on rare occasions, and then only if I'm able to wake up naturally. If I'm woken up by a squawking alarm or a person stirring on the sheets beside me, I move from the unconscious to the conscious too quickly. Floating in the buoyant semi-consciousness of my Imaginarium is much softer and slower, and certainly more magical.

There is no entrance and no sense of beginning, so I can't just find my way into the Imaginarium. It's like an unexpected summer shower while there's still blue sky overhead. The first droplets feel the same on your skin as the air. After a few moments, however, you realize that the moist, cool sensation that remains on your shoulder and face is something different than what was there just before. You're asleep and you're not quite asleep, but like the next drop of rain on the door of your consciousness, you sense something shifting.

Because the mind is able to stretch time in the Imaginarium, you can live entire lifetimes within a few seconds. It's not a dream, but it's dream-like, and it's not the thinking mind, but you can track your thoughts if you're lucky. It's a place where everything you know melds with everything you hope to know. It feels like a sacred place between time and space, between the real and the unreal. It's you, and it's the part of you that isn't limited to you. It feels a little like you've caught a glimpse of something behind the scenes—like perhaps the sleeping brain didn't shut down its offline function fast enough and you've gotten a peek behind the conscious curtain. It's a strange and wonderful thing to occasionally observe one's mind in the midst of this shift change.

From inside the Imaginarium, I grab the tail of the question regarding my forty-ninth birthday and pull it through to full wakefulness. The question travels with me along with its answer—or part of the answer, at least.

The components of that question were probably tossed into the corner of my conscious mind earlier this week. My second cousin Anne and I are planning a trip to Europe together. As we share our preferences and she offers wisdom from her vast experience in travelling abroad, we settle on October as the perfect month to go to Italy. The summer tourists will be long gone but the weather will still be pleasant, even optimal, for visiting cathedrals and wandering aimlessly down ancient streets. Since Anne will already be on vacation in Turkey with her husband, a plan is hatched for me to fly to Europe to meet her there. Since I don't want to spend any of our precious time together suffering from jetlag, I decide to fly out a few days before we meet up, since she will already have fully adjusted by then.

While Italy is on the list of places I long to see in my lifetime, the list of sites I feel I absolutely can't miss is short. I eagerly listen to Anne's recommendations on which cities will offer the most diverse culinary and cultural experiences. She and I share a common desire, not only in the type of adventures we want to have but in how we both prefer an unhurried pace when we travel.

The only other time I've been to Europe was a couple years earlier when I took both my daughters on a whirlwind twenty-three-day trip. We spent time in the town of Kampen in the

Netherlands, our ancestral stomping grounds, followed by a week in Ireland to visit my daughter's friend, and ended our trip staying with my cousin and her family in Germany. The trip was memorable, albeit exhausting due to the schedule we kept.

When Anne offers to research accommodations and book our activities, I gratefully give her my full permission to plan our itinerary. All I need to do is book my own flight. I decide I will adjust to the significant difference in time zones in Venice, an iconic Italian experience that didn't make it onto our itinerary. I find a flight from Vancouver that connects through London, but before I am able to complete the booking, I need to know my return date. It seems best to find the closest available option to Anne's return flight so we can travel to the airport together, perhaps even arrive home on the same flight. This will bring me home a few days before my forty-ninth birthday. But something stops me from completing the booking.

That night, my unanswered question goes where questions go in the mind. One part is immediately handed off to my Internal Safety Council. Travelling abroad means I'm a long way from home and things could go wrong. Other parts of the question arrive at the doors of Reality Check. The trip with Anne is already a significant decision in terms of time and finances, and the current plan is perfectly wild and wonderful as it is. Adding anything else will certainly be deemed overly indulgent.

Another part of the question is shipped to the shoreline of my Ocean of Possibilities, the place where obstacles stay on land so Potential can take a few tentative steps into the cool water. Potential scans the horizon and wonders what kind of celebration can be dreamed into existence for my forty-ninth birthday.

Another piece of the question makes it to the station that is tasked with Resolving Niggles. What is it about turning forty-nine, which is actually the start of my fiftieth year, that is setting off a beacon of familiarity? As my brain flips through the archives of my mind, I get a match from my Bible school training some thirty years ago. I recall that the Year of Jubilee happens every fifty years as a way to hit a reset button in the community. I can't remember exactly how that happens; I just know I need to find out. A sticky note is attached to that file and delivered to my conscious mind when I wake up the next morning.

Where do I want to be on my forty-ninth birthday? An answer comes back so forcefully that it shakes any remaining sleep from my eyes: "Not at home."

I require Anne's sage advice, so I ask her if we can meet.

"Well, where do you want to be?" she asks, her eyes gleaming with intrigue. "Somewhere in Italy?"

"No. Italy is our adventure. Somewhere else." I haven't even researched a map of Italy's neighbours as I hear myself say that. The destination seems less important than continuing on with my adventure.

"As much as I'd like to extend our trip, I have to be back home before the end of October," she tells me.

I assure her I have no expectation of her joining me; I just know that I need to do this. "It's the fact that you and I will already be immersed in European ways, giving me a chance to exercise my travel muscles, that allows me to even consider staying longer," I add, feeling suddenly emotional as I see the flowing storyline. "Without our plan in place, my mind wouldn't have had a space to expand into."

Surprised at my clarity when I hadn't really thought it through yet, I find myself fully trusting the evolving plan that is being directed from somewhere deep inside me. "I would like to have a home base somewhere in the European Union for the month of November," I tell Anne with increasing confidence. I watch her face beam in support. Dreams are very fragile when they first show themselves, so like handing over a newborn baby, the first person we tell needs to be someone who knows how to cradle the tiny new idea, protecting it in the places that haven't fully developed yet.

For me, one of these people is Anne. While she and I grew up in the same church and were both raised on farms in the Fraser Valley, it was my recent move to the rural town where she lives that launched our friendship. We find it easy to fill any amount of time together with delight and delicious ideas, from afternoon walks to weekends away at her cabin.

Anne reminds me that our grandmothers were actually twins. They were known in their village in the Old Country for their polar opposite personalities. My grandmother was dubbed "the lion," and Anne's grandmother was "the lamb." It was my grandmother who always spoke up on behalf of her much meeker sister. Anne and I muse how something of that twin spirit must have gotten blended into the genes that were transferred through our mothers and then passed on to us. The more time we spend together, the more I see how our personalities complement one another in incredible ways. When I need help, she's confident; when she wavers, I step up fearlessly. It all flows from this mysterious genetic glue that creates an unbreakable bond between us that endears and endures.

So when Anne puts on her trip planning hat again, I know that whatever catches her attention and her heart will be perfect for me. She quickly deduces that due to the time of year, I should stay in the south, as it can be quite cold further north by November. This rules out the United Kingdom and any Nordic countries. She asks how I feel about Crete, a large Mediterranean island off Greece, the most southerly destination in the European Union. She has heard about a town on the west side of the island that people rave about.

In no time at all, her recommendation to stay at Iason Studios in the town of Chania, on the island of Crete, makes it into my inbox. I can rent a well-kept room that includes a small kitchen and tiny balcony for an entire month at a very reasonable rate. The suite is one of four in a quaint building with a rooftop terrace, run by a woman named Despoina. This rental is located in Chania's Old Town, where I can stroll by the ocean and enjoy countless restaurants near the inner harbour just outside my front door. I know almost nothing about this part of the world besides a few household names like Socrates, Aristotle, and Plato. As the joke goes, it is all Greek to me. And with surprising ease, I realize I don't need to know more yet. I believe all will be revealed once I arrive. I am learning to trust each step in its time just like I encourage my coaching clients to do. For now, all I need to do is say yes to being away on my forty-ninth birthday, book my flight, and confirm my accommodations on Crete.

As Anne places papers with dates and names I can't pronounce in front of me, she surprises me with one more treat—she has negotiated with her husband for a couple more days away so she can fly from Italy to Crete with me to see with her own eyes where I'll be staying for the month.

In the spirit of my ancestors, I feel the lion and the lamb dance their balancing jig inside me. The gentle lamb is able to listen for subtle prompting, and the fierce lion is clearing any obstacles out of the way of my dreams. Everything is flowing. Even my budget, which I had already decided wasn't going to derail my plans, is easily managed with one fearless conversation. I am ready to take on the world. My parents, on the other hand, don't see it the same way.

My father walks into his office to retrieve the family globe I remember from childhood. He places the globe on his lap, moving it in slow increments to allow his eyes to scan its surface. He finds the Mediterranean Sea and then points his finger just below a small island surrounded by a lot of blue. He holds it up so Mom can see it too. She takes a quick look, but it doesn't change the expression of disbelief on her face. I've just told them that I've decided to not only travel to Italy with Anne but also stay for another month in a place she's never even heard of—and I'm going to do that part alone!

As the years have passed, especially after leaving my marriage six years earlier, my decisions are no longer open for debate the way they once were with my parents. I am no longer interested in being talked out of anything or guilted into anything.

As my mother keeps touching her reddening cheeks and putting her hands over her head, behind her aging face I begin to see a young child in distress. Her last intercontinental trip, apart from short vacations to Hawaii, was the traumatic trek from her small village to Canada as a child. I see her shudder at the thought of ever voluntarily returning to the part of the world that is stamped in her memory as a place of terror and loss. It seems unimaginable to her that her own daughter would travel alone as a single woman so far from home because in her mind this means putting oneself in harm's way.

The globe my father is holding was the first representation of the world I ever saw as a child. I recall him spinning it on its axis and stopping the rotation with his finger to point out to us kids where he and Mom were born, then placing another finger to show us where we lived. That place in Europe was almost as far away from where we lived in Canada as you could get on the orb. I studied the globe and tried to imagine the life they'd described in their stories, so different than the one I was living. Their tales of war made every place on the other side of the globe seem scary to my young mind. Even back then, I knew the world must be a big place, despite the way this colourful representation sat unobtrusively on its golden base at the far end of our dining room table.

It strikes me that my determination to take this trip might be important for another reason. This journey is for me, and it will never undo the awful experiences my mother endured at such a tender age, but is it possible that my growing trust in life could help bring some balance to her overt distrust of the big, bad world? Just like one person's fear can be contagious, could the clear answer I received in my Imaginarium to stay in Europe for my forty-ninth birthday set in motion a healing ripple effect?

LEFT BEHIND

With care and attention, I pull each item, in turn, out of my suitcase in order to decide its fate. The pile that will not be joining me on the next leg of this trip is slowly growing in the corner of the hotel room. Anne and I have loved Italy—and been loved by it in return—for the past month. After staying in six vacation rentals in as many cities all over the boot-shaped country, tonight we've booked separate rooms in a hotel that offers airport transfer for our early-morning flight to Crete.

It feels like forever ago, and only yesterday, that I stood in front of my own closet back in Canada, trying to figure out what to pack for this two-month adventure. Any extra space I had in my suitcase has been filled with purchases from quaint shops dotted throughout small Italian villages. Tomorrow's flight to Crete will be on a small economy plane, and unless I want to pay a hefty overweight fee, I need to lighten my load.

The first few items that land in the discard pile are easy: a sweater I've hardly worn, a top that doesn't really go with the bottoms I wear most often. The two new stunning hand-dyed scarves I purchased in Orvieto make it easier to leave behind most of the ordinary scarves I brought from home. I eye the small pile on the floor and realize that I'm going to have to dig deeper if

I am going to make it under the airline's weight restriction.

I lift up a pair of pants for consideration. I've owned them for years. They are neither wide-legged nor overly fitted, so they slide under the radar of seasonal fashions. These pants are the perfect balance of classy yet casual. They are neither lightweight nor too thick, and the material never shows creases. They are a lovely charcoal grey colour that pairs just as well with light summer blouses as with heavy black sweaters in winter. I love these pants. I've often been complimented on the fit and feel of them. And now I'm trying to decide if they are worth abandoning halfway around the world, realizing the amount of money I'll save is significantly more than I paid for them in the first place.

I wore these pants when I first arrived in Venice, the most northerly stop on my itinerary. Since then, the temperatures in the south have stayed consistently warm, and the forecast for Greece is showing unseasonably warm weather all the way through November. I doubt I'll wear these pants again on this trip. Is it worth lugging them around for another month just to bring them home, where they'll hang alongside a long row of other fine options? Or perhaps they've done their time and are now ready to be sacrificed? I hug the pants to my chest and wonder why letting them go feels so hard.

The soft but sturdy texture of the pants under my fingers reminds me of how far I've come. They saw what I saw. They were with me when I landed at Heathrow airport and got sweaty running to catch a bus to Gatwick, where there was no time to spare before breathlessly boarding my next flight to Venice. When I landed late in the evening, they were with me as I walked, my eyes heavy with fatigue, my exhausted brain out of ideas as I attempted to locate my rental amongst the maze of pedestrian bridges connecting the heart of the city. With no working mobile phone and no payphones in sight, in desperation, I entered a store at the end of a dark alleyway. I was enveloped by the smell of rich Italian leather while a young store clerk allowed me to use her personal mobile phone to contact the owner of my rental. When the clerk wouldn't accept payment as thanks, I promised to come back before I left Venice to make a purchase in this store.

Feeling like I had just completed a marathon, I landed with a thud on a nearby curb to wait for the owner to meet me. It had been thirty hours since I left home and had any sleep. I lay my head on my lap and wiped tears of relief and gratitude against the soft fabric of my pants.

As I reviewed my first dizzying hour in this new city, I found that most men had dismissed my requests for help with a wave of their cigarettes. It was the support and kindness of young women around my daughters' age who stopped to answer my questions that got me moving in the right direction. These angels took a middle-aged woman who spoke no Italian and could no longer think straight under their wing to guide her and her grey pants to safety. Fairy tales may claim that male chivalry shows up when there's a maiden in distress, but this evening, it was the generous care of other women that came through for me.

The pocket of these pants held my two-day entrance ticket to La Biennale international art exhibit. We got a little lost together, the pants and I, as I wandered along the waterways, curious where the next footbridge would take me. They watched along with me as gondoliers used their legs to push off sea-stained buildings to steer their boats down ridiculously narrow passages. They walked with me around St. Mark's Square as pigeons, in the shadow of the looming basilica, waited to see if I would share a bite of my freshly baked croissant. My pants witnessed me take things in stride and helped me find a new pace for international travel. They agreed that I'm at a perfect age and stage of life to move about the world with grace and ease—I can blend in and still bend, I'm not seen as vulnerable or venerable, I'm neither a threat nor a promise.

I hold the pants up at arm's length one more time and then, with appropriate reverence, place them on the top of my discard pile. I've never left behind a piece of clothing that I still love, and my fingers are poised, ready to grab them back at the first hint of regret. These pants have fulfilled their duty over the years, and now they will be remembered for their part in this new story. The next part of my journey requires a lighter load. I have noticed that to release what's no longer needed is the very best way to make space for what desires to come. If I slack off in the uncomfortable act of letting things go when it's time—whether that's ideas about heaven and hell, relationships, or even pants—I know life will not flow as well.

With my suitcase at the correct weight, confirmed by the scale in the bathroom, I turn out the light beside my bed—but my mind is still racing. Tomorrow isn't just another new town; it's a new country, a new culture, and for all intents and purposes, a different trip. Anne is flying over with me and staying for a few days, and then I will be alone for the month of November, including my birthday. I'm scrambling to remember why I thought travelling alone for a whole month was such a good idea when I came up with the plan.

My time with Anne in Italy has been idyllic. Our ease and joy in travelling together never wavered. We wandered ancient streets, laughed till our stomachs hurt, ate hazelnut chocolate gelato every afternoon, and talked our hearts full every day. I marvelled at how we created just the right balance of activity and rest. We roused at our own pace and spent the first part of our morning in our own bedrooms, enjoying time for yoga, reading, or writing. This was followed by a huge, homemade breakfast before we ventured out for the day. By late afternoon, we were always ready to head back to our rental for a glass of wine and something we coined "feet up time." It gave us a chance to absorb what we had seen that day and check our messages as friends and family were just waking up to start their day back home. With renewed energy, we made our way to whatever restaurant had caught our attention on our walk that day.

We decided from the beginning of our trip together that we would order everything to share, which allowed us to enjoy a greater variety of iconic Italian and Roman cuisine. We also came up with the idea of using a "common purse," a small wallet that acted like a joint account to pay for meals, admission tickets, and groceries, which freed us from having to keep track of who paid for what. I'd returned to the leather store right before I left Venice and picked out a soft leather wallet the colour of the sea. The young clerk who'd graciously offered me her phone that first night wasn't there, but I kept my promise to her anyway. I didn't know yet that this purchase would be like another gift from that angel—the common purse would tag along with Anne and me to more continents than either of us could yet dream or imagine.

As I stare at the soft glow on the ceiling of the dark hotel room, I remember that I will have to figure out my own excursions and order my own food once Anne flies home. It isn't that I don't think I am capable of doing it; I'm just not convinced that it will be as easy or, frankly, as much fun once I'm on my own. There is comfort and companionship in having a travel mate, and there is safety in numbers. There were times when I saw a sign when Anne didn't and days when she felt a strong pull to see a sight that I would have missed had it been only my decision. In Italy, although my pronunciation would routinely miss the mark, I could still look at a map and identify the name of a place with ease. The Cretans use an entirely different alphabet and language. I'm not sure how I am going to navigate my way around, let alone order dinner. I feel like I am about to throw myself overboard into an ocean, without a backup plan, to find out if I can swim—and from this hotel bed, the heaving waves look foreboding.

Uncertainty crawls into bed with me and wakes me up every hour as we toss and turn together. I feel like I'm taking a test without having studied, and I fear I've bitten off more than I can chew. There are too many things I just don't know yet, and as I lie in the darkness, my mind is desperate to fill in the glaring blanks.

By morning's light, I'm not feeling any more confident, but I have a plane to catch. I zip up my suitcase and glance back at the grey pants on the floor. I could still grab them, roll them up tightly, and carry them under my arm. While I'm at it, I could cram one of those scarves from the pile into my pocket.

Familiar things bring comfort. But they also take up space. My body needs to be free to embrace whatever comes next, and I remind myself that I've done this before. In fact, I've done a much harder version when I left the marriage and the life I knew to start over. How could leaving behind a pair of pants bring on such a strong wave of uncertainty when there's so much evidence from my life that I will be okay?

I feel the answer as I pull on a sweater against the chill in the morning air. I'm nervous because I've added a thick layer of expectation. Planning a trip like this means I've created the space for something significant to unfold, but there's no guarantee this will happen. Surviving a month alone in Greece is not the same as having "the trip of a lifetime," as everyone back home keeps referring to it. It's not that I require every moment to be complete bliss, but at this moment, I'm afraid I might not be able to find my way through this new Greek maze in one piece, let alone make it amazing.

I open the door and pull my suitcase through. There's a hotel employee in the hallway, and I let her know that I've left some clothing behind in the room. The pants need to stay, and I need to catch the shuttle to the airport. Right now that's all I know—and actually, that's all I need to know. Trusting each step as it comes into view instead of trying to control the outcome is exactly how I got this amazingly far in the first place.

KALIMERA

As our European adventure unfolded, I noticed a distinct background noise layered into the soundtrack of my trip. It was a unique, percussive duet—the hollow clack of modern, plastic wheels bumping against the low, resonant thump of each cobblestone—as luggage was pulled or pushed down the ancient streets. Every place we've stayed, I could practically tell time by the clickity-clack of travellers leaving to catch flights in the morning and another wave of incoming clatter as tourists make their way to their accommodations in the afternoon.

Today my cousin's suitcase joins the chorus as she pulls her luggage toward a waiting taxi. She and I have exchanged countless words over the month we have travelled together. I regularly joked that someone should invent a device that, in addition to tracking one's steps, it would keep a record of how many words one speaks in a day. And these were not just surface-level conversations. Sure, there was the occasional "Hey, look at that!" but the bulk of our exchanges ventured into topics that sliced deliciously through all the layers of our lives. Like Michelangelo, who carved away excess stone to reveal the David—a statue that evoked great emotion when we stood in its presence in Florence—we used words as our tool to design our futures, chipping away at endless possibilities to speak our desires into being.

I am so grateful that Anne extended her trip by a few days to allow her to experience Crete firsthand so she'll know exactly what I'm talking about when I regale her with stories later.

In our time together in Crete, we've wandered and eaten and marvelled at how different the food tastes and the people seem from our time in Italy. On our last day together, we arranged a ride in a glass-bottomed boat with a handful of other tourists. As we circled a nearby island, inhabited by a band of wild goats who clambered up the impossibly steep embankments with relative ease, I spotted two goats mating while perched precariously on the side of a cliff. The risk of plunging to their death during the act while enjoying a striking oceanfront view must have been exhilarating—and it was apparently a successful approach, given the size of their community.

Nick, the captain and owner of the boat, a fair-haired, fit man around our age, deftly navigated the boat into a cove and lowered the anchor. Then he jumped into the Mediterranean Sea wearing a mask and flippers and yelled instructions to those opting not to don snorkelling gear to gather around the viewing glass at the centre of the boat. He dove down again and again, displaying a live octopus, sea urchins, and an assortment of other unique local creatures that he held up for us to view through the glass. These views, however, came a close second to the laughs he elicited from the silly grin that the seal of his rubber mask created on his enthusiastic face. He looked as much a creature from the sea as any of his outstretched offerings.

As we made our way back to the main island at the end of the tour, I wondered if the first civilization on Crete rightly assumed they were the centre of the universe. Land. Sea. Sun. Cretans had everything they needed for a good life on their beautiful island. But they ventured out anyway, compelled to discover what was beyond their immediate world. People throughout history have felt driven to see what else might be "out there" on this impressive planet and, more recently, in deep space. We have a common hunger that tugs at the tassels of our curiosity. Although I've spent much of the past decade venturing into the uncharted territories of a life that was different than the one I was raised to live in, I'm still very new to venturing off my own continent.

I grabbed onto the side of the boat as Captain Nick sped up for the final crossing. As my body moved in time with each bounce of the boat and the wind whipped my hair away from my face, I noticed a gypsy spirit stirring inside of me. I felt buoyant, my body floating up to join the effervescence of my spirit.

In that moment, I realized for me, this is the sensation that signals I'm truly celebrating—the way I wanted to feel, but didn't, at my fortieth birthday party. Celebration can be prompted by all the ingredients of a standard party—balloons, food, presents, people—but so often is not. If I try to force it, it feels contrived, like the taste of overly sweet icing on a store-bought cake. Celebration, for me, reveals itself most profoundly at the moment when things come together. It can show up in the breathless connection of lovers joining more than just their bodies, in the gentle bounce of a baby in one's arms, or in standing alone while the moon crests the horizon and pours forth her wisdom. Celebration can feel like a swing reaching its apex right before it descends—or softer, like a gasp of awe at the depth of a new thought that expands my insides. The sensation of celebration can linger like smoke from a blown-out birthday candle or retreat as quickly as it arrives. Celebration seems to arrive most consistently when I cast my view to witness the union of beauty and banality—the ongoing meet-and-greet of the commonplace with the ethereal. Earth meets sky. Body meets spirit.

There is something rather delicious about joining two ideas together, especially when they don't obviously seem to go together. I joke that my mind was primed early for such ubiquitous unions, having spent all my formative years listening to parables from the Bible. A story told by my Sunday school teacher always started out describing something I could imagine—a house built on sand, a lost sheep, a good Samaritan—and then it took a sharp turn and became something bigger, essentially shape-shifting. This morphing seemed magical to me, like opening a door in my brain that I didn't even know was there a moment ago. I enjoyed the feeling of expansion and revelation. I marvelled at how a thing could sound like a regular note and then click into stereo with the flip of a metaphor.

And so it's not surprising that I adore metaphors and analogies. In truth, I get pretty excited by all figures of speech packaged up like little treasures to be discovered inside unsuspecting sentences. This includes but is not limited to: the always affable alliteration, the outrageous hyperbole, the head-shaking irony, the pop and crackle of onomatopoeia, both sides of a paradox, a simile like no other, subtle understatements, and most especially the proverbially playful pun.

I am enchanted by how a concept can take a seat beside me, and the next thing I know, I'm surrounded by the realization that pretty much everything can be linked together—and I finally understand that these connections happen so easily because everything has always been connected. All I need to do is gather things in, and they show me exactly where they intersect.

The boat crashed across a large wave, calling me back from my thoughts, and I looked over at my cousin, who sat peering at the horizon from her seat in the boat. Our gaze locked, and by the way her mouth was set, I suspected she was contemplating the imminent transition back to her life at home after such a long time away. It is in these random moments, with the sun glistening on the water in a place so far from home, that it's easy to imagine an entirely different life had we been born at a different time and in a different place. It is also these magical moments that allow us the freedom to continue to choose the lives we have waiting for us back in Canada.

I made my way to the front of the boat and beheld the sprawling island I was so excited to discover over the next month. The island of Crete, shaped like a kidney bean, floats in a seemingly endless sea of dazzling green-blue water, and I'm staying on the northwest side of this 160-mile-long legume. I am arriving as a foreigner to a place where everything began so long ago, but the timeless part of me also feels like I'm coming home—and if this is true, then my only task for this month is to shake off my limitations and shake up my familiar habits in order to connect with the parts of me that know how to beat in time with the universal pulse of this early civilization. I am not sure how this will happen, but I want to be more than just a tourist on this island. I already suspect that as this unfolds, I will also see where I have limited myself to being a tourist in my life back home.

Now, with Anne's suitcases safely stowed in the trunk of the taxi, she walks back to the curb where I'm standing, but neither of us seems to be able to find anything to say. We manage to squeak out a few words of farewell, our voices strangled by emotion. In the end, we hug each other close, knowing the tears we mop from our cheeks sum up everything we have already expressed during our month together. There are times when not speaking is more powerful than all the words in the world.

I wave as I watch her taxi turn away from the water and disappear behind the enormous old city wall. I blink away more tears as I make my way back up the cobblestones that lead into Old Town Chania, wandering the winding streets near the inner harbour and scanning the area with new eyes. I feel unsettled that Anne's gone, but behind the sadness I also sense something else waking up. Initially, it feels somewhat similar to when I first left my marriage—also a time where I made the transition from travelling with a co-pilot to taking charge of all the controls of a solo flight. I am back to deciding where I am going, how I am going to get there, and what I will do if something goes wrong on this trip. There is a palpable sense of freedom in the shift, but also a cloak of extra responsibility. Feeling a little shaky under the weight of this transfer, I find a bench near the water so I can sit for a while.

It's still early in the day, and I watch small vehicles back up to unload their freight at the restaurants that line the waterfront. I read that there are limited times, generally the beginning and end of each day, when vehicles are permitted to make deliveries in Old Town; the rest of the day, this part of Chania is restricted to pedestrian traffic only. My eye follows the long arc of the massive boardwalk, where museums, restaurants, and buildings of every shape, constructed over centuries, are crammed in, all facing in the same direction. Like the crowded front row of a rock concert, they all look adoringly at the most prominent feature of the harbour—a grand lighthouse, which stands proudly at the end of a long breakwater. Looking from above, the harbour is shaped like a giant eye. As I trace the lower lash of the boardwalk back around to the upper lid of the breakwater, the lighthouse is the all-seeing pupil, keeping watch over all the comings and goings.

If I walk a few blocks in any direction away from the inner harbour, like stepping off a movie set, I smack headlong into the glare and traffic of a modern city that is home to 150,000 residents. I will venture beyond Old Town regularly but feel relief at the thought that every day I get to return to this quaint, cobblestoned haven alongside the ocean.

I have less of an actual list and more of a leaning toward what I want to do while I am in Greece—and at this moment, I'm strongly inclined to find a place that serves good coffee and will allow me to stay for a while so I can write down all these new thoughts and fresh feelings that desire to be collected. Words, written or spoken, cannot possibly corral everything, but buzzing bits of thoughts are beginning to zing off in every direction; writing gathers them in and gives them a place to land. First, they rest on my page, then they become fodder for deeper understanding, and eventually they serve as a delicious archive for my memory.

I recall seeing a coffee shop with outdoor seating that faced the ocean on a walk a couple days ago, so after collecting my computer from my room, I wander in that direction.

Once I am seated, a server approaches and greets me with "Kalimera," the equivalent of good morning in Greek, followed by a string of other words I haven't learned yet. I pull an apologetic face and respond with, "English?" She scrunches her face and replies with a popular line in return, "A little bit." I have learned this may mean she only knows a handful of phrases she can use in taking my coffee order, or it could mean she is currently working on an English doctoral thesis on ancient Greece in her spare time. Today, it is the first. Fortunately, I am able to point to two items on display on a table nearby that delight me as soon as I see them. She returns with a lovely caramel-coloured coffee, a small container of thick cream, and an even lovelier chocolate croissant.

The Cretans lost many battles to other countries over the centuries, including to the Venetians. While it may be a tragic part of their history, it's had a favourable impact on their culinary diversity, which makes this the opposite of tragic for me as I take my first bite of the flaky croissant, reminding me of similar delicious offerings in Venice. With time to write while I sip from my steaming cup between mouthfuls of buttery goodness, any residual concerns over how I am going to manage alone on Crete slowly dissipate.

My only other decision this week, besides where to dine, is how I would like to celebrate my forty-ninth birthday. I'm still drawn to the idea of using the concept of the Year of Jubilee as a template for my celebration, and I'm curious to figure out how this barely remembered celebration from biblical times could intersect with my life today.

My initial web search for "Jubilee" brings up the British monarchy's use of the word. Their traditions seem stodgy, and I can almost smell the scent of mothballs lingering in ball gowns pulled from dank palace storage rooms to complete the image. Besides, their Royal Jubilee is a gala event, and I'm interested in a different way to celebrate.

The only mention of the "Year of Jubilee" in the Bible is way back in the Old Testament. It's found in the hard-to-read book of Leviticus, sometimes called the Book of Laws. This particular part of the Bible makes me especially nervous because of how often its mandates are still weaponized against people today. This Book of Laws is too often used as righteous fuel to pass judgment and incite violence. It makes my stomach turn to hear self-appointed believers hurl rules from Leviticus like rotten eggs into the distraught faces of those simply tending to their own lives.

The Bible was such a huge part of my life growing up, including four years as a student of theology. In the past decade, however, my Bible has gathered a lot of literal and proverbial dust. I haven't rejected the heart of the story, but I find the way the Bible is often interpreted from the pulpit or in religious podcasts a heartbreaking departure from its original intention.

I look up from my computer screen and widen my focus to

where the blue sea meets the bluer sky. Over my right shoulder looms a massive wall that was built around Old Chania in the sixteenth century, and when I peek over to my left, I see the roiling sea through the remains of a building that no longer has walls. The structure is only recognizable as such because of its foundation and the posts that still hold its frame. There is nothing remotely close to this kind of history back home. In fact, Crete's museums showcase artifacts that predate even the Bible. Time contracts and expands as I breathe in the fresh sea air and continue to research an old mandate in an old book while surrounded by all this visible ancient history.

It's a challenge to pull out the core of the Jubilee verses when only a basic outline of the story is available in the Bible. There's a lot of room to fill in the blanks—the walls—and the spirit of the people from that time. Being here, however—on an island that birthed one of the earliest civilizations—helps me to put this biblical storyline into perspective. I'm the first generation of my family's clan to be born in Canada, a country that's only 150 years old. My experience of living, let alone celebrating, has not really been tried and tested in history. The rituals brought from the old country where my parents were born often don't resonate with me, and the traditions of longtime Canadians seem overly commercialized by comparison. Finding a way to celebrate that feels authentic to me is going to require a gentle touch and an open heart.

As I review my notes about the Year of Jubilee, there is an obvious connection that starts the ball rolling. In Leviticus, the Jubilee Year was based on cycles of seven that were a big part of their rhythm. Every seven days there was a day of Sabbath rest, and every seven years, a mandated sabbatical, which basically meant no planting or harvesting in order to let the soil rest. The culmination of seven years multiplied by seven cycles resulted in the Jubilee Year, a time of super-sized rest and year-long celebration. 7 cycles x 7 years = 49. Voila! To personalize the math, this equals the start of my fiftieth year of life, which begins in a few days on my forty-ninth birthday. This Jubilee celebration was to be observed every fifty years and for the entire year. Most birthdays are celebrated every year for one day. Some people stretch it out for a week, perhaps even a month for a really special birthday—but claiming an entire year to celebrate is taking it to another level.

The original purpose of the Year of Jubilee was to keep balance in the community as well as the land—both components of a healthy economy. Back then, their currency was largely their land, which would grow food and provide work for the people. Every Jubilee Year, the land was to return to its original owner. Original owners were not individuals; they were families or clans. Land that was leased out in the interim years due to debts that couldn't be paid would be prorated for the Jubilee Year. So, if land was leased in the forty-third year, the term would be for six years before it returned to the original owner. The intention was to safeguard against the imbalance of power, as this reset created regular checks and balances, which was the best way to keep the economy strong for everyone. Recent global uprising against the reality that one percent of the population controls ninety-nine percent of the resources shows exactly the imbalance that the Year of Jubilee was intended to avoid.

In addition, those who found themselves in debt, known as slaves at that time, were to be set free during the Year of Jubilee. This way, bad business decisions or poor crops didn't mean a person would be doomed to a lifetime of slavery.

I easily form two questions from the heart of the Jubilee concept to guide me as an individual. First, what is my internal land that requires a reset of rest and celebration? Second, which inner slaves need to be set free during my Jubilee Year? Filled with ideas plucked from these questions, like a bouquet of colourful thoughts, I close my computer and walk into town to prepare for my upcoming birthday.

Once I see the front doors of a large, modern grocery store located outside the perimeter wall, I return the printed map left for me by Despoina, the owner of the room I am renting, to my bag. The map includes the English spelling for street names and prominent landmarks, but I'm noticing that most of the actual signage, especially in Old Town, is in the Greek alphabet. I may be able to read what the sign says on my map, but trying to confirm it on the street takes some doing.

As with creating new rituals for myself or learning to navigate uncertainty in my life, I end up resorting to something more intuitive. When my mind doesn't know or can't be sure, it signals for assistance, and then curiosity takes over and I feel the inner party begin. This is when all my senses are coaxed out onto the dance floor. I move to the sounds and sights all around me and inside me. My senses encourage me to stop and savour as I log unique places on my route like a trail of cookie crumbs within my body. I'm tickled to be building my confidence in filling in the blanks with a combination of what works for my brain and what works for my body as I wander farther afield every day.

This goblet of new adventures isn't always my favourite vessel to drink from. Familiarity has flavour notes that taste, well, familiar. But the uncertainty of travel—and the endless uncertainties of life—offer constant opportunities to try new things that may eventually be embraced as familiar, or at least nostalgic. Sometimes the worst meal is as memorable as the best. This push into new territory expands not only my actual taste buds but also the tentative places in me that initially resist being exposed. Trying new food is one thing; trying a new approach to celebration, especially when I'm flying solo in a different country, is quite another.

BIRTHDAY BLISS

I wake with a soft knowing that this day is going to be wonderful. My eyes follow a narrow stream of sunlight that carves a distinct line along the floor and up the wall of my rental suite. Once I swing open the shutters, the whole room will be showered in the sun's brilliance, but for now this narrow blaze of contained light is a gentle way for my eyes and my heart to enter the day. Birthdays are a great time to practise moving to the slow dance between the heart and mind, I muse. It's the quiet, gentle moments of celebration that often slip past our shuttered minds while we're busy anticipating grander gestures. I imagine this beam of sunlight as my very own birthday candle and slowly exhale my wishes for this year into the room.

This year's Jubilee concept isn't the only way to have a wonderful birthday, but my gut tells me it's a particularly perfect way for me to gather in my past and call in my future so they can join me right where I am. I'm grateful I already know that arriving into the present moment is always the very best gift I can give to myself any day of the year.

I throw off the covers so I can stretch my limbs, then lift my legs to the ceiling, followed by my arms. Then I bend my knees so I can wrap my pointer fingers around my big toes and draw my legs inward. In yoga, this pose is called "happy baby." How appropriate for my day of birth, I think with a smile. I feel especially good in my skin these days. I feel better now than when I carried less weight on my frame ten years ago. A friend back home is doing an ongoing photo series about loving her body the way it is. Her project is called "Be Your Own Beloved." Like a roadmap, my forty-nine-year-old birthday suit has scars running up my arm and varicose veins running down my legs—but instead of cursing these perceived imperfections, I'm learning how to honour the story they tell.

I run my fingers through my hair but decide not to apply any makeup. Setting the timer on my camera again and again, I capture my limbs in various positions. Instead of looking back at pictures of my youth, wishing I had appreciated my youthful body then, I'm anchoring memories by taking pictures of the beloved skin I am wrapped in today so I can appreciate my evolving body as time goes on. I run through a mental list of all the places on my body that have been instrumental in displaying my evolving character. With a click of the camera, I capture the arch of my feet, the soft acreage of my inner thighs, the length of my hands, my subtle lips, my thin white thyroid surgery scar at the base of my neck, and the undulating scar along my elbow.

I feel a moment of melancholy for how long I equated beauty with the lack of a story on my body. I am humbled to finally see how blemishes, bumps, and bulges provide an intriguing backdrop. At this point, five decades in, I already have a hunch that even more scars and wrinkles on the outside will come along with deepening access to my spirit on the inside. That truth is harder to capture in a snapshot.

Ready for food after my impromptu photoshoot, I cut luscious fruit into a large red bowl and add a generous dollop of thick yoghurt. I purchased the bowl and two other vessels yesterday at a shop in Old Town filled to overflowing with colourful pottery made by local artisans.

When plotting how to keep this Jubilee celebration alive for an entire year, I realized I needed something that would help me remember my intention on a daily basis. Since eating is a daily requirement, I decided that for the entire year, I will eat exclusively from this special pottery—beginning today, on my birthday.

I'd taken my time looking through the unique handmade pottery as I'd imagined every conceivable meal I might make in the next year, finally narrowing it down to three pieces: a cup, a plate, and a bowl. As I'd looked through the stacks of different sizes and colours of ceramics, I'd allowed the vessels to choose me and to tell me what they represented.

The ocean-blue plate represents the Mediterranean's infinite sea of possibilities. It reminds me that there are always options, even during turbulent times, and that the very best of these options will arise when I ensure there is buoyancy in my spirit.

The grey cup is a warm reminder in my hands that life is so much more than right or wrong, good or bad, white or black. There is a calm, neutral centre that knows that an occasional storm is only a repositioning of energy, despite the threat of grey skies above. I will drink from the well of experiences that I have already accumulated over the years and sip on new thoughts every day.

And finally, the blood-red bowl, with its small swirl of gold on its inside base, will be a daily reminder to follow my passion's fiery ability to know my yes and my no. And in this stage of life with shifting hormones tap-dancing inside my premenopausal body, I will feast on the wisdom that flows from this bowl.

I cradle my beautiful glazed red bowl, which fits perfectly in my hand, as I finish the last of my fruit. The dregs of Greek yoghurt leave a swirl around its inner circumference like frosting from a devoured birthday cake. I look at the clock and realize it's time to get dressed for my next treat.

I arrive at the hammam just in time for my appointment. I still cannot believe my luck that there's an authentic Turkish hammam right here in Chania. It's a holdover from when the Turks invaded the area. I had never heard of this eastern ritual until my friend Pam, who shares the same day of birth with me, invited me to join her at a hammam in Vancouver a year ago. After my initial discomfort with being completely naked while my entire body was scrubbed and washed, I noticed that, once I relaxed into the experience, my body remembered the freedom of infancy, a clean slate. I felt a striking sense of reconnection with my body after that first hammam experience, so it seemed like a perfect activity to add to my celebration today.

The steam in a traditional hammam is different from other steam rooms I've visited. I find it easier to breathe, as the mist is intense but lighter somehow, and the room is hot but not overwhelming. Like my thoughts, the steam slowly dissipates and then rolls back in again. I cannot see past my nose—but just like the steam, I also know that my lack of sight in this moment regarding the future of my coaching business or whether I'll be in another relationship one day doesn't mean the uncertainty will last forever. It is exactly the things I cannot see or understand just yet that require trust—and the more I trust these cycles of knowing and then patiently waiting to know more, the more magnificent the outcome seems to be. I didn't know I'd be in a steamy hammam on Crete last year or even last week and when this mist clears, I'm certain the next piece will show itself. Worry means I'm trying too hard to peer through the fog when it's actually the perfect time to rest so I'll have energy for the next step when it's finally revealed.

No one has come into the steam area since I arrived, and as I wipe sweat from my brow, a cough clears my lungs and echoes off the tiled mosaic walls that surround me. Since today there will be no traditional party with cake or singing, I decide this is the perfect time and place to serenade myself. I sing a slow, soft version of "Happy Birthday" as sweat joins my tears and streams down my face. The tears come from a place of joy that knows precisely where to find itself because it recognizes itself. It's the part of me that is so filled with awe and pride for where I am at this point in my life that I am the best person to give and also receive this personalized praise. No false humility. No explanation. No obligation. Just pure love pouring out of every pore.

Sometime after my serenade ends, a young woman enters the steam room and invites me to follow her to the next part of the hammam experience. As I lie face up on a heated marble table, she places a soft towel underneath my head. Then she slowly begins the rhythmic process of exfoliation, and I feel my blood rush to the surface everywhere she removes skin cells that are no longer needed. She asks about my time in Chania, and I tell her about my Year of Jubilee and what brings me to the hammam today. She is in her early twenties, around the age of my daughters, and confides how much she would love her own mother to gather the courage to live as fearlessly as I appear to be doing. Her comment reminds me how tempting it is to dismiss the tough climb it took to get to the mountaintop moment I am enjoying right now. I share how hard it was on my daughters and the rest of my family when I took the first steps, and that while this path has led to somewhere amazing, it's been anything but fearless or pain-free.

When the cleansing soap is applied to my natural birthday suit, the lack of covering means there are no obstacles to impede the movement. Her hands glide from my shoulders through to my feet in one long, intentional motion. The flow, as she repeats this many times on all sides of my body, knits me together in places I didn't realize were apart. I feel connected and reconnected. My arms and torso, my legs and feet aren't separate entities anymore; they all hum the same tune in rhythm. I can feel myself as an infant, an adult, and an old soul all at the same time. Bridging the gaps I wasn't even aware had formed, my being now vibrates as a whole again, and this sacred consolidation brings on another wave of emotion. My tears join the warm water that is hosing off the last of the soap residue from my body. I feel youthful. I feel wise. I feel complete.

The final step is massage. This part is dessert. I've enjoyed the main meal; with my body satiated, now I get to savour the delicious things I have relearned during this hammam experience. I get to sample the wisdom that's been unlocked and released inside my body. Massage feels like a sweet treat for the muscles that work to move my soul from place to place every day.

Leaving the hammam feeling almost numb with bliss, I walk into a clothing store located downstairs. I am greeted by a smiling saleswoman who seems genuinely happy to help me find the perfect birthday outfit for my newly rejuvenated birthday suit.

In a fitting room, I pull on the dress I spied on the mannequin at the front of the store and am thrilled that the quality and cut of the dress is a perfect match for my forty-nine-year-old body. I also pick out a light knitted sweater that requires some demonstration of all the ways to wear it. The long sections that hang from the front of the sweater compliment the bell-shaped cutout of the unique hemline at the front of the dress. I twirl in the mirror and watch how this combination flows and hugs my body, a rather stunning match to how my spirit feels supported and free in equal measure.

I exit the shop wearing my new birthday clothes and walk onto a shaded outdoor patio two doors over that boasts free wifi and cold beer. I order calamari to go with a frothy drink and feel a sudden urgency to record all the memorable details that are flowing through this special day.

Although I'm at peace with being alone on my birthday, that doesn't exclude spending some online time with my friends and family back home. Jubilee literally means to shout, or "yowl," forth a proclamation of celebration. A ram's horn was used to trumpet the beginning of the Year of Jubilee in Leviticus. While I don't plan to stand on a street corner yowling, thanks to social media, it's easy to proclaim my birthday joy, even from halfway around the world. I open my laptop and see the first of many birthday messages as people wake up back home. It's like getting to start this stellar day all over again as the birthday greetings stream in.

Birthdays usually include gifts, and I've already showered myself with many today, not to mention the ultimate gift of this two-month trip. It feels like the best way to honour this flow is by giving a gift from this overflow of gratitude. As part of my Jubilee Year, I decided to take the year off from my coaching business, but the idea of being able to support another person in their desire for a more celebratory life feels perfectly aligned with my year's intention. The day before, I had the idea of giving away a twelve-session coaching package to one lucky winner; today, I put the finishing touches on the offer, upload it onto my website, and shout it from my Facebook page. Joy, like a river, requires momentum in order to remain healthy. Giving as well as graciously receiving helps create this flow for me.

"It's my birthday!" I gush to the server upon arriving at the restaurant I've chosen for my birthday dinner, a mere thirty-second walk from my rental.

"Well, then we must give you the best seat in the house!" he says, swinging his open hand to direct me toward a small table at the centre of the restaurant. The walls fold open on warm evenings, creating a seamless indoor-outdoor space that spills out onto the cobblestoned road. You cannot see the ocean from this establishment, but the way my chair straddles the place where the restaurant meets the patio reminds me of the shoreline. I feel giddy—not so much about what might happen, but about what is happening. I ride this wave, enjoying the tingle of celebration and the cool, calm waters of contentment gently pulling and pushing me within their tide.

"You would like red wine to start, yes?" Since there are only two employees at the front of the house on any given evening, he has been my server on a previous visit and apparently pays attention to such details. I smile my affirmation with my whole face. This restaurant doesn't battle for the tourist dollar since they easily fill their tables by their reputation. Their food is fresh and innovative, and their prices are better than the restaurants that line the harbour.

The restaurant has no English signage, so I didn't know its name the first time I dined here. I asked the waiter to write the English name into my journal when I couldn't make out his verbal attempt. KALDERIMI, he slowly printed out on my page, stopping twice to try to translate the Greek lettering into the language I could read.

I did a search later and felt something stir inside when I learned what *kalderimi* meant. It refers to a network of cobblestone trails built for foot and hoofed traffic dating back to the Ottoman empire and used as the main means of travel in rural areas throughout Crete until the 1960s. The *kalderimi* network consists of thousands of kilometres of these two-metre-wide mule tracks that criss-cross the island and link every village, hamlet, chapel, and even sheepfold.

Unlike modern roads, which tend to connect one coastal town to the next coastal town, the *kalderimi* network runs almost exclusively up and down the mountainsides. The people who live in the mountains want fish from the coast, and those who live by the sea require the olives grown in the hills. The article I read said modern roads have significantly changed the way the villages relate to each other.

I was initially surprised by the idea that something as mundane as a system of roads can change how people relate to each other—and the thought that came next gave me goosebumps. This *kalderimi* network shows us the best way to be in relationship with each other. We all have certain strengths and gifts, fish or olives, that we bring to the communal table—and if we don't expect ourselves to do everything, but instead, graciously give and receive from the bounty available because of our differences, then everyone wins. If we stop sharing our resources—the gifts and talents we are born to contribute—the whole world will not function as well.

The *kalderimi* is also such a perfect image for the network within our brains. When there are open communication channels between the places in our mind that are designed to protect us and the area that's really good at creating and imagining, then life feels balanced. If we tire in our discipline to keep these channels open and opt instead to travel the convenient highway of someone else's version of life, we effectively change our relationship with ourselves. It was when I packed up my mule—my grey SUV piled high with inherited beliefs and overstuffed boxes of shame—and finally ventured out on less travelled, sometimes treacherous roads, guided by my own heart, that I found balance inside of me and harmony with the world.

A dog lets out a short bark and calmly walks past my table and into the restaurant. My waiter places a glass of wine in front of me and then turns to respond in Greek to the dog. I admire his gentle tone, considering there's a dog loose in the place. This isn't the first time I've watched locals interact patiently with the dogs that run free all over town, almost like one might with a drunk uncle or elderly person who is a bit confused about where he is.

I cannot tell if these dogs have owners or if they are collectively taken care of by the locals. It's the same way with cats. One evening on my way home from dinner, I hear a man's voice softly cooing encouragement. As I round the bend, I see bowls of milk placed in a circle for a shockingly large group of meowing felines. The display of care and camaraderie made me slow down to marvel for a moment.

The striking part, to me, isn't that people interact with the animals who amicably roam their streets; it's that cats and dogs seem to live in harmony with each other too. It's not a stretch to imagine that children find this a safe town to wander freely as well. I've noticed that how a town treats its vulnerable citizens— its animals, children, and elderly—is the most accurate assessment of its moral code. Rules don't make a town safe; people's values do.

I notice where my own values show themselves more fully when I'm in a new culture. Travelling shows me what's important to me. Without familiar faces or routines, I get to watch my actions and reactions play out against an ever-changing backdrop. When I first arrived in Venice at the very beginning of the trip, I stood in a grocery checkout line, and when it was my turn to pay, the woman at the till yelled at me in Italian. I didn't know what I had done to get that reaction. Instead of getting angry or embarrassed that I was being dressed down in public, I looked around for assistance. A handsome man with expensive shoes and a sweet smile used his broken English to explain that I needed to weigh and label my fruit before I came to pay. I didn't enjoy being yelled at, but I truly valued the way help swooped in to assist me so sweetly in that moment.

The server places my birthday dinner in front of me, and I breathe in its essence. I've ordered sea bream, a tasty local white fish that is served whole with fresh vegetables. I ask if he'll show me the best way to fillet the fish. He points to where I should make the incisions to work around the fish bones. I follow his directions and smile at how far I've come. Before this trip, I likely wouldn't have ordered a dish that I didn't already know how to approach with confidence. Just like all the times I couldn't immediately find my way or read a menu, it's become less about having the knowledge and more about soliciting the confidence to ask a question that most often opens the world to me. Questions are like doors, and sometimes really brave questions allow doors to appear that weren't visible a moment earlier.

"Would you like another glass of wine?" asks the server when he comes to take my plate, then adds, "On the house?"

"Why yes, I would," I say, pulling out my journal.

I'm thoroughly enjoying my view from the shoreline of this restaurant. A crowd-pleasing moment occurs when an old man moves his chair so a car has room to pass on the narrow cobblestone roadway. He pretends the car had driven over his foot, yelping out in mock pain to garner an eruption of laughter from the other patrons. *That gag works everywhere*, I muse, laughing along.

Soon after, two young men sitting side by side, just in front of me, are speaking a stream of words at each other in Greek, often talking over each other unless one momentarily stops talking to take a drag from his cigarette. It's only when an attractive young woman walks by that they both fall silent for a few moments. That response to beauty seems to be a global commonality as well. For all the times I see and hear things I may not understand, there are so many moments where I'm in on the joke despite being a visitor.

When the waiter returns with a full glass, he asks how my birthday has been.

"Quite remarkable, actually," I say, not sure if he has time to hear more. "I am writing about celebration," I offer, "and when you have a moment, I'd like to ask you a question I've been asking everyone I meet." He nods, willing to play along. "What's your favourite celebration?" He looks in the direction of the kitchen and holds up his pointer finger, indicating that he'll be right back.

The next time he walks by my table, he tells me, "I have an answer for you," looking calm and collected despite the hustle of a busy evening at the restaurant. I hold up my pen to paper and look up at him expectantly as if I plan to record every word. "I don't know what you call it," he begins. "The day where everyone dresses up like someone else."

"Oh!" I blurt, admittedly a little surprised. "Do you mean Halloween?"

"Yes, yes!" he nods enthusiastically. "We have another name for it at a different time of year, but yes, that one." I didn't want him to feel like he had to justify his answer, but with my curiosity piqued, I ask him why it's his favourite celebration. "Because," he stammers, taking a moment to translate his thoughts into English, "for that one day, people can be anyone they want."

As I walk home at the end of the evening, listening to the rhythmic footfall of my shoes keeping time on the ageless cobblestone, I already know why the waiter's answer took my breath away. It lands so close to the heart of the matter for me. I feel like a kaleidoscope, the gems inside the tube all pieces of me, with each new turn, every click, each new adventure, allowing me to recreate myself. Change is inevitable, which means that every day can be Halloween—not because I want to be anyone else, but because I get to discover amazing new aspects of myself. And this also means there's something to celebrate virtually every day— not least of all today, which has been my best birthday ever.

KALISPERA

I pull on a light sweater and lift a small bag over my head to position it across my body. I made the decision the very first night I was here that I would lug my compact laptop around with me to coffee shops during the day, but for dinners out, I would bring only a pen and a small notebook. The time of day seems to make a difference in what I write about and also in how I want to capture it. Scribbling down a few thoughts as I wait for food to arrive is a great way to catch the day's highlights. Just as people reminisce over drinks with their dining companions, I share my thoughts with an attentive piece of paper while sipping a beverage. Pen and paper are significantly more portable and certainly more elegant than the harsh glow from a computer screen competing with the candlelight and the softer flicker of thoughts that draw my interest at this hour.

I skip down the three flights of stairs from my room, each step echoing in the cavernous stairwell, and push open the large wooden door at the bottom. In less than a minute, I've wound my way down a narrow walkway lined by multistory buildings on either side that elbow out most of dusk's lingering light. When I reach the main boardwalk, a ring of lights trained on the lighthouse cast a warm glow against her shapely form, giving the whole harbour a romantic ambience.

I slow my pace a bit on the wet cobblestones. The harbour walk is vulnerable to rainfall, but tonight it's the wind that has muscled its way past the breakwater to create swells that lap over the edge onto the walkway and then just as quickly recede back into the harbour. As forecast, it's unseasonably warm despite the wind—even for this part of the world.

I admire the string of lights that connect one restaurant to the next along the boardwalk. As I follow the flow of people, who seem to be in no hurry to choose from the many dining options, I've noticed that if I walk on the far side of the walkway, then the touts—those hired to convince tourists to come eat in their restaurant—don't engage me with their overenthusiastic invitations.

A cruise ship docked on the island this afternoon, and for a few hours, a gaggle of tourists poured onto the streets of Old Town Chania. As the throng of tourists, easily identifiable by their bright clothing and hurried pace, make their way up and down the streets, the shop owners—those with a door to their establishment and even those who pull down a wire gate to secure their wares overnight—seemed to stand up straighter for the arriving company. It's the end of the long tourist season for them, and I notice that even after such a short time on the island, I no longer consider myself just a tourist. Shop owners and residents from the area where I'm staying smile and shout "*Kalispera!*" ("Good evening!") and wave in recognition when they see me pass by. I'll always be a potential customer to the locals, but familiarity adds a personalized element to the interactions that warms my heart.

As I make my way through the crowd that moves like a slow, steady swarm, I remove my sweater and drape it over my arm. Without a companion at my side, I am free to focus my attention on the ever-changing scene. Instead of feeling alone in this mosaic of people, I feel engulfed in the energy in motion all around me.

The next section of the harbour is much quieter, with fewer outdoor seating options—and therefore fewer tourists and fewer touts. Tonight, with the wind coming off the water, I prefer the idea of dining in a quiet space where I can reflect on the day. I push open the door of a small place that hosts a handful of other customers seated in small groups.

After ordering, I record a few thoughts on how I choose where to dine on any given evening. The very first night on Crete, I attempted to order prawn souvlaki, my go-to order for Greek food back home, but as I described a skewer of prawns on a bed of rice, the server simply shook his head with a blank look on his face. It quickly dawned on me that even one of the more popular Greek dishes in Canada might not be part of the Cretan food culture. I do, however, recognize many of the familiar luscious ingredients from my previous experience with Greek food—including a vast array of fresh seafood as well as olives and their trademark oil—that are the heart and soul of this island. I haven't had a disappointing meal yet.

Knowing I'll enjoy the food anywhere, the decision falls to less obvious criteria for solo dining. Some evenings I like seeing a familiar face, even if it's a waiter who smiles in recognition. Other evenings, I like the adventure of trying a new place tucked away in the corner of the city. Some days I find myself hankering for a specific meal I've already enjoyed. And although I feel safe in Chania, a lifetime of messages about the danger of a woman walking alone keeps me from venturing past a certain point for dinner because that would mean a long trek home in the dark. The decision on where I'll dine any given evening comes into view when it comes. It's more intuitive than planned, but as the month clips along, I know I'll run out of time before I run out of great options.

After finishing another delicious meal that I can't pronounce, I begin the stroll along the length of the harbour toward home. Tonight, the moon is waxing in the night sky and my mind travels home to my loved ones. My daughters were so happy for me when I told them about my plans for this trip. Their support means the world to me as I set out to see more of it. Not just for me, but for them, I feel determined to make the most of my time here—but what "makes the most" of a trip like this, I wonder? One thing I already know is that this month is not about how many attractions

I see or how many keepsakes I bring home. I feel compelled to submerge myself in this culture so I can gently tap into our ancient common ground. Until now, I've never considered myself much of a history buff—but as I hold up the parts of me I already know against this long line of humanity that goes back to early civilization, I hear the past whisper in my ear.

The half moon's watermelon shape becomes a storyboard for my thoughts. The whole moon is there—it's never not there—even when clouds invade the night sky. But tonight I focus on this visible slice of moon that hangs suspended in a sea of stars. I grin at the thought that this partial moon grants me celestial permission to claim any half-formed thoughts I still have about how I fit into the greater whole. I am a singular entity moving independently in the world, yet I'm looking up at the same moon as those who first wandered this island. I am separate only to the extent that a cell is a separate organism in a body. I can't immediately tell if that is comforting or confounding, and I'm still pondering this when a voice breaks my train of thought.

"Heeeyyyy," says Nikos as he makes his way toward me on the boardwalk. "You are beautiful," he adds in a sing-songy voice. "You are amazing." His comments elicit a good-natured laugh as I wonder where this persistent tout learned that phrase and how many women he regales in the same way. For tonight, I am simply content to be one of the "stars" he has decided to woo.

"You come for a drink," he insists, more a statement than an invitation. I follow him—not for the first time since I arrived on the island—and wonder what this odd meteor of a man who keeps crossing my path might reveal.

When I first arrived in Crete, this tout, a man somewhere in his early forties with short dark hair and exceptionally muscular arms, snagged Anne and me and wouldn't take no for an answer. When his initial tactics weren't successful, he tried to convince us to stay based on how fresh the restaurant's fish was. He led us to a row of fish chilling on a bed of ice near the kitchen and explained that the secret to confirming their freshness is in the fish's eye, poking a fish in the eye to prove his theory. His English was good but his accent was thick, so we understood most of what he was saying, but not everything. He finished many of his sentences with a question, but I wasn't sure if we were supposed to respond. "The fish is very fresh, you see it is, yes?!" I couldn't tell if this was a cultural thing or a tout thing, a way to create engagement and agreement. When we still didn't look convinced, he held a fish up to our faces, urging us to smell it. I could sense the rest of the staff were trying to keep straight faces, but were we the joke or did even they find Nikos's approach over the top?

When Nikos lowered the fish, he looked at me for a moment as if seeing me for the first time, then simply stated, "I like your nose." Those words had never been spoken to me in my life. I have what might be called a significant nose, in combination with a long, slender face. My face in profile has a distinctly crescent shape to it, and since I don't have a strong chin, my nose appears even more prominent. I have disliked my nose ever since I can remember but have worked on accepting it as part of what makes my face mine. My nose is perfectly functional. It is not so mountainous that people stop in the street to point at it. I regard it as something that keeps me humble as well as a distinctive feature that makes me recognizable. I've also reasoned that the length of my nose is in proportion to another feature I sometimes struggle to accept about my body: my uncomfortably large breasts. To have this man, with fish juice dripping from his fingers, choose to draw attention to my nose over other body parts leaves me feeling vulnerable and a little curious.

He didn't say that I had a nice nose; he said that he liked my nose. The tone he used when he said it was softer, almost sincere, compared to his tout voice. I quickly landed on two possible explanations for his comment: Either he already suspected I might not like my nose and was using this as a way to make inroads with me or the notion (which struck me as unlikely) that men in this part of the world, or this man in particular, held a broader set of criteria for beauty than the men in my homeland.

That same night, my curiosity about how I was seen through local eyes was sustained through an interaction with our waiter. He asked where Anne and I were from, and we encouraged him to guess. The waiter—a young man from Albania, a country farther north along the same sea—looked at Anne first and quickly assessed she was from somewhere in eastern Europe. While Anne and I have only ever identified as Canadians, as confirmed on our passports, it was sobering and a little exciting to realize that our facial features made it possible for a relative stranger to connect us to our ancestry. Then the waiter looked at me for a long while, biting his lower lip. Despite seeing an endless stream of tourists from all over the world flood in and out of this restaurant, he was struggling to place my nationality. "You," he finally said, "look like you're from everywhere."

Tonight, Nikos seats me at a table with two other staff members who are at the end of their shift, both of whom I met another time I visited the establishment. I listen to their banter, joining in between sips of beer from their signature boot-shaped glass. (Among many other things that have changed in the past decade, I drink beer now.) Slowly, more staff join the table; two of them still have customers, but no one seems in a hurry to end the night. I've learned that as a customer, you have to make a discernible request for the bill at the end of the meal or the server will allow you to sit there indefinitely without coming to check on you once the meal service is complete. I've decided it's a show of respect— once you're seated, there is no pressure to leave. From what I can tell, lingering is an expected part of the dining experience.

I catch myself wondering if I'm in a strange and wonderful dream as the moon makes its way across the sky. I get to be more than just a fly on the wall around this table tonight. It feels good to be welcomed into a group after being alone and in my own mind most of the day.

Vesna, a tall, blonde woman closer to my age than most of the touts are, sits down across from me. She is married with two children and lives a few miles down the coastline. Her English is significantly better than the servers from other countries. When she discovers I am single and that I recently had a birthday, the topic around the table turns toward celebration.

In the Greek Orthodox tradition, they celebrate "name days." One's given name, usually after a saint, is celebrated once a year, and this day is considered a bigger deal than the anniversary of one's birth. Those who move here from other countries quickly rename themselves from a long list of traditional Greek names in order to fit in and participate in name-day traditions. I wonder if it feels different to celebrate an identity rather than a date on a calendar. Had I chosen the historical Year of Jubilee as a way to personalize my celebration and infuse it with more meaning?

Vesna asks what I did on my birthday so far from home. As I share the highlights of the day, I hear in my voice how proud I feel that I created a celebration that wasn't reliant on having a party or receiving presents in order to feel celebrated. Vesna looks at me sideways, finding it difficult to believe I would choose this. She asks again, more seriously, if I'm lonely being away for so long. With unexaggerated confidence, I say that I feel less lonely at this point in my life than ever before. In fact, I admit to the group that I decided to stay longer precisely because it was my birthday. Judging by the faces around the table, I see how unusual and possibly antisocial it sounds. How could it not? It sounded the same to my friends and family back home too. But I know I'm exactly where I need to be right now.

A tall, clear bottle filled with *raki* (also known locally as *tsikoudia*) arrives at the table. A complimentary serving of *raki* is offered at the end of the meal in every place I have dined on Crete. It is a distilled spirit, made in the fall from grapes and their skins. Families produce it over open fires in large copper stills for their own consumption. I receive a noncommittal answer when I ask, but I am getting the distinct impression that restaurateurs make special arrangements with their grandfathers and uncles to produce extra *raki* to serve to their customers. It is almost impossible to find a store-bought version that tastes as good as what is served every evening in restaurants. Distinct from *ouzo*, which is the anise-flavoured spirit known back home as the preeminent Greek specialty, *raki* is by far the most popular drink on Crete. It's served as a digestive support after a meal, and I've learned firsthand that the reason *raki* is favoured over *ouzo* is because one can experience all the added joy *raki* brings to an evening without a hint of the hangover *ouzo* hands you the next morning.

Raki is poured for everyone around the table, and we raise our glasses, joining in a chorus of *yamas* in the same spirit "Cheers!" is shouted back home. As everyone sips at the strong, clear liquid, Vesna decides this is the perfect time to share a great solution for women who find themselves without a partner in bed. She looks over at me and winks. The young waiters perk up, hoping to glean some advice from a knowledgeable source. She leans forward in her chair and lowers her voice to draw everyone in. First, she offers, the single woman shouldn't shave her legs for a few weeks. Then, she must shave only one leg so that when she wakes up in the middle of the night feeling lonely, all she has to do is rub her shaved leg against the hairy one, and she'll think there's a man in bed beside her. Everyone erupts with laughter, except for one of the young waiters, who is built like a husky linebacker. His English isn't strong enough to follow the story, so his buddy quickly translates for him. When they get to the punchline and a massive smile spreads across the linebacker's face, the whole group peels with laughter again.

I've always heard that humour is the biggest challenge when attempting to translate a different culture or language. Tonight, it has the opposite effect. As I sit around this table, aware of how many different parts of the world we represent, I marvel at how connected I feel within the camaraderie of this group. Some of us are farther from home than others on this moonlit night, but humour takes us to a place that's even better than home. I wipe tears of laughter from my eyes and feel my heart travel along a web of connection that stretches around the globe. I feel like the whole world is suddenly, magically home.

As I make my way back along the harbour, I watch the moon complete her path across the sky for the night, her reflection dancing in the waves of the ocean. I'd never considered that each night when I gaze at the moon's light sparkling on the water, these reflective moments are provided by a reflection of a reflection. The moon, illuminated by the sun's energy, in turn, lights up the ocean—along with my enlightened thoughts. This tag-team display confirms that my true mandate as a human being is to simply keep calling myself home. When I'm tuned in and vibrating in my highest capacity, I am able to more powerfully reflect my small part within this larger universal light show.

I already know that home is not just a specific location because a familiar roof over my head couldn't prevent me from feeling separated from myself earlier in my life. I had to yell to communicate with my heart during those times, convincing myself that the way I had to strain my voice to be heard was simply the price of being a woman and the cost of the human experience. I made big life decisions based on someone else's operating manual and had to silence my own voice in order to hear the instructions. While that path may have appeared successful initially, I had found myself alone in a sea of familiarity, unable to locate my own heartbeat. I watched myself go through the motions with my body, but my heart wasn't in it.

I've since learned there is another way—a beautifully personalized way—to do life. It's how I claimed the courage to be walking along this boardwalk on the other side of the world. My life flows so much better when I tune into the subtle vibration inside me that resonates for my ears only. This requires stillness around me but especially inside of me.

I match my pace to my breath as I turn up the pathway that leads away from the water, away from the moon's fading light, and in the direction of where I will lay my head tonight. I'm simultaneously curious and at peace about what tomorrow will bring. I won't always know the next step, but I know my way home.

KNOSSOS

"It seems to have evaporated," jokes a large bearded man, holding up his empty cup as proof. I'd never heard anyone ask for a refill in quite this way, and I let out an audible chuckle from a few tables over. The man smiles at my reaction; his partner's eyes twinkle in delight as she looks at me in mock horror over his antics.

William and Clara are making their way through Greece together. They met in Spain last year while they were both travelling alone, and quickly discovered they were from the same area in Australia. They are in their seventies; one of them boasts a recent knee replacement, and the other is waiting for a hip replacement. They have replaced their happy, full single lives for this new love. A serious "crazy for you, baby" love.

William and Clara have opted to keep separate residences but spend most of their time together. They travel as often as they can between stints of grandparenting and occasional work gigs for William, who is an environmental geomorphologist. (I ask him to say that again slowly so I can write it down and look it up later.) By now I have pulled up a chair to their table, at their invitation, and our wine glasses have been refilled twice. They are regaling me with stories of how love is greater than history (which is William's hobby) and religion (which was my area of study) and infinitely stronger than society's ideas of how retired people are supposed to behave.

The following night, I spy William and Clara on the street in front of me on their way home from dinner. They are leaning into each other with their elbows interlocked as they walk, supporting each other's ailing joints with their giddy love. As I gain on them, I enquire how their "hobble homeward" is going on this fine evening. Their laughter wakes the sleeping dogs along the street. They claim their night isn't over yet and insist on buying me a drink at Fagotto's, an after-hours piano bar in our area of town. How could I refuse? Hearing aids are adjusted as the pianist tinkles the ivories in the corner of the bar. We order a round of local wine and speak excitedly, like old friends who can't believe their luck at meeting again so soon.

I eventually ask them both the question whose answers are quickly filling the pages of my journal. "What's your favourite celebration?" I ask without prefacing the question, quietly assuming that, with their commitment to family, they will choose Christmas or Thanksgiving, with visions of a herd of happy grandchildren running amok around a large table. Instead, without taking a moment to consult each other, they both blurt out, "Us!"

"We love celebrating us," explains William after expressing his obvious delight that his answer was the same to the beaming woman at his side, "and we don't wait for a reason to celebrate. We play by our own rules. We figure at our age, *now* is a good time to celebrate!"

Still basking in the glowing energy of William and Clara's connection, I file the experience under what a relationship can look and feel like later in life. While I truly enjoy being single, I see how partnership, especially a less conventional approach like theirs, has lovely benefits. I imagine that one day, much further down the road, I might enjoy having a partner in crime, perhaps bending society's rules by living apart while being together.

A couple nights later I'm having dinner at the restaurant where strong-armed Nikos, the tout, works. I enjoy the greeting I receive from the staff and usually stop to say hello when I pass by even if I don't plan to stay for food or drinks. Now that it's well into the month of November, the number of tourists around Chania has fallen off significantly. Restaurants and shops have changed their hours, remaining closed some weekdays. And when they're open, the menu and pricing cater to locals. On the weekends, more venues bring in live music as a way to entice locals into their establishment. And while most tourist attractions are now closed until spring, the ones that are open don't have a line.

Being a tourist at this time of year means it's easier to spot other tourists, for we are few and far between. And, if I dare speak for the group, the off-season tourist is a slightly different breed. We are looking for a more relaxed experience and are often invited to pull up a seat next to a local for a more authentic peek into the culture and its people.

Nikos has been trying to convince me that he and I should spend some time together away from the restaurant. I'm fairly certain his interest in me isn't sincere. I suspect it's the idea of "scoring" with a tourist that makes him so persistent, but is that any different than the way I'm considering his offer as a way to enrich my experience of Crete with a Cretan? When I saw him yesterday, he asked me to let him show me how young I am. I was tickled by the way he worded it, but when I told him no, he looked genuinely hurt, claiming that every time I reject him I am "catastrophizing" him. I couldn't help but smile because, although that word isn't used for relationship dynamics back home, it made me wonder whether matters of the heart should be described as a natural disaster more often.

As I sip my beer and nosh on an assortment of fresh seafood, Nikos insists on returning to my table multiple times to continue his pleading. He knows my time here is coming to an end soon.

"You are beautiful." He launches into the refrain he regularly uses to greet me. "You are amazing." I smile and wipe beer from my top lip. There are other guests seated close by who have no choice but to be a witness to his brazen attempt to woo me, and I'm beginning to feel a bit self-conscious about the display. I make eye contact with the couple beside me and smile apologetically at them as Nikos continues his antics. They invite me to join them, and I eagerly pull my chair up to their table as we make our introductions.

Asgeir, a semi-retired sculptor, and Helga, the red-haired love of his life who looks to be in her early fifties, are visiting from Iceland. They are in awe at how warm it is for November compared to their home and how much delicious, fresh food is on offer on this island. They are on the last half of their multiple-week trip as well and are renting a place that overlooks the harbour. As we compare notes on what we've seen and tasted and what we hope to experience before returning home, we discover that a day trip to the capital city, Heraklion, is not checked off on either of our lists. We discuss the logistics of making the trip together over another round of drinks.

I had been working my way up to the trek to the capital city by breaking it into manageable chunks. Heraklion was a few hours away by bus, and I felt intimidated by the thought of navigating on my own to all the places I wanted to see in and around that city. Deciding to figure out Crete's transportation system first, I'd bought a bus ticket to the south coast of the island the week earlier. The two-hour bus ride had provided an interesting glimpse into the life of the Cretans who live in the mountains across the centre of the island. I describe to my new Icelandic friends the endless groves of olive trees, as far as my eye could see, that whipped by my window as the bus wound its way up steep mountain roads. The houses were humble, and many of the villagers appeared as if I'd gone back in time at least half a century. Most women were draped in long, black dresses and wore head coverings. It felt like I was suddenly in a very different country than modern Chania—until the bus reached the coastal town of Paleochora, also a tourist destination, on the other side of the island.

At this time of year, the thriving summer beach town was virtually deserted, which gave me uninterrupted space to wander around the town. Standing on the shoreline of the south coast of Crete, I realized that the landmass in the distance was Libya and its neighbouring country of Egypt, the place on the globe that boasts the earliest evidence of human existence. I try to describe to Asgeir and Helga why looking across the water at what most historians consider to be the original Garden of Eden had such a dizzying effect on me. Perhaps my brain was still reeling from all the switchbacks on the bus, but I noticed my mind was attempting to travel back that far in time now that I was physically this close to a place I'd heard about since I was a child.

Helga has not yet ventured into the ocean, and this is high on her list, so we meet up the next day for a dip in the Mediterranean. Not up for a swim, Asgeir finds a spot on the shore and digs into his satchel filled with various tools and six-inch lengths of wood he's brought from home. Anytime he isn't doing something that requires the use of his hands—including while he walks—he busies himself by working on miniature carvings of Viking men.

Helga looks nervous as we wade into the water. Other than Asgeir, who is intent on the intricate facial detailing of his latest carving, there's nobody else on the beach. I've been in the water numerous times during my stay, as the daytime temperatures were certainly hot enough (they qualify as hot summer weather for Canadians and Icelanders alike), and the salty water continued to fascinate me with its surprising buoyancy.

Helga confides just how uncomfortable she is being in the ocean. I show her how far I can walk out with the water still only waist-high. I ask her to trust me and invite her to lean back and allow her head to rest in my hands. Once I hear her breath settle into a steady pace, I encourage her to allow her body to relax as well. I can see how deep she has to dig to go along with my request, but once she is able to relax her muscles, the water does the rest. When there's no tension, her body simply floats to the surface. I slowly pull her backward, cradling the back of her neck as her buoyant body skims along the surface, light as a feather. It feels magical for both of us. After some time with her eyes closed and a smile on her face, she jumps up, waving her arms and yelling to Asgeir, asking if he's seen her in the water. She pleads with him to take pictures of her in the ocean; he happily obliges, laughing with her in her newfound joy.

In our first meeting, I learned that Asgeir is a huge fan not only of sculpting but also of Zorba the Greek. In fact, it's the reason they are here: The movie version of this story was filmed in 1964 on the island of Crete, some of it along Chania's waterfront. Asgeir shared how watching that movie at the age of fourteen with his father was one of the last things they did together before his father's death. The movie became a guidebook for Asgeir as Zorba, the main character, became his metric for what it means to be a man. Asgeir can quote virtually every line of the movie, and every occasion seems to offer an opportunity to recite at least one quote by heart.

As we emerge from the water, salt glistening on our skin, Helga and I pull sundresses over our wet bathing suits, still giggling from the glee of our time in the ocean. Asgeir stands up, shaking the sand from his trousers, and calls forth a quote that matches the moment perfectly. "Dance?" He utters the word in an incredulous tone and then he pauses for effect, just like in the movie. "Did you say dance??!" Our reenactment of the movie's final scene—in which the two main male characters, who have been through so much together, lock their arms across each other's shoulders and begin their famous Zorba dance on the beach as credits begin to roll—ensues.

As we make our way to the sidewalk, the three of us recreate the music from that scene, clapping our hands and using our voices to mimic the mandolin that starts slow and speeds up to a feverish pace. We only manage a few measures of the song before we all double over, laughing and breathless.

I notice a tall, middle-aged man walking down the sidewalk toward us, and before I have time to assess whether it is appropriate, I ask the man if he knows the Zorba dance. He admits to the three of us that he knows the sirtaki, the name of the dance used in the movie. I ask if he'd consider giving us a quick lesson right there on the sidewalk. He only hesitates for one moment before he grabs my arm and places it across his shoulder. He talks me through a series of deep knee bends and cross-over steps as Helga and Asgeir provide the music, singing and clapping in an escalating rhythm.

I feel like I'm in a movie as the sound of their voices mixes with the sun sparkling on the water and my body moves in time to their clapping and the man's instructions. The moment slows and lengthens as the exchange of delight radiates out to the ocean and beyond. This swirl of joy on a sidewalk on Crete is a portal of celebration so unexpected I can only marvel in astonishment at how all the pieces found their way into this moment.

Having thanked our gracious instructor, we make our way back to our rentals, laughing and dancing as Asgeir continues to recite lines from the movie. From that moment, if any one of us yells, "Dance??" the other two answer in unison, "Did you say dance?!" followed by mandolin voices and a flurry of flailing limbs that soon collapses into laughter.

We plan our trip to Heraklion for the following day. There are two things I hope to do in the capital city: to go to the archaeological museum and to visit Knossos. Asgeir and Helga are game for both as long as they're interspersed with stops for food and some shopping.

We board the bus first thing in the morning and enjoy the changing scenery on the three-hour ride toward the eastern side of the island. Although Heraklion is the capital, it's almost the same size as Chania, with 150,000 inhabitants, not counting the tourists. Not big, not small. Enough, and not too much.

When we arrive at the museum, we split up so the pace of our wandering can be driven by our individual curiosity. My main reason for wanting to go to the museum is to see the Phaistos Disc with my own eyes. Discovered one hundred years ago, this fired piece of clay dates to the year 2000 B.C. Even more interesting to me than its age is the way the images stamped into the clay tell a story, starting from the outside edge and circling around to the middle. While they've been able to decipher many of its symbols, experts in the field still don't fully understand the message. Those who have spent their entire careers studying this six-inch disc believe it's a set of symbols to honour "mother goddess," or, alternatively, that it was inscribed by the Minoans as a message from the goddess. It strikes me as a version of the Ten Commandments tablets, another story of communication from the heavens that humans were able to hold in their hands. The fact that the Minoan tradition had a goddess in addition to or instead of the exclusively masculine God I grew up with also catches my interest.

I make my way to where the Phaistos Disc is displayed but the case is empty. I'm told by the staff that the disc was moved for cleaning just this morning. Initially, I'm disappointed, but I find my next thought surprisingly delicious. I decide this means I must come back to Crete so I can see the disc! The idea that it's playing hide-and-seek with me ramps up my delight.

Around the same time the disc was unearthed, they also discovered an ancient Minoan palace called Knossos. Asgeir, Helga, and I arrive at the palace site around mid-afternoon and wander all over the expansive property. To the untrained eye, much of it looks like rubble with specific structures reconstructed amongst the ruins. From a distance, however, it appears like a phoenix emerging from its historical ashes. The earth is the colour of deep red clay, and I'm surprised and delighted that we are allowed to scramble around and interact so freely with the ruins.

"You want to buy the tour?" A man squints up at us from under a stained sun hat. "You will miss eighty percent of what you see if you don't," he presses. I guess from his persistence that off-season tourists are a tough crowd compared to the busloads that arrive daily during the summer months. Today only a handful of other people scamper amongst the ruins, against a backdrop of cypress trees and tired-looking hills in the distance.

As a trio, we decide to experience the Knossos Palace with virgin eyes and at our own pace instead of doing a tour. I am in the presence of imagination and ingenuity from 3,700 years ago, and I want to see what I notice first.

Our sun-hat shadow approaches us again a little later with an offer to narrate what we are seeing at a reduced price. Now he seems more driven by a desire to offer us the pearls of wisdom he holds than by hustling for his business. By now we have more questions than answers, and we take him up on a tour.

The guide explains the advanced water system and intricate sewer system that were installed under the base of the building. With obvious pride in his voice, he tells us the queen had her own chambers and a private toilet in her room that used gravity and a long, porous clay pipe for waste management. Then he leads us into some special rooms that were designed for storing olive oil. The near human-sized terra cotta urns they manufactured apparently kept the oil from going rancid for up to twenty years. The guide describes how the architecture of the buildings utilized light, air, and thick walls to maintain heat in the cold months and serve as air conditioning in the summer.

My mind attempts to filter through the barrage of information that flows from the mouth of our guide, who is missing a few teeth but never misses a beat of his delivery. He tells us about the time an earthquake destroyed the palace, which was made primarily of stone and clay. The Minoans observed how nature responded to the event, and when they rebuilt the palace, they incorporated cypress trees as beams within the walls to provide absorption and flexibility for when the earth shook next time. Nature destroyed their palace, and nature was their guide for their future palace.

Just as I catch myself wondering how knowing more about the brilliance of these early Minoans might help me live more wisely all these years later, I tune in to some powerful words from our guide. "Any culture that turns its back on nature or forgets how to honour its women will lose harmony and peace." I feel like I'm hearing the heart of what keeps any society healthy. I also feel like there's a message here about where to put my focus in this Jubilee Year.

On the three-hour bus ride back to Chania, my brain is working hard to cross-reference and organize everything I saw and heard today. There are connections aching to be made that link Jubilee and early civilizations with what I'm feeling at this moment. The threads between all three are gossamer and tentative as they span thousands of years and countless generations.

It's long past dark outside as the bus speeds along the main coastal highway, and I notice how clusters of light from the small towns along the route signal where people live in a way you can't see by the light of day. I recall having the same thought almost a decade ago while I was on a night run with Tom as we passed small towns. Back then, my plans grew out of dark nights of the soul; today, the night provides an abundance of well-illuminated ideas sprouting from a peaceful heart.

Creating this year of celebration feels like a radiant light at the end of a long tunnel, but from here I can see how darkness helped me know where to find my inner light. It's a reminder that there will always be more tunnels, more refining moments, more sparkling light—and the best part is that I know that now. Life isn't so much one long road; it's endless cycles of possibilities that crack open more possibilities. So many options can feel overwhelming when I'm not clear which question I'm using to navigate. What am I here for? What's in it for me? Who am I in this? I like the last question best for tonight's ride home.

I use the question to answer the unanswered question of Nikos. I have spent more time than I care to admit writing about the feeling of being wooed. I recently heard from some of the other staff that Nikos isn't entirely single, and I've decided this is the reason I will not take him up on his offer. It's a solid reason, but it's not the heart of the matter. What's more telling to me is that when he asks me where I am staying, I refuse to say. If I won't share where I lay my head, then I know that I am not ready to share my bed. I know what love feels like now, and I'm not willing to share my body with just anyone to try to fabricate a sloppy facsimile of that.

Besides, if it's romance I long for, there's excitement and mystery around every corner. I am genuinely thrilled by the engaging people who cross my path and join me on adventures. And these people, mostly couples, aren't prodding me to share my body. We are walking alongside each other as we allow this world of wonder to woo us.

In the stairwell back at my rental, I bump into Jim and Lillian from Montana. They are staying in the suite below mine. Jim's long white beard makes him a ringer for one of the members of ZZ Top.

Lillian is dwarfed by Jim in stature but not in her curiosity and skills of observation. They've returned to this same rental suite for the past few years and have absorbed some of the language and much of the culture. Under their direction, I discovered farmer's markets (and how to barter) as well as other new places tucked away in the city. After gushing about a restaurant up in the hills with a killer view of the inner harbour, they announce they'd like to take me there on my last evening in Chania.

We wind our way up the narrow roads in their rental car as the sun begins to yawn its descent in the western sky. After some searching and the aid of a cyclist en route who is willing to lead us the rest of the way, we locate the place perched at the precipice of a hill. Tourists call the cafe "the owl place"—an easier-to-pronounce translation of the actual name, Koukouvaya. There are owls painted on the building and sold in every style and variation in the small shop inside the cafe. My Montana friends arrange for a table on the patio and urge me to order the signature dessert, zoumera, which apparently means juicy in Greek. The fluffy chocolate cake dipped in rich, warm chocolate and topped with real whipped cream is as decadent as it is delightful. I can't tell if I am groaning more over the unbelievable view or each mouthful of cake.

I've had some practice with this by now—incredible food, stellar views, exotic music, great company. In fact, it's been a month-long feast on top of another month in Italy before that. And yet, I still find myself in awe. Whoever came up with the term "a feast for the senses" must have spent time in this part of the world.

Through my relaxed gaze, the inner harbour below looks even more like a lidded eye than when I first nervously introduced myself to her so many sleeps ago. As I trace the outline of Chania's Old Town, instead of seeing buildings and streets, I watch a slideshow of vivid memories in my mind's eye.

In my slideshow, I see the owner of a shop a few doors down from my rental, greeting me each time I stroll by, his wrinkles deepening the longer he holds his smile. Yesterday he sold me some of his grandfather's raki to take home with me, pouring out the contents of a sealed water bottle and filling it with the clear elixir from a spigot punched into an old barrel, then taping it shut in a plastic bag for transport. I am sad that dinners at home won't be followed by a glass of *raki* once I've finished this bottle. My digestive system has never been better. I know I've supported my health with a lot of walking, fresh food, and floating in the ocean, but I still suspect the *raki* has played a significant role.

Next, a snapshot of George—a short, feisty sixty-year-old Frenchman who helps run a restaurant just down the road from the shop—comes into my mind. When I first arrived in town, he yelled out, "Are you hungry and you just haven't told me yet?" When I finally make good on my promise to dine in his restaurant, George sits with me whenever he isn't helping other customers. We speak about love (it's only natural since he's French and I'm in love with my life). He tells me that to keep a lifelong marriage going, one has to be sure to meet some of one's personal needs elsewhere so as not to place too many demands on the marriage.

"Mattress is mattress," he explains, "and marriage is marriage." When I ask how he'd feel if his wife did the same thing, he claims she may be doing it too—and says that's fine with him as long as he never finds out. Discretion is the key, he emphasizes.

I didn't take George up on his mattress offer that night, but I was intrigued by—and a little suspicious of—his version of how to keep one's family intact over the long haul. I appreciate that while this non-traditional approach may not work for most people, George has found a way to live by a code that keeps a skip in his step while still enjoying weekly dinners with his extended, intact family.

As I follow the undulating road in my mind, I recall the bright expression on the face of the woman who sold me the colourful pottery for my Jubilee Year as well as the endless options on display at the leather store where I bought beautiful purses to bring home as gifts for my girls. I recall the stacks of sheepskin-lined slippers a few shops over and relive a slow-motion memory of me twirling in front of the mirror at the store where I purchased my birthday outfit.

The images come fast as I sit quietly enjoying a beverage to go with the view while Jim and Lillian sit back to take it all in as well. I see faces of people I met stopped in mid-chatter as a spray of water from the breakwater freezes at its full height behind them. With each blink of my eye, each click of my inner kaleidoscope, there is another interaction that comes into view. I see the faces of locals and tourists who took the time to tell me about themselves and ask me what made my face shine so brightly. I see the furrowed brow of the woman I met in the stairwell of our rental; we struck up a conversation and decided to keep talking over lunch. She had lost her husband and child in the same week a few years back and was still trying to find her feet under shaky legs. She ached for freedom from the weight of grief and confided that the ocean helped a little.

I see an image of Despoina, the lovely owner of my rental, who randomly showed up moments after I absent-mindedly locked myself out of my room and wasn't sure how I was going to resolve the situation.

One block up and over from my rental, I mentally enter what has become my favourite restaurant, Kalderimi. While I adored my birthday dinner there, I watch another memorable evening from earlier this week play out like a feature movie inside those rough stone walls. The plot is a trifecta of pens and a gruff man who supplies them to a damsel who is less in distress than a little put out when her ability to record her day takes a turn. The climax comes at the end of the evening when Gruff challenges the main character to keep his pen and to keep writing.

If a real movie was ever made of my life, the scene with Gruff would absolutely have to be in it. The director would likely give Gruff more backstory and would undoubtedly insist on adding some romance between us. But from where I sit looking down on this town and all its magical moments, the way it actually happened is already perfect.

I came to the island of Crete, where long-ago humans figured out how to do life, inviting myself to wriggle out of the constraints of my upbringing so I could take in a fuller view. I desired to see and knew that as I wrote it out, I would know what I saw. See. Saw. My life finds its best balance on this fluctuating teeter-totter. And meeting Gruff and his half-brother that night created a potent intersection in time. While the spirit of the gods may not wander the surrounding hills, a real, live Greek god sat beside me, gave me a clear message, and handed me the tool to accomplish it that night.

For all the words I've written and all the ideas that have sprouted as I explored Crete, it is the exchanges with other humans that have left an indelible stamp on me. Their presence reflects new parts of me back to me, regardless of what part of the world they hail from. I trust meeting me made their day better as well.

The following morning, my last day on Crete, I attempt to capture it all in a video I record of myself on the balcony of my room. I want to contain as much as I can before I get on a plane for home, where time and cabin pressure will likely fog up the glass on what I see so clearly at this moment. In the video, I remind myself of my bliss, my hard-won self-possession, and my courage—and that these qualities are recognized everywhere I go. These are not a Canadian thing or a Mennonite thing or a female thing; these qualities connect me to the universal human experience. I feel humbled by how my personal healing journey has rubbed the layers of who I am into a high shine, with any formerly tarnished areas now displaying a beautiful patina.

This trip has been a celebration as well as an opportunity to learn how to truly celebrate. I'm not surprised to learn that celebration is something I can create within any moment. In fact, for me, waiting for a special date on the calendar to celebrate actually decreases the probability that it will feel celebratory. For me, anticipation isn't actually the best agent of celebration; wide-eyed wonder is a much better guide. This requires less planning and more available internal space where curiosity can wander—and this all requires a strong foundation of trust so that when something unexpected happens, I intuitively know which wave to ride and which to wave farewell.

A few hours before my taxi will arrive to take me to the airport, Asgeir and Helga meet me for coffee. They present me with one of Asgeir's Viking carvings and express again how glad they are that we met and danced and laughed together. Then they send me off with a quote from Zorba the Greek (and its Cretan author, Nikos Kazantzakis) that is so fitting it feels like it was written into the script of my trip from the beginning.

"This is true happiness: to have no ambition and to work like a horse as if you had every ambition. To live far from men, not to need them and yet to love them. To have the stars above, the land to your left and the sea to your right and to realize of a sudden that in your heart, life has accomplished its final miracle: it has become a fairy tale."

YEAR OF JUBILEE

November 2014

I wake slowly, keeping my eyes closed so the images of my birthday on Crete, exactly one year ago, can flicker a little longer across the screen of my mind. I suspect it will always be my favourite birthday because, like a bespoke suit, it was tailored so perfectly to what evokes joy in me.

I was curious, when I boarded my return flight, how much of a challenge it would be to reinsert the woman whose body had bobbed buoyantly in the salty ocean just days before back into the rainy days of a West Coast winter. I was away long enough, and I had walked far enough, to break in a new way of being with myself in the last two months. Once I returned to the rhythm and relationships of my life here, I wasn't sure how much would integrate and how much would gently fall off like the leaves from the deciduous trees that lay scattered all around my townhouse complex as I arrived home and pulled into my driveway?

Fortunately, I've given myself the year, my entire fiftieth year, to work it all out. The trip was only the beginning. My plan for the rest of my Jubilee Year is to continue with the same intention, using the twin pillars of rest and celebration as my guideposts.

Rest includes lounging at home and lingering longer in a coffee shop, but it also holds a larger intention. I put to rest my need to have my world figured out. I put to rest my urgency to complete all my tasks on any given day. I have to sound my inner yowl regularly to remind myself of my commitment to this year. The pace and purpose of a Jubilee Year don't match anything I'd ever seen or heard of before. Up till now, I've thought that if anyone rested for an extended period of time, it meant they were unwell, old, or just plain lazy.

While I feel perfectly healthy—more vibrant than ever, in fact—I clearly remember times when this wasn't true. I've rebuilt the tangible parts of my world in the past decade, and I've reexamined my inner workings as well. Now it's time to allow it to soak into all the layers of my being. Daily micro-decisions of what to do, what to be, whether to reach out to a friend, when to stay quiet, when to speak up—these are all part of the absorption process. I need a flexible schedule and a rested mind to notice which seemingly insignificant decisions are laying the new groundwork for how I am going to live.

Unlike the uncertainty of travel, familiar faces and regular rhythms tend to put me into autopilot. That doesn't automatically make my routine wrong, but during a reset year, I want to ensure these rhythms allow me to operate from the helm of my life. Having been raised in a family where hard work and sacrifice were highly valued, this year's goal to rest jabs hard at my definitions of laziness and privilege.

I notice the temptation to chicken out by getting a job so I don't have to explain to another person why I'm not working. That is the moment I gently remind myself or release a yowl, depending upon the day, that I do not have the privilege of taking this Jubilee Year because I am more deserving than anyone else; rather, it's because I made the decision to celebrate and rest this year, and my main job right now is to honour that decision. I have to regularly remind myself that what others think about what I'm doing is not my responsibility, nor is it my business. So I turn up the volume on my wise inner voice that has made this year possible, which effectively turns down the chatter on what isn't mine.

This voice, more like a vibration, divines its choice from the options before me. Then I send that feedback up and down the communication chain between my head, heart, and gut to gather consensus on what my next step will be. And as I take that step, doors seem to swing open, often right at the moment I am about to raise my hand to knock. A friend who flits through my mind will randomly call me five minutes later. An incubating idea finds form in the words that come out of my neighbour's mouth or in a line from a book. A small, almost indiscernible desire finds an avenue of expression as an invitation to a memoir writing retreat in Maui with author Cheryl Strayed drops into my inbox. I submit my registration the very next day, Gruff's words "keep writing" still echoing in my ears. This symbiosis floods me with a wave of gratitude, a sensation that affirms to me that I'm on the right track.

Standing at my kitchen counter, I cut fruit into my red bowl, a perfect finale bookending the first time I used this bowl for my birthday breakfast on Crete a year ago. I grab a pad of paper and scan the kitchen counter for a pen. There are none in sight, but I know where I can find one. I race up the stairs and dig through the bag of keepsakes from my trip. Underneath a concert ticket stub from Venice, a map of Chania, and the cork from the best wine I tasted in Italy, I find Gruff's pen. No more than a cheap, clear plastic click pen, it is nevertheless imbued with the magic of a Greek god—the perfect accomplice to help me take stock of this past year while I enjoy breakfast.

As I spoon an assortment of fruit into my mouth, the juice from a piece of orange squirts past my lips, leaving a spray of juicy dots on my page. My taste buds seem to be directly connected to my tear ducts this past year as delicious flavours strum deep emotions. I first dab my eyes and then the moist dots on my page. I am instantly tickled at the thought that this will likely leave permanent marks on this page. Like food and wine stains on my journal from Crete, they deepen the story beyond what the words on the page say.

When random spills and breakage happen, it's common to label these as accidents—but I adore how quickly I am able to transform them into something more interesting. We tell ourselves stories about everything anyway as we judge and label our experiences, so why not decide on the most delicious version of the story? I get to decide whether a spray of orange juice on my page is clumsiness or a way for my body to give its stamp of approval. For me, I already know which version creates a "high five" moment inside me. If there's one thing I can see clearly after this Year of Jubilee, it's how many moments we miss that can make our day shine. It's effectively the same as waiting for an event that feels worthy of celebration or seizing the opportunity to create a burst of celebration anywhere and anytime.

Flanked by all my personal reflections and ongoing research about my Year of Jubilee in my journal beside me, I'm eager to see how it is all synthesizing inside of me. Clicking the green ink tab on Gruff's pen, I draw a line down the middle of a piece of paper. Then I click the red tab and write my personalized Jubilee mandates—MY LAND and MY INNER SLAVES—on each side of the line. With a satisfying snap, I click the tab for blue ink with its ocean of possibilities and begin to record what I know about returning my land to the original owner and releasing my inner slaves.

My land is my life, I write. Besides all the tangible things I've accumulated around me in my townhouse, my land is more about how I identify myself. It's all the hats I wear, my roles, my relationships, my ethnicity, my gender, my place around the table. I list the obvious ones that come to mind. I was born into this time in history, around 2000 A.D., into a female body. I was born into a family with a Mennonite heritage and faith on Canadian soil.

Looking through my lens of Jubilee, I consider where I have returned land, my identities, to their original owners this year. Where have I released the labels and roles I no longer identify with to make room to reclaim my original inheritance—a blank-slate, stardust version of myself? I laugh at how I'm reaching for the stars today and feel a little dizzy at the thought of that much space to play in.

As irony or synchronicity would have it, just as I'd returned home from Europe, my family's farm had sold. For fifty years, that land was my enduring home base, regardless of where I lived. It's where I learned to walk, do cartwheels, work, live, and love—and now, in my Year of Jubilee, I have to say goodbye to the land. This farm provided a thriving livelihood for my family, and now, all those eggs I spent my childhood collecting have become a perfectly timed nest egg. The money disbursed from the sale of the farm made it possible for me to have my Jubilee Year without going into debt. The farm's value transformed into an invaluable resource for my land and my life.

The day before the farm officially sold, I went there with my parents to gather up the last few belongings. I filled a bucket of dirt from my mother's garden and used it to top up the soil of my house plants, effectively mixing in my past with my present.

I move the pen to the other side of the page and stare at the title INNER SLAVE. In its simplest form, feeling enslaved means someone or something else has control. These days, in affluent countries at least, it seems people are slaves to a lifestyle or various addictions. As I mentally scan my life, I struggle most when I hold too tightly to any identity. Being a friend, lover, mother, daughter, writer, sister, female, Canadian, global citizen—all are wonderful aspects of my human experience, but clinging to any one of those identities as the thing that ultimately gives me worth will cause me to grip too tightly.

This thought has the effect of pressing play on a memory from a coaching demonstration during my training a few years ago. The instructor asked me to hold my pen with my palm facing down. This meant I had to grip the pen in my fist so it wouldn't fall to the ground. Then he told me to turn my palm towards the sky and open my fist. "The pen is still there. It's still yours," he pointed out. "But you have room for so much else now too." Even knowing this, I admit it usually takes heartache or fatigue to remind me to "open my fist" when it comes to my closest relationships.

I turn the paper sideways and divide the INNER SLAVES column in half. I write OPEN FIST in one area and CLOSED FIST in the other one. While my roles and relationships regularly jump from one side to the other, I know there's value in capturing a snapshot of where I am at today so I can see more clearly where I desire to go.

I begin with my identity as a mother. Within weeks of my return from Greece, my daughters and I pounced on a day during the holidays that was free in all of our calendars and drove two hours north to Whistler, where we knew we'd find a snowy wonderland. We locked arms to avoid slipping on the ice as we laughed our way across a frozen lake, catching up on each other's lives.

Laura, my older daughter, had arranged for each of us to bring a new journal along, and over hot drinks in a warm restaurant, we took turns writing what we observed in each other in the back pages of each other's journals. The words my daughters wrote about me matched precisely what I was feeling about my life. My heart soared that my courage and creativity were being recognized by the very faces who had watched my turbulent journey at the start of this decade from the "splash zone" section they hadn't asked to be seated in. But even then, I knew that continuing to punish myself for the way my desperate decision to leave the marriage had impacted their teenage lives wouldn't make it better for any of us. I worked hard to parent them with an open hand, offering them honest apologies when I messed up and enough space so they could discover their own paths and still know I was always available. Now, with both of them in their twenties, I celebrate how close our bond has become.

I write MOTHER in the OPEN FIST box. Then, without much thought, I write DAUGHTER underneath that. More often than not, I'm able to accept my parents as people who have done their best. A huge part of getting here was learning to release the judgment and anger from events in my childhood that held me hostage for so long. Seeing MOTHER and DAUGHTER in the OPEN FIST box together makes me wonder if the really hard conversations I had with my own mother resulted in me becoming a better mother. Of course there's a ripple effect between my identities, I chuckle, realizing again that feeling rested helps connect the dots faster.

The next identity that pops into my head is a harder one to label, let alone nail down. Do I use the term *partner* or *girlfriend* or maybe something fancy like life *accomplice*? I can't tell which title feels the most accurate. I was not planning on donning any of these identities anytime soon, but Jubilee had other plans.

I first met Earl at a provincial youth retreat when I was fifteen years old and he was seventeen. He lived a five-hour drive away, and long-distance phone calls were expensive back in the Stone Age, so the connection we felt didn't have an opportunity to flourish at that time. Our paths had crossed on occasion once he moved to the coast a few years later, but I was married by then with two young daughters in tow.

Recently, Earl had spoken with my father at a funeral and, when he'd heard that I was no longer married, had followed a nudge that something wasn't finished from our teen years. He'd reached out to me weeks before I'd left on my European trip, and we'd met for coffee—which had turned into a walk, followed by dinner. Our similar religious upbringings had resulted in both of us sifting through similar chaff to get to the heart of things. We'd realized with surprise that our lives, while wildly different on the outside, had taken us both on a quest for love—the big version of love, the kind that isn't limited to only revealing itself within a relationship.

We'd exchanged emails while I was away on my two-month adventure. When his father had passed unexpectedly while I was in Rome, I'd told him I would throw a coin into the Trevi Fountain the day of his father's funeral. I'd stood with my back to the fountain, closed my eyes, and—as I tossed the coin high over my shoulder—simply uttered Earl's name and allowed the coin to speak for itself. Later I'd wondered if the fountain may have heard that as a request for romantic love.

Upon my return from Crete, Earl had wanted to hear about my adventure, and we'd planned a day-long romp to multiple specialty stores in the city, an outing he referred to as *bummeling*—a term meaning "to wander around at a leisurely pace," which is exactly what we did. We sampled cheese and meats from all over the world and brought home treats from every store we stopped at. It felt like going on a trip around the world in my own city.

A few weeks later, he'd proposed that we go on a hike, which had turned into dinner and eventually ended up at my place for a healthy pour of scotch. When we'd taken his dog out for a walk in the crisp January air, prompted by a strong feeling that didn't have words yet, I had stepped in front of him to face him, stopping him in his tracks. My head had been bowed as I tried to find words, and as I'd raised it, his warm lips had met mine. Feeling like our teenage selves, who had never gotten to first base, we'd kissed under the light of the moon for hours, our lips telling all the stories we'd longed to share since the time we'd first met.

Earl had poured his life into his work. I had poured my life into people. He had a brain that could work through impressive complexities and had put it to use in the field of computer engineering. My coaching background was a perfect tool for digging into the mind. Although these extreme differences sometimes became a hurdle, we also noticed many places where his logic and my emotional range were an excellent match.

He loved to cook and had a goofy side to his personality that made creating meals together one of our favourite activities on weekends. Our shared Mennonite upbringing injected common ingredients into our communication and our meals. We made a game of plopping perfectly parsed words from our parents' mother tongue into our wordplay. When done well, intelligent banter can be exceptionally engaging.

When we'd first noticed that this thing we were doing had its own momentum, regardless of the fact that neither of us was looking for a relationship, we'd compared notes on what we each desired for the future. My twenty-year marriage and Earl not being in a relationship for just as long meant we were walking towards each other from opposite ends of life's experiences. I had leftover concerns about my tendency to lose myself in relationships, and he had unanswered questions about whether he was built to be in one.

I had spent the past handful of years with my arms spread wide in an open-hearted relationship with the whole world. Would closing my arms around one person, committing to a relationship again, change the flow of my love? Am I better suited for the "big, wide world" version of love or the kind where each pore on my nose and every emotion that leaks out is witnessed by the same person, who is standing a few inches away from my face?

We'd ultimately decided that instead of calling what we had a relationship, weighed down by all the assumptions and obligations inherent in the title, we would get creative. So we'd jumped into a "ship," our version of a relationship that isn't a relationship, and set out to sea to see where the winds of love would take us. We hoped this less tethered approach would keep us buoyant, even when storms might knock us around the cabin. We'd agreed to remind each other of the guiding principle for our time in the ship: It has to be better together than when we were apart. This wasn't a threat; it was a way for each of us to calibrate our true north after every storm.

Earl's personality has no patience for injustice and little room for error, for himself or others. His exceedingly honest, even blunt, approach regularly puts me on the defensive and sends my heart running for cover. I joke that when love has not yet tenderized all parts of the heart, she brings out a mallet—which for me is in the shape of this man.

Living apart has left us enough space to enjoy our unique rhythm as a couple and still maintain our personal preferences in daily living. I am thrilled to see him and happy to wave goodbye at the end of the weekend. I'd wanted a learning partner, someone who desires to explore love's many faces, and that is exactly what I've gotten.

This love, up close and personal, means intimacy regularly plays tag with my feelings of vulnerability. But there's no game-playing on Earl's part and, therefore, not much traditional wooing either. This allows me the space to know what I'm feeling without having to translate his intentions. Earl is good at sidestepping my unconscious emotional traps, although he falls down a few of his own rabbit holes on occasion. I'm essentially hanging out with a broad-shouldered mirror that reflects back any attempts on my part to subtly control a situation. It takes nuanced work to notice where my gentle probing questions might actually hold their own agenda. I know how to love myself, but I'm not great at trusting someone else's offers of love. I often feel uncomfortably exposed and at his mercy, even as I preach that vulnerability is a crucial part of healthy intimacy.

And for this reason, I write PARTNER exactly on the line

between OPEN FIST and CLOSED FIST. I still struggle to speak my desires boldly while being a gracious partner. I want to feel safe, appreciated, and cherished within a partnership, and when I sense I may be disappointed, I retreat to lick my wounds and find ways to meet those needs myself. Perhaps the heart of any partnership is simply rooting for each other as we continue to hunt and gather love. I shake my head at a silly cartoon image in my mind that seems to capture the contrast between Earl and me. I'm dressed in camouflage, slinking in and out of my favourite hiding places, searching for the face of love to show up; he's wearing a fluorescent orange safety jacket, gun cocked, as he thrashes and crashes through love's dense underbrush. We may be searching for the same thing, but our hunting styles are wildly different.

I continue writing, jotting down every identity or role that comes to mind, and then I straighten the paper to view it all in one glance. It seems so obvious when I see it all written out. My land is how I identity myself, and my inner slaves are how I live out those identities. Anytime I'm enslaved by one of my identities, celebration falls flat and rest is hard to come by. When I release my grip, it feels like I'm returning myself to me, and that feeling of coming home lights a candle of celebration at the centre of my being. Jubilee—back in Leviticus and for me today—is essentially a time to remember who you are, I marvel.

Rest and celebration happen well in tandem. In fact, I've noticed time and again how being rested has given me the energy to expand into celebration. Like the rhythm of the breath, when I exhale into rest, I have space to inhale celebration. My Jubilee Year hasn't been a marathon of parties and naps; it's been a time of gently opening into who I know I am, resulting in a soft, joyful place to land for the next fifty years.

SMASHING FIFTY

Standing in front of my full-length mirror, I smooth the front of my dress after tying the sweater the way the woman at the shop in Chania showed me a year ago. November in Canada means I'm going to have to add some leggings, boots, and a heavy coat—but I wouldn't dream of wearing anything but my birthday outfit today. As I feel the soft cotton under my fingers, I know that this dress is more than just nostalgic; it's become a part of the fabric of this Jubilee Year. I doubt there's a single garment in my closet that has witnessed as many coffee dates with friends, dinners out, and even walks to the grocery store. This dress wraps my body in its celebratory intention and reminds me who I am.

These revelations don't take me by surprise. This awareness of how my body fuses with my spirit is precisely what's allowed me to experience genuine celebration—a skill I've spent the last decade developing. The body is the domain of the senses, so I muse that for birthdays, it makes sense that we have traditions that engage all of them: decorations and candles for the eyes, the scent of sugary icing for the nose, cake for the mouth, the shriek of "Surprise!" and the birthday song for the ears, and heartfelt hugs to link our celebratory connection through touch.

As I look at the length of my body in the mirror, it strikes me for the first time that perhaps we hold to the tradition of shouting "Happy birthday!" in unison because it's so effective in setting the intention while grabbing the attention of the birthday person. The body can't help but react to an effective yowl. The element of surprise wakes everything up. For some, it stimulates excited feelings as they join in celebration, but for others like me who are more sensitive by nature, sometimes the chemical reaction to the shock can overstimulate the mind and body and have the opposite effect.

Like so many things in life, I wonder why it's taken me this long to figure out that experiencing celebration is truly a unique path for each person. I wasn't incapable of celebrating a decade ago; I just didn't understand the recipe that would allow celebration to flow well for me. This past year has taught me to make sure my body is involved in some way. My limbs long to be moving, and my senses need to be invited along. Most importantly, when I take the time to ascribe my own personal meaning to how I move my body and why I involve my senses, I can submerge into celebration more fully. The more personalized and intentional it is, the more celebratory it will feel to me.

I head to the kitchen to wash my cup, plate, and bowl one last time and place each one inside its own clear, sealable bag. As planned, I have eaten every meal I prepared from these vessels for this entire year—and today this ritual is complete. At the last minute, I decide to double-bag each one before Earl arrives to escort me and my bagged pottery to the party.

My daughters asked if they could plan a birthday celebration for my fiftieth birthday. They wanted to take care of the details but encouraged me to invite the guests. As I open a time capsule of memories from exactly a decade ago, I realize that there will not be a single person from my fortieth birthday party at the event today. My girls were too young, and the rest of my family wasn't invited to that part since we had a more intimate family gathering on another day. Today, my whole family will be in attendance. The guests from the party for my fortieth were linked to my former roles of friend and wife and church member. Today's guest list is more like a roadmap of soul connections within my new life.

I marvel at the difference one decade makes. I know it's not just the passage of time but how I've lived that time. It started with the smash of my elbow and the haunting loss of my neighbour. Then came the explosion when I blew up my life and brought everything down around me. That required a lot of heavy lifting, with only one working arm to help, as I sorted through the mess and discovered buried treasures in the rubble. Every small and large decision I made after that was checked by a new, evolving system that used gut instinct and heart truth instead of the old default of how favourably it was going to appear to others. I had to clean the bugs off my windshield regularly to keep my intention in sight. A surprising gift from my personalized Jubilee Year has been the delicious freedom that comes when I soften my grip on how I identify myself. I get less tangled up when I see my decisions through the lens of simply being a human, instead of clinging so tightly to my reputation or my ascribed roles—which are both, ironically, things others control.

As Earl takes my hand and leads me to the upper floor of the Greek restaurant my girls have reserved for the occasion, I am greeted by many bright faces. Since I've expanded my ability to celebrate alone, I am also more open to group celebration. There's my individual celebration experience, and there's the collective experience—where the joy I've already soaked in on my own can multiply exponentially with those who add their delight to the pile.

My time on Crete and my presence in this room bring my Jubilee Year together. I savour the exotic flavours on my plate and hear the Greek music mix with the din of people talking and laughing around the room. "Dance?!" I whisper to my Icelandic friends, wherever they may be at that moment on the other side of the world. I hear their response in my mind and notice my cheeks already hurt a little from the genuine smile that seems permanently etched onto my face. It all feels a little dreamlike to sit in the culmination of this year, but I know for a fact that I've walked every step on the path that's led me to this celebration table today.

My friend Hal stands up, a devilish grin on his face as he

raises his hand to command the attention of the room. He is the youngest oldster I know, with a mane of white hair that gallops in rhythm with his mischievous gait wherever he goes. He and I met a few years ago through his cousin, and we immediately formed an impromptu trio of language lovers, sending all manner of linguistic transgressions, as well as praise for phrases that enchant, flowing into each other's email inboxes across the ether.

Instead of speaking, Hal breaks into song. He is a man of many talents, and today he honours me with his antics and regales the crowd. I hadn't realized how much of the ancient Greek spirit flows through him, considering that he and I grew up in the same hometown (albeit years apart). And like Zorba the Greek, Hal also takes every opportunity to suck the sweet marrow out of life. The more I go out in the world and see new things, the more new connections I see in the people and places at home.

My daughter Laura announces to the guests that cake and other birthday-related activities will continue at the home of my dear friends, Leah and Derrick, on the other side of town. On the drive over, I notice the lights that line the main streets, running up and down the hills to connect the various parts of the city at night. I soften my gaze and recall the way lights dotted the undulating Mediterranean shoreline. Crete kicked off the year of celebration, but I spent most of this Jubilee Year back home. Some days it felt like my trip abroad was a mountaintop summit and the rest of the year was its knee-jarring descent. Most days, however, I've been able to catch glimpses of how everything has been weaving itself together deep inside me, much of it unseen but happening nonetheless—and I've felt less daunted, less deterred by what life has handed me. My instincts are sharper and my decisions feel more sure.

We arrive at my friends' spacious home, already buzzing with people holding drinks and viewing the compilation of pictures capturing my life, which my daughters have created for the occasion. After cake—which was specially chosen by a mentor and friend, Rae, delights my mouth and is topped with candles that light up my eyes—and a rousing rendition of the birthday song that fills my ears as well as my heart, there is time allotted for anyone who wants to say something. My cousin Anne shares a beautiful poem she has written for the occasion, reading it out loud for everyone to enjoy. I hear her voice and I feel her love, but I can't take in the words over the loud beating of my grateful heart. Likely knowing this, she leaves me the copy of the poem so I can savour it later. My sister, Ruth, tells some funny stories from our childhood and expresses her respect for how far I've travelled in my life to arrive at the place I am now. Her assessment of things has always been a solid touchstone for me. Our thoughts share a shorthand reserved for when sacred sisterhood is laced with a true friendship.

I fumble through my tears to express my gratitude for this time of celebration shared with all those who are present. With all the words I've written this year, it feels impossible to gather them into a succinct conclusion at this moment, so instead, I invite everyone outside to the backyard.

With my three double-bagged vessels on the table beside me, the night sky watching breathlessly, I lift the blue plate above my head. This plate has been my daily reminder of what I learned about myself in Greece and how an ocean of endless possibilities is available to me, even on this side of the globe. With shaking arms raised above my head, I throw the plate onto the concrete patio. The smashing sound is met with applause and a Greek chorus of "Opa!"

Apparently, the time-honoured tradition of plate smashing has been banned in many restaurants in Greece, due to the danger caused by the flying shards. I'm proud that my idea to bag them allows for this celebratory act to take place without anyone losing an eye. While it may dampen the effect a little, my strategy to contain the shattered ceramics avoids a mess to clean up—but more importantly, I already know I want to transform the broken pieces into something new. The vessels may not hold food anymore, but they will serve as a gorgeous reminder of the power of transformation.

Next, I lift my grey cup high and hurl it to the ground. This cup contained the warm reminder that life is rarely all one thing or all another. What we enjoy about a cup is its ability to carry and cradle the substance it holds. It is the wide-open space inside the hard outer edges where most of life is actually lived. And it is in this space between all or nothing, this fertile mix of curiosity and uncertainty, where my best plans continue to be planted and harvested.

Finally, I grasp my red bowl with the hand-painted golden swirl at its centre. If there's one piece I really don't want to break, it is this one. Of all three vessels, I've used the bowl the most this past year. Within its passionate red embrace, I've feasted on fruit salads and hearty soups, curry bowls and drizzled desserts. This bowl would be a perfect ongoing companion through the strong hormonal swings menopause has been serving up. And at the same time, not smashing this bowl means that I wouldn't be completing what I began. I knew how their end would come the day I bought them, and not following through would mean I'm gripping too tightly. As with most relationships, beginnings are much easier than endings. This is never more true than when a loved one passes—yet even as our hearts break from the loss, we celebrate their life. Celebration's highest purpose is to honour a cycle that is complete.

I raise the bowl above my head and hold it there for a moment. Fragments from a million memories burst through time and rush in to join me. I feel my inner yowl shriek in affirmation. My outstretched arms sweep downward through the crisp air as I release my beloved bowl and hear it smash to pieces. The momentum strikes a chord that is ancient and true. Like the spaces between the strings of a guitar that vibrate my heartsong of celebration into the night, it feels like I'm strumming moonlight.

Celebration requires little more than inviting my senses to join in awe at how I am connected to everything. This connection was present under the bright lights of this evening's party, and now, an even fuller, richer swirl of celebration envelops me as the night sky extends its tender invitation to bask in even deeper reflection. Today, on my fiftieth birthday, I celebrate the completion of a cycle, a most beautiful year, on the tail end of a wild decade that smashed me wide open.

ACKNOWLEDGMENTS

There aren't nearly enough ways to thank everyone who inspired me and made it possible for me to complete this memoir, and I'm already sure this page of acknowledgements is going to come up achingly short. But from an overflowing heart, I will spill some words here to express my sincere gratitude.

Instead of a lengthy list of names, please see yourself reflected in the multiple ways you have impacted my life and supported this project.

Thank you, most especially, to those who listened over the years, often for hours on end—only yawning occasionally—as I shared my stories so I could know more fully what I knew.

Thank you for showing up in my life while watching for falling stars, lying on a patch of sun-warmed grass by the river, asking the best questions ever, riding in a fire truck, hiking all over the mountain to find the best place to build my labyrinth, running my *bars*, helping me become a better listener, walking on railroad tracks, taking the high road, paddling your kayak while pulling mine, trusting me with your innermost, offering me your kind assistance, doing a podcast together, and sleeping on the pillow next to mine.

Thank you to those who challenged my outer limits, poked my

inner bear, and told it to me straight.

Thank you for making my life infinitely better by topping up my drink, having a decent comeback to my brilliant pun, writing lyrics to my tune, spilling your guts, strumming in time to my lead, sharing from your soul's infinite bounty, staying up past my bedtime with me, keeping my knives sharpened, whisking me away, flooding my social media feed with your inspiring comments, tripping your way through the early version of this book, welcoming me onto the mountain, reminding me that I'm good enough, and never (well, almost never) burning the food.

A very special thank you to all the angels at Awaken Village Press who held my hand and soothed my soul as I wrote it all down, laid clarifying questions at my feet, took care of the important boring stuff, breathed magic into my dubious grammar, got me to smile from my insides for my headshot, and patiently tailored the design of this smashing book cover so it fits my heart like a glove.

I love you all to the moon and back.

Made in the USA
Monee, IL
09 January 2022

88471723R00152